Praise

THERE ARE FAIRIES AT THE BOTTOM OF OUR GARDEN

"There's something about this "real time" approach that brings home a story that will inevitably play out in each of our lives as we either care for someone stricken with illness or are cared for in turn. What Evans provides here is the very thing she gave her mother: companionship. Complete with poems written by her mother, what emerges aren't so much the traces of a life lived, but footprints on a road well-traveled and the promise that it doesn't have to be traveled alone."

    - Christopher Renstrom, bestselling author of *The Cosmic Calendar and Ruling Planets*

"This work left me laughing and crying. I can't say enough for how authentic it felt. From addiction to grief. I love how Erin wasn't afraid to write the truth. This book doesn't pull any punches."

    - Jenna B. Neece, bestselling author of *Handy One*

"Fairies is a hauntingly beautiful account of family, life, loss and love. The "framily" (friends and family) that one develops in life beyond bloodline, are on standby, without judgement, extending love and support. One is drawn in page by page at the complexity of the situations and relationships between these women. Theirs is an impassioned journey that causes us to pause to think of our own familiar relationships."

    - Martha Wallace, author of *A Sampling of Life, One Taste at a Time*

THERE ARE FAIRIES AT THE

BOTTOM OF OUR GARDEN

ERIN EVANS

Author's Note

After a month in quarantine, I was told I might not have a job to come back to. It scared me to death. My parents raised me to fight through rough patches, until another job comes along. Little did I know a nationwide lockdown would give me the time I needed to write this book. One year later, I still have the job I was worried about losing, as well as the book I have dreamed of writing: my family's struggle with cancer and drug addiction.

I have expressed the idea of writing a book about our journey after mom received her grim diagnosis. When I asked her how she wanted to be remembered after she left this earth I was able to ask myself the same question. It was clear to me as to what my purpose is. I am here to help people and needed to tell our story in hopes that it would be medicine for others.

I compiled my family's journals and wrote in the morning with my furbaby, Bella, asleep on my feet. In the afternoon I did the heavy work of cleaning out my late Dad's office, chock full of memorabilia. When my husband and I moved into my childhood home, we were in such a rush to get things done; I simply put my parent's belongings into a room and shut the door. It was a place I could keep them, but didn't have to look at them until I was ready... and, ready or not, quarantine was the perfect time to go through the accumulation of both their lives. Not only was I grieving my "normal" life, I was also grieving my parents all over again.

Studying mom's journals wasn't easy. I cried knowing she had been in so much pain. During that time, I blocked a lot of it out. I was the caregiver and absolutely had to during that moment in our lives. Don't get me wrong; I wanted to feel, but the automatic reaction of letting my body go numb took over. I didn't have the luxury of feeling when I needed to be there for my parents and my sister. I had to be the rock. I didn't see any other way.

In this book, my mom's entries are all hers. I didn't change a thing.

Hayley allowed me to read the journals she kept when she was deep in her addiction. If there was a time when she didn't keep a journal, I interviewed her about what happened and how she felt. I would get choked up when I probed her because I had no idea she lived through such scary situations.

The stories she told me were surreal. I felt like she was describing scenes from a movie, not her life. Reading her journals has given me more empathy for all addicts. Her stories are raw and true. She has the least amount of entries, spread out because that's how it can be to have an addict in your life. They are in your life, they leave, and then come back again.

The first draft of this book was more methodical than emotional. I was a robot, just going through the motions. As I read my words out loud to my husband, he saw a need to inject more passion, more feeling, more me. When my parents died and my sister was struggling, I wouldn't let myself surrender to the pain. With his help, I was finally able to give in.

I hope our true story will be a salve on the soul of anyone who reads it. We all have scars, bruises and struggles. More often than not, we try to cover these up, but if anything, our pain and suffering are the bridge to helping others. I cross it now, and take your hand. Happy reading.

Table of Contents

2012

There are fairies at the bottom of our garden.

Night is full of unknown creatures.

I am awake, covers over my head.

Like a tent about to collapse.

September 18, 2012

It is a beautiful late summer morning. I am sitting on my deck remembering to appreciate my surroundings and that I'm starting to feel better compared to when I woke up. I wake up most mornings with a headache due to allergies and stomach cramps. I will make an appointment tomorrow with my doctor to figure out what is wrong. I realize I need to start taking care of myself no matter what happens.

Namaste, Jude

September 20, 2012

I am very worried about mom. She hasn't been feeling well the last couple days. She feels like she has the flu, but her belly is very swollen. She said it is bigger than ever and it is hard when she touches it. Very unusual. When mom saw her internist today her doctor said her symptoms are similar to cancer patients. She immediately made an appointment with an oncologist for next week. I really hope everything is okay.

XO, E

September 22, 2012

I had a superficial blood clot last week, ended up at the emergency room yet again. My stomach has been distended for a few weeks. I have severe gastro intestinal issues as well. Saw my internist last week. She suspects ovarian cancer, but will talk to an oncologist to determine the next step. I am not going to give in to the fear of it all. Five years ago I had melanoma and got through that fine.

I woke up early today filled with fear and dread. After meditating, reading O'Donahue and other authors I realize I do have a choice how to face the difficult situations in my life. I can choose courage and the necessity of taking care of myself spiritually and physically. I can do this. At least today!

Namaste, Jude

September 25, 2012

Off work today, which I am grateful for. Yesterday was difficult working, waiting for my internist to call with no news yet. I saw my therapist yesterday. He said I didn't have to be strong right now. He suggested leaving a time every day to grieve. Kind of nice that Hayley gave me this journal for Mother's Day. I have not seen her for almost 2 months. Is cancer a result of this loss? I wonder.

Mame had me over for dinner again. My stomach had heart burn, but went anyway. She can be so nurturing and caring. I told another friend, but she said how blessed she is- felt pity from her. Interesting what different people give me or don't. The most important thing is what I give myself. Freedom to let it all out, to bend like a tree in the wind. A message in meditation. "I'll always love you" from my mom. Having a cuppa with mom and grandma. So much of them around and in me. Remember to breathe, to live, go on until it's time to go home.

Namaste, Jude

September 26, 2012

The cancer doc is recommending surgery on Monday, Oct 1st. I was impressed with his thoroughness. He actually thought it might be colon cancer, but after looking at my records and talking to the surgeon who treated me for my blockage last fall, he decided it is ovarian cancer. He did a pelvic exam and could feel a thickening. Because of my symptoms, he feels it is advanced, and I will need to have whatever is cancerous removed, and then chemo.

I will be at the hospital for 3-5 days if they don't fiddle with my bowels. I am still in shock and terrified. Hopefully the next few days will give me the strength I need to get through all of this.

Namaste, Jude

September 26, 2012

Since Mom had her appointment with the oncologist today I made sure to keep my phone close by. When I heard the pitter patter of it vibrating on my desk a pit grew in my stomach. I knew it was her calling. I needed to know what the doctor found, but I was scared it could be worse than what we expected. Before I could even put the phone up to my ear I heard soft sobs on the other line. When I asked mom if she was okay she paused before telling me the doctor said she does have cancer. She isn't positive which type, but know it is advanced. Before they start chemo they are planning on removing the tumor that has taken over her stomach next week. She made it sound like it is curable, so I am trying not to worry too much yet. After I told her I loved her and hung up the phone I fell into my chair. How could this be happening? Since grandma died of breast cancer when she was young, mom has taken all of the right precautions to make sure she doesn't as well. She is one of the strongest people I know, so I am sure she will fight as hard as she can, but this will be an uphill battle and I will be with her every step of the way. My life will never be the same, no matter what the diagnosis is. I can either come out of this a better version of myself or let it destroy me. I am determined to not let it be the latter. I just hope Hayley feels the same and can find a way to be there for her too. Mom will need all of the support she can get.

XO, E

September 26, 2012

Mom called to tell me she has been diagnosed with cancer. I immediately started to cry and have a panic attack. I took a few Xanax hoping they would calm me down. Knowing the pills weren't going to work right away, I got into the shower to let the hot water wash over me. I sat in a ball and cried for at least an hour. I feel lost, helpless, and like I can't be there for mom in the state I am in. I don't know what to do. I knew a wakeup call was in the midst, but I didn't think it would hurt this much. Wishing and praying everything works out for the best. I love my mom so much.

-Hayz

October 1, 2012

Today was the day for mom's big surgery. Since her friends couldn't get the day off work, and Hayley didn't come I was alone in the waiting room. Her brothers really wanted to be there but live so far away they were unable to make it. Uncle John wrote me yesterday saying, "Please keep me posted on how your mom is doing by e-mail or phone. She called here yesterday and talked to Bonnie. Bonnie said your mom was crying and really concerned. I wrote to her today. Judi thinks the world of you, Erin! Love, UJ."

I brought a couple Vogue magazines with me to read, hoping they would help ease my nerves, but not even Anna Wintour and the carefully curated pages of coats for the upcoming season could get my mind off of mom. I am frightened. The doctor seems to think he will be able to remove the large tumor inhabiting her belly, but what if they find something else? What if the cancer has spread? What if it is terminal? I try to block the terrible thoughts by repeating positive mantras in my head. "I'm just stressed. She's fine! This too shall pass. They will discharge her like she went in for a paper cut." I tell myself that I don't know anything yet. For now, I am just a concerned daughter, who has taken the day off work and is sitting in the waiting room. But as the hours tick away in the drab room all I do is squirm, and continue to tease myself that I will read the stack of Vogue's in my lap.

Eventually, I am joined by one of mom's closest friends, Mame. She has been such an amazing friend to mom. It was comforting to have her wait with me, but she was unable to be with me when I really needed someone; when it was time to hear the surgeon's diagnosis. She gave me a big hug before I left to get the news. I followed the nurse down a cold, antiseptic hallway to a room where a handsome young doctor, who looked like he walked straight off the set of a soap opera, was waiting for me. He looked concerned and asked me to sit in one of the two chairs in front of his desk. When I sat down I couldn't help but think that Hayley should be in the empty chair next to me. I couldn't understand why she wasn't there on such an important day. Mom and I needed her. Once I got comfortable the doctor told me the cancer had spread too much to take it out and there was nothing he could do. My heart sank! None of us had any idea she was so sick. She was vomiting and her stomach was starting to swell, but other than that she felt fine. Her internist said there was a chance it could be cancer because her swollen belly (otherwise known as ascites) was a symptom, but no one had any idea that it was this bad! He continued to talk, but I wasn't listening to him. I just stared at him wild-eyed, not knowing what to think or feel. I snapped out of my trance when he asked me if I had any questions. I didn't know what to say, so all I said was thank you as I walked out of his office shaking. I felt like I was in a nightmare I couldn't wake up from. I wished dad or Mike was standing in the hallway with me. I needed someone to hold me and tell me everything was going to be okay, but no one was there. To keep from falling over I leaned against the stark white wall to process what I was just told, but couldn't. I didn't want it to be real.

As I walked to mom's room to wait for her to get out of surgery I thought about how I was going to share the bad news with everyone. She had made a list of people for me to call once she was out of surgery. We both thought I would be spreading good news, not that the cancer is too big for them to remove. It wasn't going to be easy, but I needed to figure it out soon. When I stepped into the room I was surprised to see two of mom's best friends, Mame and Carol. Tears started to come to my eyes as I divulged what the doctor had told me. We cried and held each other until mom came rolling in. She was very out of it from the anesthesia, but she was awake enough to ask me if they were able to remove the tumor. I held her hand and smiled. I wanted to be strong for both of us, but I couldn't help the overflow of tears. In a groggy voice, she asked why I was crying. I took a deep breath and told her I was happy to see her. In her state of mind, she wouldn't have understood anything I said to her, so I figured it was best to keep it simple.

Once the anesthetic began to wear off mom was laughing with her friends. I felt like this was a good time to excuse myself to start making the dreaded phone calls. Family was first. Uncle Phil and Aunt Becky are planning a trip to be with mom to help her after her procedure, so I thought I should let them know as soon as I could. When I told them the prognosis, they said they might cancel their trip, but I asked them not to because she was really excited about them coming. Their visit will give her something to look forward to.

I called Uncle John and Aunt Bonnie next. They were distraught to hear the news, and said they will come to visit as soon as they can. The other people on the list were her many, many close friends. Mame took over making phone calls, which I was grateful for. It started to get a bit overwhelming. I sat next to mom's bed while she held my hand and slowly drifted back to sleep.

Mom had a lot of visitors in the evening, so I took much needed break. Mike and I walked mom's pups, Sophie and Ossie around the block for a little outdoor therapy. It's hard to believe we have been together for 8 years! I know he wants to get married, but I hadn't felt the want to be someone's wife, until recently. Mom being so sick has made me realize life is short. Since I was feeling pretty vulnerable my emotions were on high, so I asked what seemed like the most important question on Earth. I took a deep breath and on exhale said "do you still want to get married?" His big brown eyes lit up as he said "Of course!" This may have been the first time I had brought it up. He has been so patient with me wanting to wait, but after seeing my mom so sick, and knowing there was a chance she wouldn't be around much longer, I knew I would want her at our wedding if we decided to tie the knot. And what a perfect thing to look forward to? Whether you have cancer or not.

XO, E

October 1, 2012

Mom's surgery is today, but I am not in the right state to be there to help her or my sister. I am stuck in a single wide trailer with 5 people who are like strangers and don't know what's best for me. I know my family is only 20 minutes away, but I feel like they are on a different planet, and I am unable to reach them. I am stuck with nowhere to go, with no one to turn to. I am scared.

-Hayz

October 3, 2012

Today was the first appointment we had with an oncologist. When mom sat down in my car, I could tell she was nervous by the way she was fidgeting with the leather handles on her handbag. We knew it was bad, but we didn't know the specifics. I placed my hand gently on hers and told her I am here for her no matter what he says. Mom and I are very optimistic, so I know we will able to find the light in whatever he has to say.

We only had to wait a few minutes until a young nurse called mom's name. She led us to a room where she took mom's vitals, and asked how she was feeling. Mom said, "Okay, just a little nervous." I was nervous as well, but since I am mom's rock I needed to stay calm for both of us. The nurse smiled and said she would let the doctor know we were there. A short 5 minutes later, an older man entered. He looked tired and near retirement. He was not very warm, which can be good and bad, but he could have been a little kinder when he uttered the scariest words I have ever heard anyone say, "You have stage 4 cancer and you only have a few months left to live. There is nothing we can do."

Mom and I were stunned. Of course, there is something they could do! There always is. He said she has about 9 months to live if she did chemo, but if she decided not to go ahead with chemo, she would most likely live for only 3 months. Mom started to cry, and I was angry. She squeezed my hand while I wondered how someone could be so insensitive? This is my mom's life! Maybe he has told so many people grim news; he has learned that it's best to just pull of the band aid as fast as you can.

I told him I wasn't taking his diagnosis for an answer. We were going to get a second opinion. As we walked out, tears rolled down mom's cheeks. She was visibly shaking and crying when we reached the car. I wanted to cry with her, but didn't feel like I could. Instead, I soothed her while trying to ease my anger over how we had just been treated. It took everything in me to hold back my tears, but I needed to be strong for her and not show how upset I was. At that time being strong was the only option I had. I wanted to do something that would make her happy, so I asked her if she we would like to go to lunch and talk about the options she has. She nodded yes as I pulled out of the parking lot to drive us to one of our favorite restaurants, Ruth's.

It was a gorgeous fall day and the patio was still open. As we relaxed under the golden leaves, in the beautiful surroundings of the mountains, we talked about what we were just told, and what we were going to do about it. Her spirits lifted when I told her I would start calling different doctors to see if they would take her insurance. There is a wonderful cancer institute in our own backyard: Huntsman. I told Mom that's the first place I'd call.

Lunch was wonderful and getting some Vitamin D really helped. As we drove down the canyon 'I Will Wait For You' by Mumford and Sons came on the radio. I rolled down the window to allow my hair to dance in the wind and breathe in the fresh mountain air moving throughout the car. It was a reminder to take one breath at a time. At that point I knew I would associate that song with this day forever.

I dropped mom off, went home, and immediately called the Huntsman Cancer Institute. The woman I spoke to was very sweet. She answered every question I had, assuring me that they took her insurance. Talking to her gave me hope.

XO, E

October 4, 2012

Quite a roller coaster ride the past few days. I am looking forward to the light at the end of the tunnel. The docs still don't know the origin of the cancer, so they cannot predict treatment or outcomes. I saw an oncologist yesterday. He gave Erin and I grim news that we refuse to let in.

I'm not in denial – just trying to stay positive. They want to do a colonoscopy next to determine if the cancer originated in the small bowel. I had a small bowel obstruction Nov. 2011, and I am really wondering if there was something wrong then. The docs seem to be trying to cover their butts. Water under the bridge at this point.

Namaste, Jude

October 4, 2012

I needed to go back to work today. Knowing Uncle Phil and Aunt Becky were going to be with mom made me feel more at ease, but I still couldn't stop thinking about her during my 45 minute commute.

When I walked into work and closed the door behind me a huge sigh came out of nowhere. It was a sigh of relief. Relief knowing that I wasn't going to be at the hospital or doctor's office today. Relief that I could step away from everything, hoping to digest all that was thrown at me the last couple days. I have been so busy I haven't had a chance to let it all sink in.

With the exception of a couple emails and a few people "just looking" I had the day to myself. I was able to sit with the idea that mom could pass in just a few short months. I kept reliving the moment when the doctor told us the upsetting news. It made me furious, but the fury turned to motivation. I am determined to find a place for her to heal. Not somewhere that is giving up on her before even knowing her. She is a warrior. My parents are the most important people in my life. I can't lose her and I am going to do everything I can to not let that happen. We are going to create a possibility that anything is possible. This isn't a death sentence. She is going to be a miracle story I will be able to tell people about to give them hope. We are not giving up.

XO, E

October 4, 2012

Nothing is more humbling than when you end up in a situation you never imagined yourself being in.

When you go from having everything to having nothing.

Thankful for my family and friends.

I hope you all will understand.

I'll be back to old self soon.

Can only go up from here.

-Hayz

October 5, 2012

My brother, Phil, and his wife Becky arrived yesterday to spend a few days with me. So nice to have them here. We are going to Snowbird on Saturday to spend the night in the mountains with Erin and her boyfriend, Mike.

I came home from the hospital on Tuesday. The doctors haven't diagnosed the origin of the cancer yet. I am having a colonoscopy this morning, one of many tests I have had the past few days. The cancer has spread throughout my abdomen. Saw an oncologist the other day, and he said it's not a good prognosis for a long life. Erin and I refuse to go that route. Call it denial, but we remain positive. I am making arrangements to go the Huntsman Cancer Center here in Salt Lake for treatment and support. Recently, I have not *been happy with the treatment and care I have received at the hospital I have been in. My friend, Margaret, works in the Cleveland Clinic. She is a nurse there and knows many of the docs. I have had my records sent there for the docs to look at as well. If I need to fly to Cleveland, I will. For sure, I will be doing some sort of chemotherapy, but until they know what type of cancer we are dealing with, they don't know what chemo to use.*

Erin is a dream daughter. She is with me every step of the way. Hayley is still missing in action. I just hope she is safe and well. She has not come to see me since all this has occurred. Not like her at all.

The past week has been a nightmare I just want to wake up from.

Namaste, Jude

October 7, 2012

It's safe to say that guilt and regret are two of the worse emotions. I'm coming for ya mom. Just give me a few more days. 2 days down. 2 more to go.

I'm sorry.

-Hayz

October 12, 2012

Feeling a little light-headed today for some reason. Went for a walk with the pups and my friend, Carol, this morning. Taking it easy at home the rest of the day. Feels good to be home alone. Phil and Becky left Tuesday. It was good medicine to have them here with me. We spent Saturday night at Snowbird in the mountains. Erin and Mike stayed with me in one room and my brother and sis in law stayed in another. We went for an early morning walk, rode the tram, and danced at the Oktoberfest. I managed to forget about cancer for 24 hours.

I went to the Huntsman Cancer Center to meet with a GI oncologist, Dr. Wilson. He admitted he does not know the origin of my cancer either, but he is presenting my case before a tumor board next week, and will do more pathology tests on the specimens the other doctors gathered last week. I felt he was scientific, but caring. He recommended placing a port in my chest to help administer the chemo. I told him I had not decided yet whether I will do chemo. I explained to him that as a cancer patient, I felt powerless in many ways. Making rational decisions about my treatment that is not fear based gives me a sense of control over my life. Dr. Wilson explained to me the pros and cons of chemo in extending my life. I opted to try it and see what happens. Will it shrink the tumors; enhance the quality of what life I have left? He said there is no expiration date stamped on my foot. I could have years to live.

It's funny; I have accepted I have a terminal illness. I am not afraid to die. I know love lives on. I know death is simply a transformation. Acceptance of what is brings me peace in the middle of the chaos and blind sidedness. I asked my doctor about seeing Leonard Cohen in California. His chemo philosophy is to not center your life around chemo. He said a few weeks would not make much of a difference.

Namaste, Jude

October 12, 2012

I joined mom at her first appointment with Dr. Wilson. His office is located at 2000 Circle of Hope Dr, otherwise known as the Huntsman Cancer Institute. I wondered if Dr. Wilson knew how much hope we were going to be pinning on him.

As we walked into Dr. Wilson's waiting room I heard my British born mum let out a giggle. She was excited to see a plastic statue of Queen Elizabeth waving to us from the receptionist's desk. Mom shimmied up to check in, and before saying her name she asked where she could find this fun toy that brought her so much joy on such a scary day. She and the receptionist instantly hit if off after talking about their British ancestry and their love for the royal family.

The volunteers at Hunstman have a way of making us feel pampered. They offer free valet service and we are given no end of food, drinks and magazines while we wait. It is a small gesture of kindness that helps make us both feel like we belong there. We instantly gave it the nickname, "Hotel Huntsman" because we feel like we are in a 5 star hotel, not a hospital. Dr. Wilson's nurse is also named Judy. Mom got a kick out of the fact that they shared the same first name and were close in age. Judy was the first person we met from Dr. Wilson's arsenal and the first person to know the singer Leonard Cohen was mom's "boyfriend." He isn't really, but the hope of being able to see him perform in California was helping keep mom alive. She is worried she won't be able to go because of cancer. Getting the okay to go was one of her top priorities of this first visit.

When Dr. Wilson came in I instantly felt at ease. He isn't intimidating like the other doctor we saw. He is approachable. He has a nice smile under his white mustache and he wore a crooked blue tie that made his eyes pop. He first asked how mom was feeling and told her that he doesn't think the cancer originated in her stomach because she would be a lot sicker if it did. He treated us like she wasn't going anywhere soon. She was free to book concerts and look forward to life. It is such a relief to know Dr. Wilson and Nurse Judy are here for us. They asked all of the right questions and are willing to seek the best answers. We finally got the hope we were looking for.

XO, E

October 13, 2012

I vacillate between periods of fright, anxiety, guilt, regret and despair. Erin has suddenly become so precious. Being with her is like being with happiness incarnate. Hayley is impossible to communicate with at this time. I can't allow myself to think about her even though my soul misses her like a part of me is missing. It's like I am without one of my limbs, trying to hobble about like a cripple. Somehow I have adjusted out of pure survival. I want to live. I choose to live.

Namaste, Jude

October 13, 2012

Mike asked me if there was something I wanted to do tonight. I am still so numb from everything I told him I needed to do something that would make me remember what it was like to feel an emotion. I decided going to a haunted house would be the perfect thing. He was a little hesitant in taking me because he knows I don't like to be scared on purpose, but the thought of having adrenaline move through my body excited me. We wandered through the Haunted Village with only the light of the moon and small, candlelit lanterns lighting the way. We entered old cabins from long ago where people dressed as old pioneers and ghosts would jump out at us. I know they weren't there to hurt us, but I wouldn't let go of Mike the entire time we were there. I was too scared. At one point, a masked man came up behind me and said boo in my ear. I screamed, "Oh shit," let go of Mike's arm, and ran out of the house. Mike was close behind me laughing. When I saw him, we both started laughing hysterically. It was just what I needed. I was able to forget about cancer and feel emotions I hadn't felt in a long time. I quickly went back to feeling numb, but it made me realize I won't feel this way forever.

XO, E

October 13, 2012

I WILL BE SOBER.

I will get sober. I will be sober. I will stay focused on my health. I will look within for motivation. I am doing this for myself. I will stay positive. I will only listen to constructive criticism. I will not give up. I will meditate. I will be honest with myself, my family, my friends and my doctors. I understand that I'm sick, and I need to take the proper remedies to get well again. I will surround myself with people that want the best for me. I will surround myself with positive, goal-oriented people. I will kill this demon inside of me. I will live in the present. I will find alternatives to help with my anxiety. I will love myself. I will understand. I will open my mind. I will not allow myself to be drowned in guilt. I will remind myself that I am only human.

I will be sober.

-Hayz

October 14, 2012

My friend sent me an email about love and healing. Holding Ossie today and feeling his love and my love for him makes me realize how tangible love is. Is there a way to infuse my body, soul with love? Infuse my body with love, dogs, friends, earth, ancestors and family?

No matter what happens, may peace be with me and all those who love and care about me. May those people around me not live in fear, but learn along with me the power and undying strength of love. It is the emotion, the power that gives us strength- food for the soul- sustenance. Survival food. Love in and love out. Love is breath, love is life. Life is love.

Namaste, Jude

October 14, 2012

My hair has started to fall out unexpectedly. I first realized it a month ago when it was noticeably thinner, and it has continued to fall out since. I went to the doctor yesterday where she took a few tests that will help us figure out what is going on. I received the results today, but everything is pretty normal. She told me I had a low white blood count, which was probably due to stress (duh) and advised me to start taking an iron supplement. I am trying to handle it all the best I can, but it has been tough to say the least. I have always internalized stress. So much so that I gave myself shingles when I was only 24!

After my shingles diagnosis I realized I needed to find ways to manage my stress. Being in nature, spending time with animals, working out and music are all things I have found to ease the side effects.

Cancer seems to have taken over our lives, so to feel a sense of normalcy, Mike and I went to do one of our favorite things, and one of my stress relievers, go to a concert with friends. I have always been enamored with music. It is the only language that everyone in the world can read. It can move us to tears, to love, to act, to create and affects us in ways that other art forms can't. Whether I am playing the piano or going to a live show, I get lost in the music. The notes melt my stress away, almost like magic. I have always had long blonde hair, so having it fall out has made me very self-conscious. Since I have no idea how to style it at this point I pulled it up into a low ponytail hoping no one would say anything. No one mentioned my hair, but our friend, Tim could tell my mind was somewhere else. His dad recently won a battle with cancer, so when he asked if I was okay I felt like it was safe to tell him the news I had received about mom. He took the time to talk to me and told me he was there if I needed anything. His warmth and support made me realize that my friends want to be there for me. Cancer is scary, but the journey is going to be easier with friends by my side.

XO, E

October 14, 2012

Dad,

After thinking everything through, I have allowed my anxiety to get the best of me. I keep replaying the scenario of getting sober in an unfamiliar place. I've decided to take matters in my own hands. I am going to get sober with a friend, doing something called the Thomas Recipe. I am so disappointed in myself that I don't want you to have to pay anymore. I plan on doing the Thomas Recipe, then following up with therapy afterwards. I know how bad this looks, but I PROMISE I

WILL BE BACK BY WEDNESDAY, at the latest. I will keep in touch, and the next time you see me, I will be sober. I love you. I promise I won't let you down again, Dad. Please keep an eye on my car. I have a plan to eventually pay that baby off!

Also, please tell mom not to worry. With the cancer scare, I'm not going anywhere; I'll be right by her side. PLEASE just allow me these 4 days, and I'll be back to normal. I love you, and I will keep in touch.

-Hayz

October 15, 2012

I am a little out of it after spending the morning having a port placed under my skin above my right breast for chemo. They gave me a valium type drug intravenously for the operation. During the procedure, I asked for more "happy juice."

Hayley is still missing as far as communication and not seeing her is making me concerned. I am kind of numb regarding her. I don't have the energy to go there at the moment.

The Huntsman Cancer Center has turned out to be a blessing. The GI oncologist I met with last week offered more hope than the doctor I saw initially. I will start chemo in November after I go to LA to see Leonard Cohen. My doc said a few weeks won't make a difference as far as chemo is concerned, and the trip will offer good mojo. They still don't know the original tumor site. At least they admit they didn't know. My doc is going to put my case before a tumor board tomorrow, which is a panel of other docs, radiologists, pathologists and oncology nurses, to get their opinion about where the cancer originated. The type of chemo they give me is somewhat determined by the tumor site. I feel the center is more scientific but caring in a humanistic sort of way.

All in all, I am doing well. My friends have become a small army helping to bolster my spirits and keep me fed. My friend drove me to the hospital today and took me home. He is an earth angel to me. I'm amazed he is still with me as we have only known each other since July of this year. Erin is fiercely positive and always with me at doctor's appts.

Namaste, Jude

October 17, 2012

Mom has continued to work through all of this, which has been a good distraction. She loves her job, her patients, and the dentists she works for adore her. The tumor panel met yesterday, and decided mom has stomach cancer/gastric cancer. We saw the oncologist today at Huntsman to chat more about treatment. They asked us to come early so they could do some labs, where mom and Jamie (the lab nurse) had a great time.

Jaime said she loves working with people, and mom said that is one reason why she wanted to be a hygienist. At one point, Jamie said how hard it is to find veins. When she's at the gym she even looks at people's veins to see if she could poke into them. Mom asked her if that hurts her dating life, and she told us a story about when she was cuddling with a guy who had bulging veins. She couldn't stop touching them. He was very surprised and asked her what she was doing. We had a lot of laughs with Jamie – so much in fact, another nurse walked in, asking "where's all of the love?"

After labs, we went to the doc and chatted with Dr. Wilson's assistant, Dr. Sam about the diagnosis and chemo. Mom said she didn't want to know the statistics on how long she had to live. She only wanted to hear about what chemo cocktails would help. He said they have three options to choose from. One is more toxic than the others, but the ones that are not as toxic give her a better chance of living longer. Dr. Sam told us patients on chemo live about 13 months longer than those who opt out. It all depends on how the cancer responds to chemo and the person.

Dr. Wilson walked in as we were finishing up with Dr. Sam. He waited patiently by the door for him to finish. He is mom's main doctor, but does not let his ego get the best of him. He is a very kind and gentle man.

He told us most people who have a gastric cancer do not live past three-six months without being treated. He added Mom's cancer seemed unusual because they think she has had it for quite a while. Mom begged him for miracle stories about patients living with gastric cancer. I piped in and said, "you already are one" as Dr. Wilson smiled.

Although the doctors have told us this is incurable, I am going to stay positive because I know mom can make it through this. Also, I'm just not ready for mom to leave. I know Hayley needs her too. She can't go yet. I am going to help her fight. I know how much it hurt her when grandma died of breast cancer at such an early age. She misses her terribly. She told me she doesn't want Hayley and I to feel the same pain she has by not having our mom in our adult life.

XO, E

October 19, 2012

Looking forward to seeing my brother-in-law Bill next week. He emailed me after talking to my ex, Mike, and said he had been thinking about me. He even rearranged his scheduled so he could make a stop to check on me and visit with family. I went to a birthday party for one of my niece's daughters last Sunday. So wonderful to be with family. The girls are growing up so fast!

The doctor told me last week the primary tumor is gastric cancer, stage 4. Not great news, but at least we know what chemo cocktail they can give me. I have surprisingly little pain at the moment. It is almost surreal knowing I have cancer, I'm not feeling poorly. I am grateful for that. Not looking forward to chemo, but I know I can have extra time if I do it. My sister- in-law, Marcia, is a great cancer mentor, considering they gave her a terminal diagnosis and she is alive and well. My spiritual practice of meditation and mindfulness has served me well during this and Hayley's situation. She is still missing in action. We heard from her the other day through a text message. At least I know she is alive.

All in all, I have accepted the cancer diagnosis.

Namaste, Jude

October 20, 2012

I woke up early to run errands; one of them was to talk with my hair stylist, Shane. Tears welled up as soon as I saw him. I hadn't told him about mom yet. Honestly, it's so still fresh I find it hard to tell people I know who care about me.

Shane checked my hair and when he confirmed it was indeed falling out the tears started to travel down my cheeks. He gave me a big hug and recommended a special kind of shampoo and conditioner to help. I felt a little better after talking to him, but also scared. I had no idea the stress of my mom was affecting me so much that my hair would fall out! He said I needed it to grow back healthy, and the only way to do that was to not do much to it, so no blow drying or curling at all. I have always had long beautiful blonde hair and have taken such good care of it. For it to fall out is traumatizing, but I am trying to see it as a sign that I need to take better care of myself. I have let mom's diagnosis and the absence of my sister get the best of me. I really need to find more ways to relieve the pressure. So, I decided to meet Mike at a U of U football game.

We love college football and go to as many games as we can. Since Mike was partying with his friends at the tailgate lot I waited for him outside the gates. I wasn't in the mood to party. After getting confirmation my hair was indeed falling out, combined with my mom's health, I probably looked like the saddest girl in the world. I felt like everyone who walked past was staring at me, wanting to ask if I was okay. My long hair has always been something I could hide behind. It was like a piece of armor that protected me from the stares, but I no longer had it. I felt more vulnerable than I ever had and started to think going to the game wasn't the best idea. I should be home. After waiting for what seemed like hours I heard Mike call my name. He was with a friend who lost his mom to cancer at a young age. He was very sweet and understanding, but I didn't want to be around friends right now, even if they do understand.

For the most part the game was a good distraction, but Mike continued to get drunk with his friend. Even though I was in a crowd with thousands of people I felt so alone. This is a unique time in our lives, and I really need him. I know he doesn't know what I am going through, and he isn't trying to hurt me on purpose. I am sure needs a break from cancer as well, but I need him to understand that I don't get to have that option.

XO, E

October 22, 2012

The past few days have been tough ones. Even though I am happy to be back at work I cried on my way in today. My coworkers were very supportive. They know someone who is a narc. We have the information that he needs to hopefully bust Hayley's boyfriend, Grant. Hayley texted me today to tell me a check is coming to my house from her last job for her. Her dad and I will see a drug counselor /interventionist Friday afternoon. I hope this helps.

Erin leaves for California soon. I will miss her. She is pissed about Hayley more than anything. I understand.

I spoke with my friend Mary today and invited her to come this weekend for the local Street Fair. I invited Brenda too. She will soon be out of unemployment, so I asked her if she wanted to paint my garage. Probably pay her hourly.

I am very tired tonight after the emotional roller coaster of the day. I will start going to the gym again starting tomorrow.

Namaste, Jude

October 25, 2012

I think I am grieving many losses. I received a text from Hayley yesterday. She said she is so scared and will come home soon. I cried after reading it.

Sent her a text saying how much I miss her, love her, and want her to come home. No answer back. It is almost easier not to hear from her. I need to put her on the shelf again. So little control over my life. "Eternal protection" according to John O 'Donahue.

Sun is shining this morning, snow on the ground. Feels cozy in my house with the dogs. Breathe.

I feel close to spirit these days. My mom visits often. I have much support spiritually, and from my friends. Breathe.

The candlelight, sunlight bumped me.

Namaste, Jude

October 28, 2012

I had two nice days off work. Bill visited, took me to lunch, and we walked around the new Natural History Museum. He was so much more open to me about his life in New York and his relationship with Don. One of the gifts of cancer is the realization that connection is vital to relationships that matter. Mitch came over that night. He recounted some war stories and teared up talking about his platoon mates who passed while in combat with him. I love his tenderness, and ability to be open and intimate with me. I feel so blessed to have him in my life. Yesterday, Carol went with me to Huntsman for a cat scan. I was expecting a long drawn out procedure. It turned out to be less than ten minutes. Yea! Carol and I walked around the park with the pups. I love being with Carol. I never tire of our banter and laughs together.

I feel hope and warmth. My dogs. Me personification of love.

Inner belonging and shelter of the soul.

Later on, I raked crab apples and spoke with my neighbor. He offered to help me, but true to my nature I finished myself. Peg M. came to deliver soup to me. My favorite, pumpkin soup! She stayed for an hour or so to talk. Another friend I love to be with.

Hayley text me last night, "What are your plans tomorrow?" I responded "Why?" Mike, her dad, said he got a similar text and didn't want to give me false hope.

Big breath. Mame and her friend are picking me up at 3 PM to go to the museum and to have dinner. Be nice to get to know her friend better. He is good for her. Sun is starting to shine. Pups seem tired. So grateful for:

No pain from cancer, except for my bladder, and that seems manageable.

My faith in the afterlife. Divine love and all that is.

The flexibility my bosses have shown me to work when I can.

Erin – She is a light for me on this journey- Michael too.

Huntsman – A cancer home. Place of healing. I feel good there.

My house – A safe warm haven.

Pups-Smiles – reason to live and love.

My dad – Symbol of strength and resilience and support.

Namaste, Jude

October 28, 2012

Mike and I went to California the weekend before Halloween. The day we arrived, we immediately went to Wayfarers chapel, thinking it will be a good place to get married. We aren't engaged yet, but decided to start looking at venues in case we need to rush the wedding date. We don't know how long mom has and we both want her to be at the wedding.

The drive to the chapel was gorgeous. There were huge trees to the left of us and the Pacific Ocean to the right. When I stared at the otherworldly ocean I was reminded of how I am only a small part of this big world. Watching the waves come and go on their own made me realize that nature doesn't have anything controlling it. I don't have to ask the sun rise or to set. It happens by itself. I need to remember that I can't control my life and I need to be grateful of this precious life, and all its opportunities.

I could feel my heart beat faster when the sweet voice of the woman directing us where to go on Mike's phone told us to turn left in 500 feet. I have seen pictures of the chapel, but this was the first time I was going to see it in person. I gasped when we pulled in. The chapel is more beautiful than I could imagine. It is a glass chapel designed by Frank Llyod Wright's son, Lloyd Wright. The glass, wood and stone chapel is nestled in a grove of Redwood trees. They are living walls and roof to a natural sanctuary encased in glass with view of the surrounding forest and nearby ocean. As we walked up to the front doors I started to get teary eyed. I had no idea I was going to be this emotional, so I grabbed Mike's hand before stepping inside. As I walked into the chapel a wave of electricity came through me and the tears in my eyes started to roll down my cheeks. I felt at peace there. Mike hugged me when he noticed me gently wiping the tears from underneath my eyes. While we stood there, holding one another I visualized walking down the aisle towards Mike with our loved ones in the pews. This is the place. The perfect place to get married.

XO, E

October 29, 2012

Worked yesterday. Felt good to be regarded as not someone with cancer, but as a dental hygienist. My bosses are very supportive and kind with me. I am grateful they are allowing me the freedom to work when I can. Went for a walk with my good friend, Carol around the park. So good to laugh and cry with her. Erin and Mike popped over on their way to the store. Erin looked tired. Mike is a gem. I love being with both of them.

Hayley is still estranged from us. It has gotten worse instead of better. Her dad is suffering, but remains on the same page as me. We help hold each other up. We spoke to the drug interventionist yesterday and he was able to give us some good advice. He made me realize I have been in denial about Hayley and her illness. The reality of her car being repossessed has made me understand the gravity of the situation. She is self destructing and there is nothing we can do about it.

I went to an Alinon meeting last night at the recommendation of a friend. I am so glad I went. It was pretty low key, but supportive. At least I have some tools to help me survive, and perhaps in doing so, I can help Hayley.

I lashed out at Hayley last week when she called us to tell us her car would be repossessed. My anger will not make things better. It only serves to make her feel worse about herself. I acknowledge that anger though. I have to. The grief, disappointment, fear, anxiety, anger are all with me now. Hopefully I can let them go, at least for today.

Namaste, Jude

October 29, 2012

I just got back from CA yesterday, and to my surprise Hayley came home!!! Her car has been repossessed because she wasn't making the payments on it. We hadn't seen her for a while, so we were happy when she showed up to carve pumpkins with us. I love when she is home!

Mom's doctor wanted to check her out before she went to CA herself. He said her lymph nodes look okay, and she is well enough to go. He also said there is something that keeps popping up on her lab results, which makes him think it could be ovarian cancer. This would be easier to treat.

He has been trying to get in touch with the doctors at the other hospital, but of course, they have not returned his calls. While we were there, we learned of a mix up with some of mom's samples. Dr. Wilson came to the rescue, ensuring all Mom's docs could work with her pathologist.

Dr. Wilson told mom he is worried about her, and he wants to do all he can to get her better. He is so caring. Since this was Hayley's first doctor visit, he filled her in on what was going on. She seemed to handle everything very well.

Mom doesn't want to know how long they think she has to live, but he whispered to Hayley 9-12 months without chemo. I am glad Hayley could come, but I can't help but feel a little resentment towards her. I know she is sick, but we all need her support, especially mom. I hope that her being there today will help her realize how much her presence helps all of us. We should know the pathology results before she starts chemo. Crossing my fingers that it's ovarian.

XO, E

October 29, 2012

Finally, home.

-Hayz

October 31, 2012

Today is Halloween! Hayley came to Park City with mom and the pups to hand out candy with Mike and I. Since we get about 2,000 trick or treaters at my work every year I need all of the help I can get. Kids of all ages run up and down Main Street to fill their bags with candy. Mike puts on a wolf mask while he helps me pass out candy. It is great to see kid's reactions when they walk up. Some are scared, but the majority of them think it's really cool. Mom was all smiles. Even though she is a dental hygienist, and prefers to give out toothbrushes instead of candy at her house she loves to help us pass out the sugary treats. We try to give only one piece of candy to each trick or treater because if we don't we run out of candy quickly, but mom likes to give at least three. She can't help it. She really enjoys seeing the kids so happy. We don't get many trick or treaters at our houses anymore, so it is a chance for us to see the creative costumes and hand out candy. It was Hayley's first sober Halloween in years!!!

XO, E

November 1, 2012

Beautiful afternoon here in SLC. Blue sky, snow dusting the mountain peaks, trees becoming bare but still beautiful. I drove home yesterday after helping Erin pass out candy to children trick or treating up and down Park City Main Street. She had 1400 pieces of candy this year. We passed it all out with the help of her husband dressed up as the big bad wolf. Several small children will need therapy in future I am sure. It was dusk as I was driving home. The Quaking Aspen took on an ethereal, silvery glow. Their white trunks glistened against the back drop of the darkness. I almost drove off the side of the road because of the luminous beauty of it all.

I have my kitchen door open even though the temp is only 55 degrees. My house is full of light most of the time. Especially at this moment. Big sigh. My shoulder continues to bother me. I went to an acupuncturist, chiropractor and a massage therapist all within the past week. The only thing that gives me relief is 800mg Motrin. I guess I will sacrifice my stomach to live pain free. I am grateful for all of the rest.

About to take the dogs for a walk. I was holding Oz the other day. Could feel his little heart pounding away. I think we were dog buddies in a previous life.

Hayley came home Sunday night. She is starting therapy today. So good to know she is safe. We are both so vulnerable right now. Many similarities in both of our life paths at the moment. Let the healing commence.

Namaste, Jude

November 1, 2012

Well, here goes nothing. Wish me luck!

-Hayz

November 4, 2012

I've said it once before, and I'll say it again.

Nothing is more humbling and eye opening than going from having everything you need to losing almost everything.

I am so grateful for all of my amazing friends and family for sticking by my side through these past couple of years, when I haven't been the best person and treated them with mutual respect.

One step back, 10 steps forward.

Ready to do this.

-Hayz

November 6, 2012

Leonard performed for 3 1/2 hours last night. He is an amazing performer for someone 78 years old. He wore a fedora most of the time except when his band would perform solos. He would then take his hat off, hold it in front of his chest as in homage them. So much grace. I remembered the name of the song I like so well. It is called "Anthem."

Finally home after a long day of flying. Listening to the election results with apprehension. Still not sure who is ahead. I start my first round of chemo tomorrow. The thought of poison infusing through my body is a surreal one. I need to concentrate on being positive. Just scared at the moment.

Hayley came home intent on recovery. She said she wanted one last fling. I hope she realizes the impact her flings have on me, and especially her father.

Namaste, Jude

November 6, 2012

Tomorrow is mom's first chemo appt. It sounds like she had an amazing time in CA. She said it was just what she needed before chemo starts. Hayley stayed home Sunday-Friday, but then tricked dad on Friday by saying she was spending time with her best friend, Celine. To be safe, Dad escorted her to the corner of the street before watching her walk towards her friend's house. When it started to get late he called her to make sure she was okay. Hayley surprisingly answered, and said she was having a great time being sober with her girlfriends. About an hour later, she sent a text telling him she was sleeping at a different friend's house, and would be home tomorrow. Everything seemed fine. She was acting like her normal self, until dad tried her in the morning.

She didn't answer the few times he called, so he asked me to call Celine to see where they were. Celine told me she hadn't seen Hayley, and she isn't going to lie for her. I relayed the message to dad. He was incredibly upset. I really hate being in the middle of all of this. I was Hayley's age not too long ago. She deserves to have fun, but I also want her to be safe. I know she is experimenting with drugs. I just don't know how much. After I went away to school a few years ago she stopped confiding in me. I have turned into more of a parent rather than a big sister. I decided to try calling her myself, hoping she would start to trust me again. After 5 long rings I heard a drawn out voice say, "hello" on the other line. She told me she had just woken up, and that she would call me back. I told her okay, but didn't hold my breath. I knew she wasn't going to call and nor did she come home that night. Dad was worried sick. He couldn't sleep.

Neither he nor I tried calling her Sunday. We figured there was no point. Dad seemed upset, so I asked him if he would like to go on a walk together to try to get his mind off of things. I cherish my walks with dad. We have taken them together ever since I was a little girl. Even though I have gotten older, we make sure to carve at least one hour out of the week for a stroll around the block, or in the mountains. It is a chance for us to appreciate nature without the distractions of our phones. Today the trees were showing off their fall colors. The leaves, dressed in their November gold's and rusts floated down from the limbs as we passed. For just a moment we were able to stop thinking about the drug that makes Hayley run away from the people she loves the most. But, we were reminded of it when we arrived home because she still wasn't there.

As it was getting dark I saw headlights pull into the driveway, and heard the sound of a car door softly close. It was Hayley! She had finally come home. I overheard her telling dad that a friend picked her up down the street. She never did go to Celine's house. Her friend gave her free drugs so she could have one last "hoorah." Whatever that means.

I don't think I will ever understand. She hurts our parents so much when she does this. Since she finally came home, I thought she could feed mom's dogs while I was at work. She hadn't been around all weekend, and I needed help. When I brought it up she said she couldn't do anything because she had to get in the shower, and then go out to dinner with friends. I felt so hurt. Why can't she help? I held it together while I was at work, but when I felt the privacy behind the tinted windows on my car I burst into tears. I was crying because I was exhausted, because I missed Mike, because my mom was sick, and because I felt resentment towards my sister. I needed a hug.

XO, E

November 7, 2012

I've grown more in the past 2 weeks than I have in the past 2 years. Movin.on.up.

-Hayz

November 8, 2012

Yesterday was mom's first day of chemo. Since Mike has been busy with meetings on his business trip we haven't been able to talk often, so it was nice to receive a text from him wishing us the best. Dr. Wilson filled us in on what the plan was for the day. He said they are going to go ahead and do chemo for gastric cancer and that mom is Hep 2 positive, so they can do the TOGA recipe. This is the least toxic off all of them, and it combines Hep 2, Cisplatin, and 5FU. She takes the 5FU home with her, keeps it in a bag for about 120 hours before a nurse will come to her house on Monday to disconnect her. We will get the pathology reports back on Friday to see if it could be ovarian cancer. Keeping our fingers crossed that it is.

We arrived to the infusion area about 12:00. It is a large curved room with big windows overlooking the valley. Lauren was mom's nurse today. Once mom was hooked up, Hayley and I went to the cafeteria to grab lunch, but before we could get too far a nurse stopped us to tell us one of her patients, Sylvie asked to speak to us. Of course, we said yes and the nurse led us to her where she was sitting. When we sat down Sylvie asked if we would tell her what makeup we use. She told us that she loved to get done up when she was younger, but now she is sick she doesn't have much motivation to get ready anymore. It broke my heart to hear such a beautiful woman, inside and out feel this way. When I asked her if we could do her makeup the next time she was there her eyes lit up. To my surprise, she reached inside her big brown bag to pull out a small makeup kit. Her collection consisted of a palette of blue eye shadows, a peach blush and a hot pink lipstick. Hayley and I took turns putting on the bright colors while she shared her passion for dance and told us about her late husband, who was the love of her life. We visited with her until the nurses came to take her to her next appointment. As we walked away, Hayley and I talked about forming a program to help cancer patients feel better about their appearance while they are going through chemo. So many patients experience hair loss and weight fluctuation they don't recognize themselves anymore. They have turned into a stranger. We mentioned it to nurse Lauren, and she said there is a program called "Look Good, Feel Good." She said it really helps a lot of people regain their confidence while battling the disease.

When we returned from talking to Sylvie, Lauren changed mom's chemo bags. She had to wait for the pharmacy to get all of the bags ready, so she could pump mom full of anti-nausea fluids when they were done. Hopefully the meds will make it so mom won't have many problems once she returns home.

Brandon, a volunteer, came around to make sure everyone was comfortable. When mom noticed the blue bracelet around his wrist she didn't hesitate in asking what it stood for. He smiled and gently placed his hands on mom's as he told us about his partner of 25 years passing from colon cancer. The angels came to take him away three years ago. The bracelet was from a foundation that was formed by parents who lost their 24-year-old son to colon cancer. After hearing Brandon's story and speaking with Sylvie I began to realize how many people cancer affects. It doesn't discriminate. I knew it was one of the leading causes of death in the US, but I didn't realize the toll it takes on patients and families until now. Tears welled up in my eyes as I looked around the room to see people from different backgrounds, race, gender and sexuality being infused with the poison they hoped to save their life. There are so many people who could use support. I really want do more to help others who are fighting, but right now I need to concentrate on being there for mom.

After Brandon gave mom a big hug and said goodbye we turned Ellen on the TV. We laughed so loudly a gentleman who was sitting in front of us asked the nurse why mom was at the hospital. He said there was no way she could be so sick because she was having too much fun. Mom blushed when the nurse told her, and said she was sorry, but the nurse insisted that it was a good thing. The man appreciated hearing laughter. Even during one of the scariest times of her life, mom's infectious laugh makes people smile. It was a reminder that life is to be lived with joy, not overtaken by fear.

Pretty soon, Carol stopped by to be with mom. I am so happy mom has a friend like Carol. She is like a sister and makes her laugh, which is just what we need. Since Carol was there I went home to walk our family dog, Lucy. It was a beautiful, fall day. To have the opportunity to kick through the collage of red, orange, and yellow leaves, hearing them crunch beneath my feet was therapeutic. Doing something I loved to do when I was child filled me with joy, even though the chill in the air reminded me that winter was on the horizon.

I got home, worked out quickly and ate a snack. There was so much going on I had forgotten to eat most of the day. I needed food! I talked to dad for a bit before picking up Hayley to take her to group therapy. We got there a little early, so I called my friend, Ali.

Ali works in the same building as Hayley's therapy. She and I have been friends since elementary school. She lost her dad at a young age and since she is a therapist she understands addiction. We were greeted with a big hug when she saw us and she immediately asked what type of flowers were mom's favorite. My mind was still preoccupied with everything going on, so I didn't think anything of it. I told her mom loves many kinds of flowers, but tulips are one of her favorites. It was nice to be able to take a break and talk to a good friend for a bit.

I got back to mom about 6:15. The infusion room was nearly empty, but we had to stay for another 2 hours. We were waiting on someone to show us how to do the at home chemo. We waited and waited, but the nurse never came. Luckily, another nurse was able to figure it out. While mom was getting hooked up to her 5FU, I left so I could get her prescriptions filled. On my way home, I was on the verge of crying. I felt so overwhelmed. I am working 6 days this week and my only day off was spent at the hospital. I am grateful I could spend the day with mom, but I am incredibly exhausted, both physically and mentally. I really hope I can do this.

After talking to dad I ran to the grocery store to get mom's prescription, water, ginger ale, cleaning supplies, etc. Tina was my checker. When she saw what I was buying she asked if someone was sick. She has become a friend to us, so I told her mom's first day of chemo was today. She got tears in her eyes when she said, "you are such a wonderful daughter. Please give your mom a big hug for me" and walked around to give me a squeeze. I don't dread going to the store because of people like Tina.

Meanwhile, Mom decided it would be a good idea to smoke a little weed. It is supposed to help with the side effects of the chemo, so when I got to her house she was as high as a kite. When I opened the fridge I noticed a glass vase with orange tulips on the kitchen table. Ali had dropped them off on her way home from work. She knew mom was going to be feeling pretty lousy these next couple days and thought something colorful would make her feel better. Very sweet of her to think of us. I am grateful to have a friend like Ali.

I finally went home about 9:45, showered, fell into bed and quickly went to sleep.

XO, E

November 9, 2012

Felt more nausea yesterday, but still feeling queasy and have a headache. Ate 1/2 banana and a boiled egg for breakfast and drank 32 oz of water in the past four hours. Called the doctor on call because I felt so lousy. He recommended I take Zofran three times a day, but I find pot and my anti-nausea meds are the best combo for nausea. Feeling emotional, but otherwise good considering. Took a nap and woke up to snow when a Reiki practitioner friend of Hayley's came over. After she left I was surprised by a bouquet of flowers and cards from the goddesses. I started to feel much better.

My friends have rallied like an army ready to do battle. I am moved to tears at their caring, attention and to my needs; emotional and physical. I have never been so aware of such love. For the past 10 years since my divorce I have been looking for romantic love in a man. It's funny, but this illness has made me realize how much love was always around me. Romantic love seems shallow compared to the love people have shown me the past month or so.

Namaste, Jude

November 11, 2012

The at home chemo has made mom feel very sick. The bag makes it hard for her to carry around. When I tried to find a bag online I couldn't find anything that would work, so I decided to make her one. Since she wanted something she can wear across her body it needed to be comfortable. I went to the fabric store to buy soft fleece in her favorite color, turquoise and hand sewed a bag for her to use. It isn't the prettiest bag, but it is made with love and will do the job. I gave it to her today, and she put it on right away. She loves it!

XO, E

November 12, 2012

I am sitting at my kitchen table with orange tulips in the foreground.

Outside there is at least six inches of snow, and more coming down. I bought a cheap laptop before my chemo experience. Seems to be working fine.

So far this has been my worst day as far as the nausea and vomiting are concerned. This is such a strange journey. I'm still trying to navigate it. Hayley has been staying with me 24/7. She told me I am her motivation to get well. I told her she is mine.

I did get one bit of positive news on Wednesday. Turns out I have Hercetpin receptors in my cells which allows me to take Herceptin, an antibody type drug that has been proven to prolong the life of gastric cancer patients. What was a terminal illness can become chronic one. Sounds good to me.

I sometimes think I lack the courage energy to take this journey. Tough day today. I get so emotional.

Namaste, Jude

November 17, 2012

I've lived the fast life.

Time to take it slow.

-Hayz

November 18, 2012

I am tired tonight but had a good day. Hayley has been staying with me most nights. She sleeps in what was once her bedroom, and now is my office. Tonight, she is at her dad's for dinner.

My oncologist called me Friday morning to tell me one of the recent pathology test results showed that the tumor of origin may be breast cancer. It could possibly mean better treatment options and survival.

Namaste, Jude

November 21, 2012

> *"An insincere and evil friend is more to be feared than a wild beast; a wild beast may wound your body, but an evil friend will wound your mind."*
>
> *-Buddha*

I want to pay thanks to my family and friends who gave me a second chance and continue to have faith in me. So grateful to be home and actually be present this Thanksgiving. Honestly.

-Hayz

November 28, 2012

Getting ready for my 2nd round of chemo today. The daughters are picking me up in less than an hour. Feeling a lot of apprehension about this. I am wrestling with the grim diagnosis I was given, and the idea of allowing poison to enter my body again. Fear is taking over. I have so much support, but I am afraid of what I have to face. Will I be strong enough? Will those I love suffer too? I am grieving. For the lost time with those I love.

Big breath. Trying so hard to be courageous and positive. One step in front of the other. One day at a time. Have to look at how precious the time is I have left. Feel, smell, taste every bit of it. I am alive right now at this very moment.

LIVE, LIVE, LIVE.

Namaste, Jude

November 28, 2012

Today was mom's second chemo infusion. I know she was a little apprehensive after the first one made her feel so lousy, but I am grateful she is willing to go. Hayley and I picked mom up together. We met with Dr. Wilson, who told us her tumor markers are already going down since the last treatment. Hearing this made me even more hopeful that mom will be able to beat the cancer living inside her. The cancer we were told only three months ago was going to kill her. Since the regimen seems to be working they are going ahead with the same chemo cocktail. Even though the stomach isn't the place of origin, Dr. Wilson is still treating it as stomach cancer because of the large tumor still taking residency there. I trust him, and I know mom does too.

The infusion room was just a beautiful as the last time we were there. I feel lucky mom is able to get care at such a wonderful place. After an hour or so, Angela, mom's social worker came to visit us. When Mom met her a few weeks ago, they really hit it off. Angela instantly became one of mom's biggest support systems. She listens to mom and is able to answer a lot of her questions the doctors can't. At one point, Angela asked how I was doing. I felt relieved to have someone acknowledge, and understand my situation without me having to explain it. Of course, mom is the one who needs to be tended to, but being the main caregiver has been very hard. It took everything in me to stop myself from bawling. I wanted to cry, and tell her I was stressed, exhausted, and resented Hayley for not doing more. But, I held back. I didn't want to make mom or my sister feel like they are a burden. It is not mom's fault she has cancer. I didn't want her to see how much her being sick has affected me. She is already worried about me because my hair is falling out. I don't want her to worry more. My dad is my rock, and Mike has been there the best way he knows how, but no one has really asked me how I was until today.

XO, E

November 28, 2012

> *"Character is like a tree and reputation like a shadow. The shadow is what we think of it; the tree is the real thing."*
> **-Abraham Lincoln**

Something to think about.

Round two chemo infusion today. Spending all day at Huntsman. Wouldn't wanna be anywhere else.

Eff you cancer.

-Hayz

December 10, 2012

I felt like mom could use some pampering, so I suggested we have a mommy daughter spa day. We sat down in the comfortable massage chairs, allowing them to attempt to knead our stress away. Mom laughed with the pedicurist who was close to her age. They had a lot in common, but when she lamented to us about getting older tears came to mom's eyes. She told her, "not everyone gets the chance to grow old. Aging is a gift denied by many. We need to give thanks for every year we complete." The woman stopped painting mom's toes with the bright pink polish and looked at the floor. When she raised her head I saw a puzzled expression on her face. It was like she had never thought about being grateful for the ability to become older.

We didn't say much the remainder of the appointment, nor did mom mention her life was most likely going to be cut short because of cancer, but she didn't need to. I think her comment helped this woman realize life is fleeting and she needs to be thankful for every moment. If it didn't resonate with her, I know it did with me. We need to be lucky for the opportunity to be here and have the ability to enjoy it. Getting older should be a source of happiness. Every day signifies thousands of minutes of new adventures. Every second gives us the chance to be present and share moments with others. We need to look forward to living our life instead of dreading the wrinkles that are going to appear on our faces. After all, they are just a beautiful reflection of age, formed by the smiles we have made throughout our lifetime.

XO, E

December 10, 2012

"When it rains, it pours."

This statement is exactly how my life is at the moment. Good thing, I love the rain.

And I have an umbrella.

Oh life, you silly bitch.

Bring it on.

-Hayz

December 12, 2012

How the hell am I supposed to do this?

Sad face

-Hayz

December 16, 2012

Today was our annual baking day. Grandma taught mom how to bake, and mom passed her passion for baking onto me. We have made

Christmas goodies for friends and family every year since I was young. I look forward to putting on my red apron, icing sugar cookies, and using the press to form mom's famous butter cookies. Hayley has missed the last two years of baking, but this year she decided to join. The day felt complete having her there. We sang and danced to our favorite carols the entire afternoon.

Mom has always been a messy baker, so when we were done she had flour all over her face and hair. Next thing I knew I saw flour souring through the air towards her. Hayley had grabbed a handful and threw it at mom. She let out a loud shriek when it landed softly on her cheeks and then started laughing while she put her hand in the bowl of white powder to get Hayley back. We all started taking turns grabbing handfuls and tossing it all over the kitchen. Before I knew it we were in a full on flour fight! By the end we were covered in flour, giggling. It was a much needed day to have with mom and Hayley. We were able to forget about cancer and addiction for a few hours.

XO, E

December 25, 2012

I usually have to work Christmas Eve, but since it landed on my usual day off I was able to spend the day with family. Dad asks Hayley, Mike, and I to help him make homemade chocolates to give as gifts every year. We start weeks before Christmas, so we can have a huge batch by the time the holidays roll around.

Hayley continued the tradition of sleeping in my bed Christmas Eve night. We went to bed early and fell asleep to the sounds of *The Polar Express* playing on the television. The next morning, Hayley and I had breakfast and opened gifts with dad before going to mom's for a late lunch and more gifts.

While we were at moms, Hayley heard the news that one of her best friends died of an overdose. She was heartbroken! He was her first close friend to die of an overdose, and her being so sick didn't help the situation. Mom and I hugged her while she sobbed in our arms. It made me think that this could be us crying about Hayley one day, and all of the families that have struggled with addiction. It is an epidemic many people are afraid to talk about, but it needs to be out in the open, so we can figure out a way to stop it from taking more lives. I really hope having someone so close to her pass due to an overdose will help her realize what she is doing to herself, and will give her the motivation to stop, but I am afraid it is going to do the opposite.

XO, E

December 25, 2012

Never forget to say I love you. Love you Clint Brown. You have left a permanent place in my heart. Merry Christmas everyone. With all the recent tragedy this holiday season, please be grateful for your loved ones and the ones around you on this amazing earth.

-Hayz

December 26, 2012

Mike, Erin, Hayley, and I spent the evening with Tandi, Troy, Ambria, Aric, and the little girls before my second round of chemo. We went out to dinner and walked around the temple grounds. At one point, Cosette asked to hold my hand. She made my night.

Namaste, Jude

December 27, 2012

Mom had another chemo session today. It was supposed to be about a week ago, but she asked her doctor to push it back so she could enjoy the holidays without being sick from the poison they had to pump through her body. Mike had the day off and was excited to see Hotel Huntsman for himself. When he walked out of his apartment he was holding several grocery bags and grinning from ear to ear. He came up with a great idea to pass out candy to patients in the infusion room. It was a surprise to me!

When Dr. Wilson walked in I could tell he was intrigued by the bags Mike had with him, but got straight to the point. He said the tumor markers have continued to drop, so he wants to stick with the same chemo cocktail. When he finished talking about mom he finally asked what Mike had with him. When Mike pulled out a handful of candy canes Dr. Wilson smiled and laughed. Mike found this to be a good time to ask Dr. Wilson a few questions he has had. My eyes widened as he asked about the chemo he had prescribed mom and what she can do to lessen the side effects. I didn't know he had questions. He has tried to understand what we are going through from what I tell him of the appointments, but no one really knows the reality of a situation until they are able to experience it for themselves.

As we walked into the infusion room Mike said, "Woah!" He has listened to me rave about how nice Huntsman is, but he hasn't seen it in person until today. Mom was excited to read her new book, so after she was situated Mike and I asked her nurse it if was okay if we walked around to talk to patients while we handed out candy canes. Her eyes glistened as she nodded her head yes. We each gave mom a kiss on the forehead before we started giving out our sugary gift.

Everyone was very appreciative. Several patients had visitors with them, but the few people who were alone asked us to visit, which we were more than happy to do. Everyone we met had a different diagnosis. Some were expected to beat it; others were there to prolong their life a little bit longer.

No matter the expected outcome everyone was in good spirits. I don't know if it had something to do with the holiday season or Huntsman being such a wonderful place to heal, or both. Whatever it was, I'm happy Mike and I could help make a few people's day a little brighter.

XO, E

December 27, 2012

So far this energy shift has confused me beyond words.

Grateful for the experiences.

Anxious for the results.

Growing every day.

Life.

-Hayz

December 31, 2012

I have been home since Thursday trying to pretend I have the flu rather than chemo. I also determined that the best course of action is to be as out of it as I can. Good smoke, lollipops, and Xanax help a great deal. According to my doc, they will do a cat scan in three weeks and then try oral hormone pills to shut off the estrogen receptors in my body that is feeding the cancer. Not sure about the side effects.

I am without the portable chemo pump giving me a sense of freedom and relief. This chemo round did not seem as intense as the last two, although I am still pretty light headed and dizzy. Hayley and I are going out for a bite to eat before she goes out with her friends. I plan on being tucked in my bed my 10PM.

Tomorrow starts a new year. It will hopefully be a year full of healing. I want to walk forward. Not backwards, nor to stay in one place. To take a step and trust that my legs will support me. That I won't fall and if I do I can get back up again no matter what the circumstance. I have the strength, and the courage to face the unknown. It is scary. It is unseen. But for all there is unseen there lies a world of wonder, the taste, the smell. A buffet of sensual experiences to pick and choose depending on my mood. It is spread out for me to be wise in my choosing. To take my time in choosing. To try things I have never done before. Now is the time to move forward.

Namaste, Jude

December 31, 2012

So far, 2012 has been the most influential year in my 22 years. So many events have occurred that have changed my life. Some for the better. Some for the worse. I've lost amazing people that I cared about deeply. I've also gained a lot of long-lasting friendships. Although, it has been a rough year. I am glad to say I am celebrating this New Year alive, well, and surrounded by the people I care about most. 2012, thank you for showing me what life is really about and teaching me lifelong lessons. 2013, please be nicer. Happy New Year Everyone AND BE SAFE DAMMIT.

-Hayz

2013

"Mummy" I call into the darkness.
Will she be angry or kind this time?
I wait holding my breath.
She comes and gently peels back my covers
To expose me to the night.

January 9, 2013

I am going to get out of dodge this weekend to go to southern Utah with Mame to a town called Ivins near Snow Canyon. She has a friend there with a guest house on his property complete with a hogan. I so need to get away. The temperature there is a balmy 40 degrees.

Went to my women's group yesterday for the first time since August. My good friend, Adrienne led the group. She spoke of the trees, and how the Redwoods have ancient wisdom. All we have to do is listen. One woman shared a story about her son cutting down a tree in her backyard called a Chinese Elm, supposedly a "junk" tree. When her son began to saw through the trunk, the tree's sap began to pour out like tears. She never took trees for granted again. Even when she prunes her fruit trees she does so with the utmost of care. A lesson for us all.

Namaste, Jude

January 9, 2013

Unfortunately, I have found myself surrounded by a lot of ignorance lately. Especially on a particular situation that has become pretty prominent in my life at the moment. This quote is MORE than fitting for what I've been thinking recently. I wish more people were open to looking at all perspectives of a situation rather than sharing their close-minded opinion. Experience is just as important as intelligence in life.

> *"My mother said I must always be intolerant of ignorance but understanding of illiteracy. That some people, unable to go to school, were more educated and more intelligent than college professors."*
> **-Maya Angelou**

-Hayz

January 10, 2013

We are 10 days into 2013. Mom is doing great and is continuing to do the things she loves. It's so inspiring to watch her live a "normal" life while still so sick. Just a few months ago we were told she had a few months left to live, but look at her now! Last night we went to see one of Mike's favorite DJ's at a club in Park City. It was a much needed night of dancing with some of our closest friends. Being there for mom is my first priority, but I have found it important to experience moments that allow me to love my life. I would be even more exhausted emotionally if I was unable to get a break every once in a while. I am grateful mom understands and pushes me to continue to do things I love. I think her diagnosis and Hayley's addiction have reminded all of us that life is short. We need to do what we love, and do a lot of it because we never know when it will be all over.

XO, E

January 16, 2013

Got good news from my doc today. I had a cat scan Monday. The results are promising, showing the cancer has diminished in size. My doc consulted with a breast cancer oncologist I had seen a month ago. They concurred that I should receive bimonthly injections of an estrogen blocking drug as well as daily oral hormone meds. I had the first injection today in my butt. So far, the only side effects are a little nausea and lightheadedness. After three months, I will do another scan to evaluate the effectiveness of the meds. More chemo, unless meds are ineffective. I knew intuitively that I was healing. Stomach pain is gone. So happy today. Somehow, I have found a way to make friends with my cancer. I have learned acceptance for what is. The fear is gone. At least for today.

Mame and I went to Ivins for the weekend. The folks we stayed with have property in the desert. They built several buildings 25 years ago before the building boom there. It is an oasis among snowbird homes. They are both working artists and about as eccentric as you can get. Katie and her late husband built a little three room motel on their property with a hogan close by. Each room in the motel has an animal theme. I stayed in the pig room, Mame in the donkey room. We had to use space heaters because of the unseasonably cold weather, but I had a great time.

Namaste, Jude

January 17, 2013

Today is the first day of the Sundance Film Festival! It is a great distraction from the cold month of January. We have had so many amazing experiences because of the festival. We look forward to attending every year because we never know what it is going to bring. Mike contacted our friend, T who is a publicist, to find out if she knew of any gigs during the festival. She hooked him up with a job at a private lounge. His job is to promote the brand sponsoring the lounge by passing out gloves and hats around the city. The opening night party was tonight and they asked us to come. It is the biggest lounge I have ever seen! From what I can tell, this will be one of the best Sundance's yet.

XO, E

January 18, 2013

After talking to a few friends who volunteer for the Sundance Film Festival, mom decided to sign up this year. She is very excited about seeing a few movies, meeting new people, and getting the jacket only Sundance volunteers get. She and I were able to get tickets to, *Austenland*. I don't know how we did it, but we were lucky enough to see the premiere and hear the cast speak at the Q&A after the film.

Mike called me as we were leaving the theater to invite me to a private concert at the lounge he is working at. Mom had to get home, so I rushed over to catch the show just as it started. Since there weren't many people I had a great view of the beautiful, acoustic concert. During the guitar solos I would close my eyes and let the notes take me into another world. A world without cancer or addiction.

XO, E

January 20, 2013

Feeling great about life. Everything is on the up and up. Ahhhhhhh.

—Hayz

January 22, 2013

Tonight, I took dad to see *In a World*. He hadn't been to a Sundance film before, and I really wanted to take him. Lake Bell wrote, directed, and starred in it. One of my favorite Sundance movies to date! After the Q&A, Lake Bell was in the lobby talking to people. I wanted to talk to her, but it was after midnight and I didn't want to ask dad to have to wait. I already regret not saying something. There are not many female directors who are chosen to show a film at Sundance, let alone write the script AND play the lead. She is truly an inspiration. I wanted to tell her how much I admire her and how much I loved her film. Maybe one day.

XO, E

January 27, 2013

I connected with a woman I know who teaches sculpting in her home. I have arranged to take classes from her on Wednesday mornings before work. She has students do a bust or a flat piece initially. I was hoping it would be more free form. Maybe it's like painting. You have to learn techniques and such before plunging in. I am a little intimidated by it all. Will it be a good growth experience? I am also taking a writing class once a week for a couple of hours. Funny, I am not as intimidated by a writing class.

Namaste, Jude

January 27, 2013

A few years ago mom, Mike and I decided it would be fun to see the closing film in SLC the last Sunday of the fest. We continued the Sunday movie tradition with mom today by seeing, *The Words* starring Bradley Cooper and Zoe Saldana. None of the cast was there, but the director stayed to do the Q&A. Afterwards, we went to have a cup of tea and finger sandwiches at the Beehive Tea Room. I love being able to keep traditions with mom. It's important for all of us to have things to look forward to.

XO, E

January 27, 2013

I love my friends equally. EVERYONE makes mistakes. Nobody is perfect. Let's have the will to forgive. And live together as one. Only human. Don't let your struggle become your identity.

−Hayz

February 8, 2013

Hayley has been living with me and has helped around the house, including helping me shovel my driveway today, but I had to ask her to leave. She is using again. She took my credit card out of my wallet without my knowledge and used it to get $500 at several different cash machines for drugs. I found out about it through my e-mail notifying me of cash advances. I immediately called her, and of course, she denied it. Eventually, I calmed down, confronted her when she came home, and asked her to leave. The credit card company forgave me the cash advance after I told them what happened. I was tempted to file a police report. A few of my friends advised me to press charges. The next day, I told her I was thinking about filing a police report. She became hysterical, telling me I would be ruining her life. I let her sit with not knowing if I was going to file for 24 hours. I finally told her I wouldn't. I just couldn't do it. I think asking her to leave was enough. She still has no job and I can't afford to support her. I am a little sad, but mostly relieved. I *really need to concentrate on myself and healing. Although, I am worried about her mental state at the moment. She is living with her dad. He is more absolute with her than me. Hayley did tell her therapist she relapsed. Sometimes I feel like someone else inhabits her body.*

The writing class I am taking is taught by a lovely young woman who has her MFA and teaches at the university. She is giving us a lot of freedom. We did some free writing during class for ten minutes.

"I remember life before cancer. When the future lay before me like a blank map waiting for me to plot my destination. The map is gone. I no longer know how to navigate through my future. The signposts are gone. Now, yes. Now is the most important aspect of life. The Here and Now. Dealing with the pain, loss fight, not to fight. The advice from well-meaning friends and family. "Sugar feeds cancer." "You should be juicing." "Have you heard about this cancer clinic in Mexico?" Please, I want to live MY way. I want to discover a new plan for navigating my life filled with courage, hope, and grace. I want to find the wealth of inspiration that is within me. I want to experience all those things I have put off. Life is now. I want to smell, taste, walk, and see those places, things I have dreamed of. I want to nurture relationships with the ones I love. I want to leave a legacy I am proud of. I want to leave a part of myself with people I hold dear, so they can hang on to or hold that piece of me when I am no longer on this earth in human form. I want to love with an open heart, free of judgment and conditions. I want to experience compassion for myself and those who suffer. I want to learn and learn. Life goes on whether I am here or not. My value is the light I leave for others to see and use as a torch to navigate their way." Pretty raw huh?

I prefer not to change this in any way for some reason. I am going to concentrate on writing as though I am composing a blog. The sculpting class is peace producing. I am working on sculpting an Egyptian gold piece of jewelry that was found with King Tut's remains. It is inlaid with pieces of turquoise, lapis and carnelian. It spoke to me. My friend tells me I am a "natural" with a good eye. I absolutely love the feel of the clay in my hands. Using my hands to create after all these years of cleaning teeth gives me such a taste of freedom. Loving it! I am reading one of Pema Chodron's books, When Things Fall Apart: Heart advice for difficult times.

"Getting the knack of relaxing in the midst of chaos, learning not to panic-this is the spiritual path. Getting the knack of catching ourselves, of gently and compassionately catching ourselves, is the path of the warrior." Can so relate and find comfort therein.

Namaste, Jude

February 9, 2013

Feels so good to wake up on a Saturday without a hangover. This not drinking stuff is kinda nice, after all.

-Hayz

February 10, 2013

Mom called me the other day to let me know Hayley had been stealing from her. I was shocked! I knew she needed money for drugs, but I never thought she would take from our sick mother. She is already having a hard time paying her medical bills. Hayley is now living at dad's. She has already snuck into his office, searched through his desk and stole a role of Sacagawea dollars grandma had given him. He was so upset when he saw what Hayley had done. They were one of the last gifts he received from his mom. I know it's the drugs that make her act this way, but I still don't understand. For Hayley to feel like it's okay to take from our parents is not like her. She is not herself. I hope she can get through this and recover who she once was. Someone who can be there for the people she loves the most.

XO, E

February 12, 2013

Randomly, in a really good mood tonight. Life is good people. Really good. Really, really good.

-Hayz

February 15, 2013

My cancer doctor is treating me for breast cancer even though everyone thought my primary tumor was stomach cancer. Breast cancer is actually good news because if they are right, my survival is much better with the drugs available now to fight breast cancer. I had three rounds of chemotherapy at Christmas time. Now I am taking oral medication to block the estrogen that stimulates the growth of the cancer. No real side effects so far. As a matter of fact, I feel better than I have in years. I have confidence that I will be able to live to hopefully play with future grandchildren. After I was diagnosed last year, Erin asked me where I have always wanted to travel to. I told her that I have always wanted to take her and Hayley to my birthplace, Kingston upon Hull. We then started to plan a trip there. I still have not decided whether to rent a car in Manchester or purchase a rail pass. John emphatically told me not to DRIVE. He can be somewhat bossy at times. The girls will leave for the US while I go to Ireland to stay with my friend, Becky in her cottage in the country.

Namaste, Jude

February 15, 2013

Mike and I have started the loan process to buy our first home. It's a buyer's market right now, so there is a lot of competition. We have narrowed it down to only look at homes in two of our favorite neighborhoods. They happen to be two of the most desired areas to live in Salt Lake, which adds to the competition, but we are willing to wait. We first need to get approved, and then we can look more seriously.

Even though we aren't engaged yet, Mike put together an excel sheet to help budget our wedding. He is very excited. So far we are under budget, but I am sure there will be plenty more expenses we don't know of. We are not using a wedding planner to save costs. I am paying for the majority of it myself because I don't want to ask my father. He has already done so much for me. Mike is trying to help, but it's mostly me. Mike's parents said they would give us some money to help with the wedding, but we feel like it's more important to put it towards a down payment on a house.

Before mom was diagnosed I wasn't excited about the idea of getting married. Even though I am in my early thirties I still don't know who I am. I didn't know if or when I was going to be ready to make such a big commitment to someone. The thought of going back to New York to get my graduate degree was in the back of my mind and I wanted to see as much of the world as I could. But now things have changed. I can't be selfish anymore. I am going to stay put for a while so I can be here for mom. I have always put family first, but her diagnosis made me realize even more how important family is. Because of that I feel ready to make that commitment to Mike and maybe start a family of our own. Such an exciting time in our lives!

XO, E

February 16, 2013

I am looking through my office window at the melting snow leaving patches of brown grass. I never thought seeing brown grass would feel so good. Through all of the dark days the past year, I have become my own good friend, going within, finding strength, peace, grace to carry on. Sure there are lonely times, but in the midst of it, a deep knowing that whatever happens, all is well.

Saw my cancer doc yesterday. I am doing so well I can go two months before seeing him again for another cat scan to evaluate the efficacy of the current medication regimen I am on. If there is no metastases, I am good to be on it for another three months. Have experienced no real side effects from the meds. I have been feeling the best I have felt in a few years.

Namaste, Jude

February 17, 2013

How you live your life today affects who you are to become tomorrow.

—Hayz

February 22, 2013

We found out yesterday Hayley is still using. We ended up taking her to an inpatient detox hospital where she will stay for 3-5 days, and then maybe longer depending what the doctors tell us. I am feeling a lot of stress and sadness.

Namaste, Jude

February 22, 2013

I received a call from dad on my way to meet my good friend, Lexi for dinner yesterday. He told me they were taking Hayley to detox that night. I was surprised because I didn't know she was willing to go. Every time someone mentioned the idea of detox or rehab she would get defensive. He said I didn't need to come home, but I called Lexi to ask her if she wouldn't mind rescheduling. Of course she understood, so instead of heading to the restaurant I drove straight to the detox center.

I was blinded by the fluorescent lights when I walked in. I found my family by following the sounds of my mom's sweet voice. Hayley was talking to the therapist while we waited patiently in the light blue waiting room. I could tell mom and dad were nervous. None of us knew if Hayley was ready. When Hayley walked out she looked exhausted and scared. My sisterly instinct could tell she really didn't want to be there and if she didn't want to be there this wasn't going to do her any good. She would just form more resentment towards our parents because she was doing this for them, not her. The therapist told her she could give us one last hug goodbye before she couldn't have contact with anyone from the outside world for a few days. When I gave her my hug I whispered in her ear that she was strong and she could do this. She looked at me with tears in her eyes, making me think that she wasn't so sure she could. When she hugged dad it seemed like she didn't want to let go because she was squeezing him so tightly. He was the one who arranged for her to be there, but she still loves him. It hurts dad to see her like this. All he wants is for his little girl to get better.

XO, E

February 22, 2013

Grant had a way of making me feel inferior to him. He made it seem like he was my only option, my only source of help and my only shoulder to lean on. By making me feel less confident and bullying me down he gained control over me. He manipulated me to the core and has shaken my confidence to this day. Another reason why my addiction is so bad. In order to conquer my confidence fear, I need to address the pain from Grant and move forward. Grant made me not love myself, so it led me to self-destructive behavior. In order to move on, I need to learn how to love myself again. When I love myself, I'm able to love others and treat them right. I have been mistreating everyone so badly, including myself.

I just realized a year ago today, Grant was arrested and put in jail for 40 days. We would talk on the phone every night, and I remember how painful it was to talk to him because I missed him so much. For some reason, I've been thinking about him a lot tonight. Just so happens that my roommate has been on the phone with her boyfriend talking about how much she misses him. It just seems all too familiar, and far from a coincidence. I know Grant and I are bad for each other, so maybe this is a test. Either way, I would rather be lonely than disrespected. And so it turns out, I'm lonely, but now I'm the one disrespecting.

-Hayz

February 23, 2013

Hayley has called her father to complain of conditions at the detox center. I hope we are doing the right thing. She will need intensive inpatient rehab afterwards. Her addiction has become so much bigger than she can handle. On a happier note, I had my last writing class today. My teacher and I formed a special bond, one that I hope to continue through e-mails. Today there were only two students because of the weather. She introduced a couple of different organizational structures to aid in planning. I have enjoyed this class and look forward to writing more perhaps through classes at the university.

Namaste, Jude

February 23, 2013

I realize the reason I've been so depressed is because I don't feel like myself. I haven't been myself for a while. I just wasn't aware of it until now. I cannot wait to feel completely sober and have EVERYTHING out of my system. It will be the first time in a long time that I'll be able to feel ME again. I'm still trying to find the motivation to be sober and to want to stay sober. It really is an all-over behavioral change that I'm going to have to put into play. Change phone number?

I wish I had something left to fight for. I've lost everything. Trying to find the strength within me.

-Hayz

February 26, 2013

Going to pick up Hayley from inpatient detox today. She has agreed to outpatient intensive therapy from 9-4 each day. I don't know what I think about all of this. It is so much bigger than me. Addiction at this level is beyond my comprehension.

Namaste, Jude

February 26, 2013

Hayley is home from detox. She was very unhappy there. Like I said before, I don't think she was ready. She isn't fully invested in getting better. It's almost like she went to get mom and dad off her back. Her few days in detox gained her more time to steal from them, and continue to use. I really hope I am wrong.

XO, E

February 26, 2013

Welp, that sucked. AYYYEEE BEETCHES.

-Hayz

March 2, 2013

INDEPENDENCE

-Feel like a 16-year-old with a curfew, no car, phone/internet rules, etc.

-Can't leave my house to hang out with anyone for a while.

-My dad loses sleep when I don't sleep at home.

-My sister lost her hair due to stress when I was using.

-So I understand why they expect me to follow such rules because it helps with their anxiety and they don't worry as much.

-But I don't feel free. I feel locked up in a sense.

-My recovery is up to me. I'm 22 years old I should be able to do it by myself.

-I know a solid support system is one of the main components of recovery.

-Is this crossing the line of support?

-Level of codependency?

LONLINESS

-I hardly get to go out of my house with friends anymore. My friends come to me to visit.

-Sometimes I feel forced to hang out with my family.

-I feel like I don't have a choice with my daily routine.

-I know I fucked up big time, and I respect my parents a lot, but I feel like their needs are being fulfilled by me agreeing to whatever makes them comfortable, but it is making me feel like a teenager again. That lacks freedom. Is it appropriate for me to ask for leniency?

SELF ESTEEM

-I am without a job, a car, and a boyfriend. This is the first time since I was 16 to without one of these things, let alone all 3.

-The sense of accomplishment you feel when you complete a day's work or when you pay your car payment. The feeling of comfort when your boyfriend hugs you and calls you beautiful. All of these things used to motivate me to do better, to want a good life for myself and to be healthy! Well, I have lost all of them.

-My motivation and the feeling of wanting a better life for myself has not only diminished, but it seems to be gone. I lack in confidence, and I am extremely lacking in drive.

-I don't know what it going to make me feel worthy again.

-Hayz

March 8, 2013

The day your Erin was born. She came into this realm full of grace and beauty. She is a wonder. You are so blessed to be her mother. You know that she needs you more than you can ever understand. Her light is just beginning to glow brightly. Seeing your journey with such courage gives her the courage to try new things. She is what you helped her to be. Hayley too- She's not finished. She will turn heads and minds. You'll be around to see her succeed in life and love. Be persistent, positive and open. Open to the possibilities of that is now.

Namaste, Jude

March 10, 2013

We just got back seeing one of our favorite DJ's headline a small music festival in CA. Our friend asked us to go a few months earlier, and when I saw that the show was on my birthday it was a no brainier. I talked to mom about not going. She and Hayley are both very sick, so I didn't think it was a good time for me to leave. I told her that she and I could do something else to celebrate while Mike went with our friends, but she insisted I go. She knows traveling and music are therapy for me. She is not the only one trying to navigate cancer.

We flew out on Thursday and stayed at our friend's apartment in Hermosa. Mike had to get up early to move the car because a local farmers market uses the parking lot we parked our car in. He woke me as he walked in the door holding a bouquet of fresh flowers and my favorite fruit, raspberries, from the market. I was so surprised! I squealed with delight, jumped up and gave him a big hug. It was very thoughtful and the perfect way to wake up on my birthday. We went out to breakfast at a nice restaurant on the beach with friends before heading to the Getty Villa in Malibu.

I was feeling a little under the weather, so Mike put the top down on the convertible we rented. Feeling the natural remedy of the hot sun and the smell of the ocean breeze helped a lot. The Getty Villa is gorgeous! Greek, Roman, and Etruscan artifacts are displayed within a mansion inspired by Roman architecture and Roman-style gardens surround the villa. After walking through the old mansion we made our way to one of the gardens that overlooks the ocean. As we walked through a hallway of pink roses, butterflies started to fly around my belly. I was sure Mike was going to propose. We designed an engagement ring together in December. I didn't know when he was going to ask, but since we have been talking a lot about our wedding I figured he was going to ask soon. Being in such an amazing place on my birthday would be very romantic. Mike took my hand and led me to the fountain the middle of the garden. He stopped to give me a big hug and whispered that he loved me in my ear. This was it! I was getting ready to say "Yes, a millions times yes." But instead of getting down on one knee he asked me if I wanted a picture. I smiled and posed for the perfect pic before we took a quick selfie. As we drove to meet our friends I couldn't help but feel a little confused. I wasn't upset, but couldn't understand why he didn't ask me there. It would have been perfect. Knowing Mike, he has something even better planned. I just need to be patient.

XO, E

March 10, 2013

I am taking a break from preparing a lesson I am presenting for the Women's Sacred Circle Tuesday evening. Hayley seems to be soldiering on. She told me today that she isn't missing partying with her friends as much as she thought. I feel like we are all on a balance beam that could teeter either way. I am trying to distance myself. I went to an acoustic concert last night. A folksinger, finger picking musician performed. Erin turned 32 on Friday. She spent a long weekend in LA visiting her future brother in law and various friends. I am so grateful for her support of me the past six months. She has been to every doctor's appointment I have had. What a rock.

Namaste, Jude

March 11, 2013

I was sad I wasn't able to be with my family on my birthday, but we had a great time celebrating in CA. To celebrate with my family, we went to dinner to our favorite sushi restaurant. Dad, mom, Hayley, and Mike were all there. We then went to dad's house to have cake and ice cream and open gifts. Mom always makes a homemade chocolate cake with chocolate icing for my birthday. I feel so lucky that even though my parents are divorced, they find a way to be together for birthdays and holidays.

XO, E

March 11, 2013

I just want to apologize to the group as a whole. Due to medical reasons, I wasn't able to come to group, and I know if I were on your guys end I'd be thinking, "Who does this chick think she is? Just coming in and out of group when she pleases." But, I do take this very seriously, and I'm coming to complete the program.

-Hayz

March 15, 2013

Dad, I hate the person I have become. I have destroyed my life and taken you, mom, and Erin down with me. I don't value life anymore, nor am I valuing the life I've been blessed with. You are such a great dad to me, and over the years I have crushed our relationship. I have done a lot of reflecting on these past couple years, and quite frankly I am disgusted with myself. As you know I've been reacting solely on impulse over the years, but especially over the past few months. With mom's condition and the relationship I've ruined with you, I want to get better. The difference this time from the past few times is that I'm doing it to better my relationships, and to be happy again. When I went to the detox center and to rehab, I was doing it to make you guys happy and comfortable. Don't get me wrong, I WANTED to get sober, I just wasn't ready. I truly wanted to take it seriously, but the addict mentality was still in me. I couldn't stop reacting on impulses. My lying has gotten out of control, and I can't live life like this anymore. Somewhere inside me, I'm still a good person. I'm still the person you raised me to be. I just need to get over this addiction. I am so sorry for putting you through this; I will never forgive myself for what I have done to you guys.

The reason I have decided not to detox this time around is because again, I would be doing it for you guys and I'm afraid it wouldn't turn out the way we all want it to. I feel like I need to learn how to value life and appreciate all you do for me. I feel like I don't deserve to come home yet. Detox takes care of the physical withdrawal from drugs, but I need to put myself through this to take care of the mental part. I can't keep relying on you to always save me. I'm going to do this independently so I can learn how to live again, to take care of myself. I know you may not understand and please know this is the hardest decision I have had to make. But I need to do this independently or it won't work. I love you so much dad. I'm going to do this. I will live the life you deserve to see me live.

-Hayz

March 16, 2013

Hayley is out there sharing couches with friends. Her dad told her she can't live with him until she is serious about becoming well. Tough love. She called me the other night to tell me she is safe. We both cried on the phone. One of these days, I will have happy news about Hayley.

Namaste, Jude

March 17, 2013

Mike and I woke up to a dreary, Saint Patrick's Day. For no particular reason we both love St. Patty's. Maybe because it's a good excuse to go out with friends, which we love to do. We usually spend every Sunday together, and we like to start our day by walking up to a beautiful canyon, and ending our walk with a visit to nearby dog park. We stop to admire all of the dogs, and talk about what our life will be like when we are ready to adopt a furbaby.

When I stepped outside I felt like the world's spin had slowed just enough for us to notice our breath floating in mid air. I wasn't prepared for such a wintery walk, so I suggested that we go back inside for a cup of hot chocolate instead. Mike said he really wanted to go, and promised we could indulge in a hot beverage when we returned. It would be something to look forward to. As we walked up the steep hill my body started to warm up and my mood changed. Even though the skies were grey, it was a beautiful day to be outside. The green grass was nestled underneath a freshly fallen blanket of snow, and birds sang us a love song as we walked through the tree lined pathways. Mike held me as snow flurries started to fall and I forgot why I wanted to stay home. I imagined we were in our own snow globe where nothing could harm us. I was happy Mike insisted that we go. We talked a lot about the house, the wedding and how much fun we had in California. It was hard to be back to reality, but knowing we had a lot to be excited about made it easier.

As we neared the dog park Mike stopped on a stone bridge. He smiled at something behind me. When I turned around I saw a familiar dog running up to us. It was Lucy! When I knelt down to greet her I noticed a little red box tied to her collar. In the past, I mentioned to Mike how cute it would be if a dog delivered the ring when he proposed. The butterflies came fluttering back. This is it! When I unhooked the box I heard dad call Lucy's name. He smiled as he and Lucy walked away to give us some privacy. Mike was on one knee when I turned to face him. As he opened the box with the ring inside he asked me to marry him. The ring is more beautiful than I imagined. I couldn't wait to put it on, so instead of saying yes I said "put it on." He laughed while he slid the ring onto my finger. He stood up, gave me a big hug and kiss before yelling, "you can come out now." Next thing I knew mom, Mike's parents, Mel and Barb came running out from behind a nearby building yelling "Congratulations!" It was perfect!

Saint Patrick's Day was a great day for Mike to propose. It is our lucky day!

XO, E

March 21, 2013

I just bought our tickets to England! Mom was born in a small town, Kingston, upon Hull. She has dreamt of showing Hayley and I where she was born for years, so we figured what better time than now? She came over on the Queen Elizabeth II with Grandma Joan, Uncle John, and Uncle Phil, when she was only 5 years old. Grandpa Ron came to the states a year earlier to find a job and home for his family. He decided Cleveland, Ohio, was the best fit for them and worked as an engineer. Mom had a wonderful childhood. I love when she tells me about the times grandpa would wake her up before sunrise to take her sailing. When she was a teenager, after a night of drinking with her friends, he would still come in her room early in the morning to wake her up, but always made sure to have a hot thermos of coffee waiting for her on the boat to help nurse her hangover. If they weren't sailing, they were taking vacations, ice skating, hiking, and just being a family.

Mom continues to visits OH regularly to spend time with grandpa and her brothers. She also talks to them on the phone every week. Even though grandpa has dementia, he remembers mom when she calls. She has always been his "favorite."

XO, E

March 22, 2013

Dad decided he has had enough and suspended my phone service for a while. I am so upset with him. How am I supposed to talk to my friends? I hope people don't think I am ignoring them.

-Hayz

March 25, 2013

Now we are officially engaged I couldn't wait to start looking for a dress. As someone who has always turned to clothing to express myself creatively, finding "the dress" was important to me. I fell in love with "pretty dresses" at the age of three. Unable to ignore the embroidered details and the ripples that formed in the fabric when I twirled, I wore them almost every day. Mom would have to fight me to wear anything else. I have fond memories of going to the dress shop with my grandma and mom to pick out a new dress for the holidays. I would walk out of the dressing room and spin around until I was dizzy.

I asked mom, Aunt Marcia, my soon to be mother-in-law, Barb, and Lexi to go with me to my first appt. Hayley was invited but didn't make it. It hurt not to have her there. I want to be able to share these moments with my only sister. We met at a small boutique in our neighborhood, The Bride's Shop. I have admired the dresses gracing their display windows since I was a young. I have dreamt of what I would wear on my wedding day every time I drive past the big windows adorned with white gowns. There was no other store I wanted to go to. The woman helping me was named Lisa and she was wonderful. I told her it was my first time trying on dresses and I didn't know exactly what I wanted, so she filled the dressing room with several different silhouettes. When I walked into the large dressing room full of white tears came to my eyes. It all started to feel so real. I am getting married.

As I stepped into the first gown a wave of goose dimples covered my body. Lisa laced up the back and asked me to look into the mirror before walking outside. My eyes were literally sparkling. I looked so happy. When she opened up the curtain all four ladies gasped. Mom started to cry and asked me to do a twirl, just like she did when I was her little girl.

XO, E

March 26, 2013

Beautiful morning here in SLC. The grass is greening up. The forsythia bush is blooming bright yellow blossoms near the front of my house. My mother used to have a row of forsythias in her backyard. I remember squinting my eyes because the color was so vibrant. This time of year symbolizes new beginnings and hope to me. Here's to all of that and lovely friendships.

Things have been up in the air because of Hayley. Erin bought her a plane ticket to England, but we have no intentions of taking her. Erin is trying to get the ticket transferred to her fiancé's name. The airlines are giving her the run around. It may be just Erin and me coming or the three of us.

Erin is engaged and planning to be married on Sept 1, 2013. She and Mike are planning a small wedding here in Utah. We went bridal gown shopping yesterday. She looked beautiful in everything.

Namaste, Jude

March 27, 2013

Hayley is unable to come to England due to her addiction, so I am negotiating with the airlines to get the ticket transferred to Mike's name. They have different circumstances when it comes to changing the name on the ticket, and one of them is illness. Having a family member suffer from addiction, I now see it as an illness, but I know a lot of other people don't. Mom is very upset Hayley can't go. She really wants both of her girls to see where she was born, but if Hayley is away from the drug for too long she will become very sick from withdrawals. We thought a trip to England would be a perfect motivation for her to get better, but she is not ready to give it up just yet.

Now she has gone to few different rehab facilities we finally understand it is up to her. Rehab isn't a magical place where she will come out sober. She has to be ready and willing. We can't force her to get better. If she isn't ready, there is no point in making her go, but it's so hard to watch her slowly kill herself. My parents, especially my dad, continue to try, but they also know they have to give her tough love. It is the hardest thing I have ever had to watch anyone do. She is their child and the last thing they want is to see her suffer like this. In a lot of ways, addiction is harder than cancer. Mom is following doctor's orders to try to live a longer, quality life, but addiction has taken over Hayley's life. She doesn't want to get better and hasn't figured out how to get her control back. We heard she has to hit rock bottom. I just don't know when that will be. Hopefully sooner than later; for my parent's sake.

XO, E

April 12, 2013

Good news. Preliminary cat scan results are good. No ascites or metastasis. My doctor is very pleased. I still have cancer, but at the moment it will not kill me. Happy news! I have been asked to submit a blog piece to the Huntsman Cancer Institute's website.

Just got back from working out at the cancer hospital with my trainer. I actually have gained weight, but feel so much stronger. My legs are taking me much further when I walk. I don't hold onto the stair railing anymore. My goal is to get up gracefully off the floor. My trainer is actually working on strengthening my leg and core muscles to enable me to do just that.

Namaste, Jude

April 15, 2013

Guess who's back, back again, HAYLEY'S back. I just took a little break from everything.

-Hayz

April 17, 2013

I have gone from living alone to having my friend, Monica stay with me until she finds a job, which she has as of yesterday. Now she needs to find a place to live. I have given her until mid-May.

Hayley is living with her drug dealer boyfriend. She managed to e-mail her dad last week to let him know she was alive and safe. I am trying to think of her being away at school or on an extended vacation to keep my sanity.

I have a cat scan on Thursday, and then see my doc on Friday with the results. I am surprisingly not nervous about it. Whatever happens I will deal with it. I have been feeling very good most days. Mame had to cut several inches off my hair last week. I think it is getting thin from the cancer meds I am taking or maybe it's just old age. I miss my long hair. I can still put it in a tiny ponytail if I need to. Tumor markers are down as well as cat scan looking good. Time for celebration!

Namaste, Jude

May 3, 2013

Mame picked us up to take me, Mike and Erin to the airport about 11AM. We had no problem checking our luggage. As a matter of fact, people went out of their way to be helpful. The flight was uneventful. We are sitting in the Atlanta airport at the moment, waiting for our flight to Manchester at 8:25PM. Hard to believe this is really becoming a reality.

Namaste, Jude

May 4, 2013

We arrived in Manchester about 9AM. Had a rough night trying to sleep on the plane, but I didn't really expect to sleep well. Jean, Andrew, and their neighbor Danny met us at the gate. I drove to Hull with Jean and Andrew. Erin and Mike with Danny. We got ourselves settled. Went shopping at a local market and agreed on chicken for dinner. We went to see my cousin's, Kim and David later on. Their kids, Thomas, Laura, and her boyfriend were there as well. I had a great evening laughing and getting a little drunk. Mike fit right in. He and Andrew watched the Hull City football game that afternoon.

Namaste, Jude

May 4, 2013

We made it to England! It is so nice to have Mike with us. He really helps mom. We are staying at Andrew and Jean's house for the next few days. Andrew is a childhood friend of Uncle John's. After spending time with them a few times while we were both visiting family in Cleveland they quickly became friends of ours as well. I am so happy to spend some quality time in their hometown. They live in a home in the middle of Hull city with a beautiful backyard full of flowers. It is just what I pictured a home in a small city of England to look like. It costs a lot to call the states from our cell phones, so I have been emailing dad to keep him updated. He always worries when I travel.

Mike and I are planning on going to the football match between Manchester City and Chelsea tomorrow. Mike is very excited. We haven't been to a professional football match in a different country before. When Mike ordered tickets off of a resale site online we asked that they be mailed to Andrew and Jean's, but they hadn't been delivered yet. Andrew was very worried. He is a retired police officer, and was afraid we had gotten scammed. After a few phone calls they were able to figure everything out. Apparently, George, the man who sold us the tickets accidentally sold them twice. To make up for the confusion he is going to give us better tickets for the same price at the game tomorrow. Mike and I decided to give him the benefit of the doubt and reserved seats on a train going to Manchester first thing in the morning. We have learned to make it work, so I am not concerned. Looking forward to our first England adventure.

XO, E

May 5, 2013

Had a great night's sleep. Erin and Mike off to Manchester United game on the train. Jean and I went to get railroad tickets to Newcastle on Tuesday and walked through the mall downtown. Came home, had a bit to eat and went to Jean and Andrew's daughter and son in law's house. They have two girls and one boy. Beautiful children. Went home, had dinner and went to George's for a visit. He looks very old, but he is 93! Lives by himself and still drinks, YIKES! Erin and Mike made it back from the game after having a wonderful time.

Namaste, Jude

May 5, 2013

I woke up to the smell of a full home-cooked breakfast. To my surprise, Jean had made us toast, eggs, sausage, baked beans, and of course a wonderful pot of tea. She and I had a really nice chat while we ate breakfast and enjoyed the view of her beautiful garden. It was a perfect way to start the first full day of our vacation. After we finished eating, Andrew drove Mike and I to the train station. Neither of us thought it was a good idea to try driving on the opposite side of the car and the road, so we thought it would be safer for us to take the train. Andrew insisted on us taking his cell phone in case we needed to call George. He told Mike he would like to pick us up at the train station and drive us to the stadium. I was a little weary, but George felt so bad about the mix-up he wanted to do something to help make up for his mistake.

As I watched the rolling hills, old stone cottages, and sheep pass by I thought about how lucky I am to be able to be in England with mom. We have dreamt of taking this trip for 15 years now! I am grateful we were finally able to make it a reality. It took a cancer diagnosis to do it, but we are here, and that's all that matters right now.

We found George outside of the train station. The stadium wasn't far, but we appreciated the ride. We were pleasantly surprised to see that we were sitting two rows behind the home team, Manchester United. Everyone around us was so sweet. Many of them have season tickets, so they know each other well, and welcomed us with open arms. It was such an amazing experience for our first European Football match.

After the game, we went straight to the train to go back to Hull. Even though it was late, Andrew was waiting to pick us up from the station, and Jean had a pot of tea ready for us when we got home. Mike and I were still excited about our day, so we stayed up and chatted with Jean and Andrew while drinking a few British brews. It has been nice getting to know them a little better.

XO, E

May 6, 2013

Left around 10:30 for York. Andrew, Jean, Erin and Mike in their car. Kim, David, Thomas, and I in their car. It was a beautiful, warm spring day. We drove through the countryside until we got to York. Outside of York, we caught a bus to take us to the Shambles and York Minster. Everyone was hungry, so we ate at a pub with an outdoor patio called the Yates Bar. I had yummy fish and chips. First of my trip to the UK. After lunch, we took a walk through the Shambles, a shopping area with many shops dating back hundreds of years. Mike and Thomas snuck into Guy Fawkes pub to have a pint. We found them after wondering where they were. Cool, quaint pub. We then made our way to York Minster. I have fond memories of going there 40 years ago when I was 20 years old. I remember music being played by some musicians under the minster. So magical.

After spending a bit of time freshening up, we took Jean and Andrew out to dinner at the Beech Tree, a pub/restaurant. The home I lived as a child was nearby. I was a little nervous to go because I didn't know if I would remember it, but as we pulled up memories of learning to ride my bike outside and seeing the Christmas tree in the window came to mind. I almost started to cry when I saw the home I knew so well. I felt like I was seeing it for the first time and in a way I was. I hadn't been there since we moved to the U.S. I was anxious to knock on the door to meet the new residents, hoping they would let me take a tour of the inside, but the windows were dark, so I opted to stay outside. It meant a lot to be there with Erin. I have wanted to take her to my birthplace for a very long time. I am so happy we could finally make it happen. I just wish Hayley was there too.

Namaste, Jude

May 6, 2013

We had a wonderful day in York and didn't want to leave. On our way home we drove by Staveley Road, where mom was born. Since Andrew grew up nearby he knew which house was hers. When we arrived mom started to get teary eyed. She hadn't been to her home since she was young. I am sure it was emotional for her. We stepped outside to walk around a bit before taking some pictures. In typical mom fashion, she almost knocked on the door so she could see inside, but decided it was best not to.

We had a busy day and were exhausted from all of the walking, but we stayed up to have one last evening chat with Jean and Andrew before heading to New Castle the next morning. They have been such amazing hosts. I really hope they can make it to Utah soon so we can return the favor.

XO, E

May 6, 2013

Grant and I got in a huge fight tonight. We fight on a regular basis, but not like this. I feel bad I am not in England with my mom and sister. I wanted to see my dad, but Grant wouldn't let me leave. He never allows me have any contact with my friends or family. He said that they are the bad guys, but I know they aren't. All they want to do is help. I have had enough of his bullshit, so when he stormed out the door to meet his family at the movies I called dad from a neighbor's phone. I started to cry when I heard his voice. When he asked if I was okay I only said, "I need you to pick me up." I didn't know how much time I had until Grant came home, so I had to get straight to the point. There was no time for small talk. I rushed back to the trailer, franticly packed a small backpack of my favorite clothes and ran to the gas station where I asked dad to pick me up from. I ran like I never had before. I didn't want Grant to see me or realize I was gone so soon. I needed to get away as fast as I could. When I made it to the gas station I smoked a cigarette to try to calm my nerves. I was relieved I had made it to the meeting spot without any problem, but I was scared. The anxiety started to worsen as I saw dad's brown Subaru pull into the parking lot. When I sat down in the soft, heated leather seat my anxiety turned into a full blown panic attack. I was terrified because it was the first time I experienced something like it. I didn't know what to do and continued to tell dad I was going to die. He calmly told me to take deep breaths. After a few deep inhales and exhales I started to feel better. I was panicking because I am scared of Grant. I have wanted to leave the trailer for a while, but he wouldn't let me. He has a manipulative control over me. He told me that if I left my life would be terrible. He would give me guilt trips and sometimes even threaten me. I am so happy to be safe with my dad, but I don't know what Grant will do when he sees that I have left. I am still so scared.

-Hayz

May 7, 2013

Left for Paragon station at 8:30AM. David helped drive. So good to see and connect with him again. Jean and Andrew were so very hospitable. Train ride uneventful until we got to Newcastle, and we didn't realize we should have kept our tickets. Chris was waiting for us and the ticket taker let us through. He took us to a nice pub on the Tyne river side where we ate outside in the sunshine, another beautiful, sunny day. Chris took us on a nice tour of Newcastle. We walked up the castle keep stairs and he paid for us to take the tour. The bridges of the Tyne are spectacular. I was so impressed with the city, its buildings and vibrancy. We walked around downtown, and it was busy with shoppers, even on a weekday. We then went to the beach of the North Sea. Beautiful area. The Tynemouth Priory ruins were spectacular. People were actually swimming in the sea. We sat and had a cup of tea on the beach. Drove to find Lumley Castle. The Northumberland countryside was beautiful, like a British sitcom. Daffodils grew wild on the side of the road. We started to go over a very narrow bridge when all of a sudden Chris's tire went flat. He saw a pub straight ahead. We parked, and Chris called the British version of AAA to have his tire repaired. Fortunately, there was a tire shop across the street! We joked about a symbolic relevance between the bridge and the tire shop in town. Ate dinner at the Adam and Eve Pub then off to find the castle. I am sad to see the kids go, but looking forward to spending some time with Chris.

Namaste, Jude

May 7, 2013

Hayley called right after we spoke, and she's home now. She's very skinny and was starving, but she is OK. I'm not sure what to do next, but she's agreed to see a therapist. I guess we'll take it from there.

Love you, Dad

I saw dad's email right after another beautiful breakfast by Jean. I am glad Hayley is home, but I am worried about her and dad. When she comes to live with him it can be hard. I know he loves to have her, but it can be stressful for both of them. At least we know she is safe. David came to help drive us to the train station. When we said our goodbyes Mom and Jean both started to cry. They really are like family to us. It was hard to leave, but we were excited to see a little more of England.

Mom's friend, Chris picked us up from the train station and drove us to downtown Newcastle.

Mom met Chris when she was backpacking through Europe when she was 18. They fell in love and have managed to stay good friends. They have kept in touch by writing letters, talking on the phone, and now emails. Both have been married, had kids, and divorced.

We ate lunch under the Newcastle Bridge, toured an old castle, and walked around the city. We then took a drive to the coast of the North Sea to explore some gorgeous old ruins. We made our way to a cute little restaurant on the beach where we each had some tea. There were a few people swimming in the cold water of the North Sea, so Mike and I dared each other to go in. We figured this could be our only time to be in the North Sea, and if cancer has taught us anything it is to live life to the fullest. We ran up to the water like we were ready to jump in, but came to a halt when we were only a few feet away. We could already feel the cold coming from the deep blue sea. We cuffed up our jeans, held one another's hand and inched our way closer to the waves coming towards us. The water crept up to our ankles as we both let out a little squeal. We enjoyed the icy water for only about 30 seconds and then skipped back to Mom and Chris who were laughing at us while pouring us cups of hot tea.

As the skies started to darken we thought it was a good time to drive to the hotel where Mike and I staying for the night, Lumley Castle. The woman who checked us in didn't hesitate in telling us that the property is haunted. Mike told me it was all a story to frighten me, but I could definitely feel a presence while we were there. It was too late for dinner, but we had a drink in the bar. The majority of the guests were older locals who frequent the bar and hotel for a "staycation." We cuddled into a cozy corner booth where we had a couple glasses of wine before heading up to bed. Old sculptures and paintings lined the hallways. I felt like I was in the Haunted Mansion in Disneyland, and was ready for one the busts to break out into song. Our room was decorated in medieval decor. There was a huge canopy bed covered in red, satin linens. To get to the bathroom you had to step into what looked like an armoire. It was like a secret passageway. Mike fell asleep the moment his head hit the pillow, but I had a hard time getting to sleep. The wine had relaxed me a little, but it wasn't enough to get me to stop worrying about Hayley. We have been so busy on our trip I didn't have much time to think about her, but when I heard from dad earlier today it reminded me of the troubles we have at home. I feel like I should be home to support them, but instead I am thousands of miles away. Sure, I am taking care of mom, but I also want to be there for her and dad.

XO, E

May 8, 2013

I had a fairly goodnight's sleep except for the alarm clock going off at midnight for some reason. Chris came over about 10AM, made me eggs, mushrooms, toast, and tea. We talked about past experiences. Chris showed me photos from when he was little and showed me a super old image of myself that I hadn't seen before. We set off for a city near the banks of Tyne. We got the tire replaced, and I made small talk with the guys while we were waiting. We then made our way to the new art museum, The Baltic. It was raining like mad and very overcast. I saw several exhibits, but my favorite was done by a French artist. It had piece of writing on the walls. Sheets were hung up on several clotheslines with random drawings and writing. We were encouraged to walk through them. There were several wooden sheds. We were instructed not to go inside, but we could open the doors and peek in. Another shed had a prism with many rainbows shining on the walls. Fun exhibit. The other floors were a little obscure. We then climbed more stairs to the symphony hall. The nickname for the building is "the snail." Chris says it is the most acoustically constructed building in the world. Still running. Next, went to the new arts/cultural center and stopped for a cappuccino at a pub where Chris's group from Jamaica is playing on Thursday night. Also went to a small farm for children next door. It stopped raining and the sun came out. Pretty place. So much history in Newcastle. I asked Chris about a pottery shop, and he took me to a gallery showcasing local artists. Went back to Chris's flat to rest before dinner.

Chris took me to his neighborhood pub for happy hour where I met a group of his friends who were mostly older than us. They were very interested in what was going on in the US. Next we went to a Japanese restaurant. We ordered small plates, appetizers, rice salad, sushi, and two glasses of wine. Chris knew the owner. He is responsible for the Chinese dragon Chris uses for a local music festival. Feeling a bit drunk, we left for another pub near the Tyne. Chris knew the owner who was a former roadie of his and said a lot of bands perform outside in the summer there. Drank a beer and went back to Chris's place. We smoked a bowl and watched old clips of bands from the 70's. We both reminisced about when we fell in love years ago. Chris said not many people find love like we did sometimes throughout their whole life! So true. Chris and I reconnected as friends who love each other.

Namaste, Jude

May 8, 2013

We heard there was a good chance we would be able to see the Queen of England in London this morning, so we got up early, ate breakfast in the dining room of the hotel, and caught the 7:00 AM train to London. We really wanted to walk the grounds of the castle because we were unable to enjoy the hotel the day before, but we thought seeing the Queen of England was a once in a lifetime experience, so we rushed out as soon as we could.

When we arrived to our hotel in London we asked the receptionist if we were too late to see the Queen. She smiled when she said she had passed by just 10 minutes earlier, we wouldn't catch her in time. We decided we still wanted to try, so we dropped our luggage and ran down the street. Since we didn't have any idea as to where we were going we figured we should run towards Buckingham Palace. We started to get tired after traveling all morning, but seeing her carriage in the distance made us run faster. We were determined. Her carriage pulled into the palace gates just as we arrived. We barely missed her!

Since we had already made it to Buckingham Palace we decided to continue our self-guided tour of London. I visited London when I took a class in college where I toured the four fashion capitols in Europe. I spent a week in London, Paris, Florence and Milan. Mike hadn't been to London before, so I made sure we saw everything he wanted to see. We went to Big Ben, Westminster Cathedral, Shakespeare's Globe Theater, and simply explored London.

For dinner, we had a great Italian meal in the middle of the city. The waiter was so much fun and the dessert was one of the yummiest desserts I have ever had. I told Mike it was "orgasmic." I don't know if it was because the dessert was THAT good or if it was the few glasses of wine talking, or both. After dinner we made our way to a cabaret show at a little speak easy. We had a few martini's before stumbling back to our hotel. We quickly fell in love with London and can't wait to explore more of this amazing city with mom tomorrow.

XO, E

May 9, 2013

Took the train to London from Newcastle. Got to King's Cross early, pouring with rain and windy. Found a cab to take me to Horse Guard Hotel. Beautiful, stately hotel on the banks of the Thanes. From our room and balcony, you can see the gorgeous garden filled with tulips and statues. Erin and Mike found me in the room. Erin a little worried about me. Found out Hayley has come home. My ex, Mike said long story and will tell us later. I have mixed feelings about it. Took off for the Orangery for high tea. Decided to take the tube rather then walk. Very busy because it was rush hour. The gardens around Kensington Palace were absolutely stunning, even in the rain. We were able to get a table and sat down for high tea. The walls were all white ornate plaster with very tall windows. We asked our waiter for a gluten free menu for Erin. He assured us that it was available, but he was a little difficult to understand. He brought Erin sandwiches that looked a lot like mine and Mike's. We had asked the hostess earlier if they had a gluten free menu, and she must have remembered because when she saw Erin eating the sandwiches, she stopped to let us know they weren't gluten free. The manager came over to Erin with a very concerned look on his face. She assured him she wouldn't get sick right away, and it's not a serious allergy. She wasn't upset. He told us not to worry about paying for the meal. He was very nice about everything. It did not spoil our experience there. We took the tube back to our hotel to get ready to see Mama Mia, the musical, and then to a nice restaurant afterwards called The Steak House.

Namaste, Jude

May 9, 2013

We went straight to The Orangery at Kensington Palace for high tea after meeting up with mom this morning. It was the one thing she requested we do, so we made sure to go before seeing more of London.

The traffic moves at a different direction than at home. Since mom isn't used to it she looks the wrong way when we cross the streets. Mike has had to grab her a few times to stop her from walking into incoming traffic. Thank goodness he has been observant because we have had several close calls! Mom doesn't seem to care. When Mike gently takes her arm she just squeals, "oh" and proceeds to laugh and laugh about it.

To save money we shared a hotel room. Mike and I had the king size bed while she slept on the fold out. At about 3am, Mike and I woke to a loud noise. It was mom snoring! It was the loudest snore I have ever heard! Mike and I put the covers over our heads and giggled like little kids. We laughed so hard it woke mom. She said, "Guys, stop," but then started laughing at herself before going back to sleep. I have really enjoyed traveling with mom and Mike. I was afraid there were going to be some disagreements, but it has brought us closer than before.

XO, E

May 10, 2013

Slept in a little. Made our way by river taxi to the Tower of London. When we got there, people were gathered around the fence. Platoons of soldiers were in formation, and then began to play. We got there just in time to see the procession. The line to the Crown Jewels was very long. We took a great free tour instead led by a guide dressed up in a beefeater uniform. We ended up in the chapel of the Tower and were able to sit down. The guide was both informative and funny. Got something to eat, Cornish pastry for me and got in line for the Crown Jewels. Wait wasn't too long. The Crown Jewels were pretty spectacular.

I started to get pretty tired. We were supposed to meet my cousin, Sarah at the hotel at 5PM that day. The kids had tickets to ride the London Eye, so they went to ride it while I met Sarah at the hotel. I waited in the lobby and Sarah came right to me. We chatted for almost an hour until the kids came. It was very easy because we have a lot in common. We had to take the train to Sarah's home. We had a very tough time navigating the stairs and crowds with large suitcases, which made me pretty grouchy. Sarah's home is over 100 years old! Her two adopted children and her son's girlfriend who is 4 months pregnant live with them. They have an elderly cocker spaniel, Snoopy, and a new little rescue dog from Eastern Europe, Angel. Her husband, Phil, came home, and we took a drive to an artist's party at a huge home near where they live. The party had all sorts of art for sale as well as martinis to drink. Had a beautiful yard that went on forever. We went to an Indian restaurant afterwards for dinner. Had a great time! Mike and Erin getting along with Phil talking about the Sundance Film Festival in Park City. They went to the pub while the rest of us went to bed.

Namaste, Jude

May 10, 2013

After touring the Tower of London, I read another email from Dad.

Hi Sweetie,

I got your message, but the phone didn't ring. Thanks for calling. I'm glad all's well.

The bank debit card fraud department left a message for you on the home phone, nothing specific. Have you had a problem?

Hayley seems to be doing well and trying although it's a long story. She has seen her therapist and is supposed to go to group tonight.

See you soon.

Love, D

It makes me happy to hear Hayley is doing well at home. I don't get to see much of her, and want to help dad out as much as I can. I have had a wonderful time away, but I'm ready to come home.

XO, E

May 11, 2013

Slept well on a mattress in Sarah's front room. The kids had their own room in the attic. Sarah made bacon, eggs, and toast for breakfast. Phil drove us to London because he had an appt. at the Apple store. He dropped us off at Covent Garden. I loved all the different stalls with a variety of homemade crafts. Bought Hayley and Becky a scarf, and then went to Oxford Street for the remainder of the day. Erin was very happy shopping at all of the different shops. We found a great restaurant, China Noodle House for lunch. I could not believe how many people were on the streets. It felt like Christmas time in Salt Lake City. Mike wanted to buy his mom a hat, and we found a great selection at Marks and Spencer's. We needed to phone Phil and Sarah and asked one of the store clerks if we could use her phone. She gave us to her manager who proceeded to help us to the point of suggesting we meet

Phil at the pub around the corner. She found a gentleman who worked there named David to help us find wine and flowers to give to our gracious hosts. He was about my age and very friendly to me and the kids. He took us to the pub and gave me a kiss good-bye! Sarah made a wonderful roast chicken dinner with homemade bread and ice cream! We gave her flowers and Phil wine and beer. So happy I could connect with her and meet her family.

Namaste, Jude

May 11, 2013

We decided to spend our last day in London shopping. I love shopping in different countries because I find treasures I can't get at home. When we arrived, Mike could tell how excited I was to be there. He told mom, "she's in her element" and stood back to let me shop. We all bought things for ourselves, souvenirs for friends and family. I even found my going away dress for our wedding at a small boutique. After a nice lunch we made our way to the large department stores. I was in heaven! They were huge and had every brand I could think of. I forgot how amazing the department stores are in Europe. What a great way to spend our last day in England.

XO, E

May 12, 2013

Got up early to go to the airport. Phil was kind enough to drive us. The kids were flying out of Heathrow, and I flew out of Luton, opposite parts of the city. I got to know Phil a little better while we were alone in the car together. Flew to Knock, Ireland, to be picked up by a crying Becky. She thought I had missed my flight. Very, rainy cold. She drove us to Westport to pick up groceries. Quaint little town. I paid for the groceries, and we drove to Drummin where she lives. So beautiful. Lots of sheep and lambs everywhere. Stone walls bordered the fields. Becky's cottage is away from town. Her closest neighbor is ½ mile away down by a country road. Becky gave me her room. Her cottage is cozy and has everything we need. The fireplace takes up one wall. *A wood stove insert with a glass door helps heat the house. The house is 200 years old! We had cheese and crackers and some wine. Then went to a local pub. The scenery was beautiful, rolling hills and views of the Atlantic Ocean. While we were sitting at the pub, a boy about 8 years old started to do some Irish dancing by himself in front of the pub patrons. He then went behind the bar serving customers.*

Namaste, Jude

May 12, 2013

Mom is headed to Ireland to spend a week with her good friend, Becky in her cottage in the country. I was invited, but I felt like mom could use some alone time with one of her closest friends. We gave mom a big hug goodbye and wished her well on her next adventure.

A feeling of gratitude flooded my body as we climbed into the clouds. I couldn't believe we were able to make one of mom's dreams come true. It was a special trip none of us will ever forget. As I nodded goodbye to the green landscape below I decided that one of my goals was to help make the upcoming years some of mom's best.

XO, E

May 13, 2013

Have had an amazing time connecting with family, but so happy to be in Ireland now with Becky at her home. It is more beautiful than I imagined. I slept in until 10:30! Left around lunchtime to go to the Croagh Patrick museum. Becky took the scenic route along a loch. The weather is rainy and five minutes later it will be sunny. Everywhere I looked there was a photo op. We went to the museum, and then ate at the Tower Pub in Westport Patrick. One of the bartenders is originally from Salt Lake City, and he fell in love with an Irish girl while he was in Chicago. Our meal was very good. I had fish n' chips and Becky had beef stew. We shopped in Westport for some gifts to take home. Found two beautiful wool blankets for the girls. One of the shops we went in, the shopkeeper, Nick, told us many stories of this trip to the US with his boss for a trade show. Becky really related to him well. Made our way home stopping at an old church along the side of the road. Took some photos. Hayley came home, although, I don't want to know the long story until I get home. She is in therapy, but living at her dad's.

Namaste, Jude

May 14, 2013

Slept well again, Spent the morning pulling weeds and planting flowers in the garden. Still raining on and off, very chilly as well. Becky made us a great breakfast of eggs, veggies and toast. Her coffee is the best I have had on this trip. We had plans to meet friends for dinner in a little town about a half hour from Drummin. Another spectacular drive, but this time we went around the shores of a lake with several green islands. One of the islands had an old pirate's castle on it. We stopped in for a drink at Keane's pub. A young man asked if he could film us drinking Guinness and giving each other a toast. He was making a documentary about Irish pubs! We made our way to Cong and on the fringe of town there were ruins of an abbey with the river close by. One of the small, stone buildings was a fishing hut where we took lots of photos. We met friends at the pub. One of them is from Salt Lake and the other is Irish. They are a couple who have been together for 6 years. Delightful women.

Namaste, Jude

May 15, 2013

We had a lazy morning and then went to a neighbor's for tea and sandwiches and jam tarts and Cadbury fudge for dessert. She is very warm and welcoming and works three nights a week at a local pub in Drummin. We spent the afternoon cleaning the cottage, gardening, and getting ready to leave on Thursday. We decided to drink the rest of the wine that evening, almost two bottles! Had fun singing along to Joni Mitchell sitting by the fire.

Slept well. Feeling lucky that I was able to get away to see family and friend. It was a much needed trip.

Namaste, Jude

May 18, 2013

I am supposed to be starting suboxone in a few days. Which means I will no longer rely on opiates to get me through. I have now been using opiates on a daily basis for three and a half years. Most of those years were pain pills and eventually moved to heroin. I am nervous, excited, and anxious to start my suboxone regime. I have literally felt like my life was out of control for years now. The drugs took over my life and everything I was sure I knew about myself went out the window. I am a new person now. Some things have changed for the better, some for the worse. All I know is, I'm ready. I'm ready to live the life I deserve to live. My life has been built on lies for far too long. It's time to start with a clean slate and to look at my addiction as a mere disease. A disease that will take a lot of work daily. But I know I will do it.

Of course, I do have my reservations or a "fear of the unknown," if you will. I have had opiates a part of my life for so long now to think that I will no longer need or want them is terrifying, yet amazing. This demon has haunted me for far too long. It's now or never, I can't waste anymore time. I'm excited to have myself back again. To be the hardworking, smart, and beautiful woman that I know I am deep down inside.

I now realize that doing the right things in life will always be more challenging, but the outcome is what makes the challenge worth it. I'm starting from scratch, building my life from the bottom, and moving on up.

-Hayz

May 22, 2013

Hayley is living with her dad again. She just called me to say she has a job interview as a server for a local Mexican restaurant. I feel like I hold my breath when I am with her for fear she will disappear again. Living in the present with no thought of what the future may bring. Kind of like cancer. I see my breast oncologist on Friday. I have not seen her since December. I am still feeling great with no symptoms of anything wrong.

Namaste, Jude

May 24, 2013

Hayley is still home, which has been nice for everyone. She went on a hike with Dad and Lucy to the Uinta Mountains yesterday, and joined mom and I at Huntsman for a doctor's appointment. Mom is now seeing two different oncologists. One who specializes in stomach cancer, and one who specializes in breast. Today we saw the breast cancer doctor. Everything seems to be going well. Her tumor markers haven't gone up for a while, so she is sticking with what the doctor has prescribed until her body develops a defense against it. I am so grateful the cancer hasn't gotten worse. She is happy, experiences minimal pain or discomfort, and able to live her life.

After the appointment, we went to lunch before going to try on more wedding gowns. Hayley wasn't able to come to my first appointment, and I really wanted her to be there to help me find "the dress." My friend Ali met us there. We are close friends and great shopping partners. She recently got engaged and is planning a wedding a week after ours. When we made these plans, she wasn't engaged yet, so it wasn't our intention to try on dresses together, but it made it so special to be able to share such a memorable moment with one of my best friends. I tried on several dresses, but didn't find anything I loved. Ali tried on a few and when she walked out of the dressing room in the last dress she was glowing. The saleswoman put a veil on her, and she began to cry tears of joy. It was "the one!" I can't wait to see her in it on her wedding day.

XO, E

May 24, 2013

I wake up every morning feeling guilty, and like I need to redeem myself to my loved ones. I feel so incomplete every day. I need to find something to occupy my mind, and to take place of the drugs. I am done being this person. I feel like a really, really bad person when I'm using, and I hate it because that's not ME!

I am a good person who can make the right decisions. It's time to change my ways, time to succeed and live a normal life. No more lying, especially to my family and close friends. No wonder why I'm so afraid to be myself. It's all lies. Lying to my parents is some teenager type shit. I need to stop allowing a drug (an inanimate object) control my life. No more impulsive actions, no more stealing. GET MY MIND RIGHT!

-Hayz

May 26, 2013

Moving slowly this morning. A friend came over yesterday to help me work on the deck. I am grateful for his help because my back, legs and shoulders are sore from bending over and scraping. I have lived in this house for eleven years now. There is still so much work to be done. I should have spent the money from my trip on my house. No regrets. The gifts I received there are intangible, but oh so precious. I can't put them into words at the moment. So much to process.

One of the side effects of the meds I am taking is joint pain. My oncologist suggested acupuncture. The pain is particularly bad when I am working. Most of the time I try to ignore it, or find other ways of holding my instruments.

Hayley seems to be doing well. So hard to know for sure. She did get a job as a server/busser at a local restaurant. Holding my breath.

Namaste, Jude

June 7, 2013

We usually go out to dinner for mom's birthday, but this year she planned a trip to a little town called Ivins in Southern Utah. She is going with her goddess group, the Women's Sacred Circle. Mame took her to Ivins at the beginning of the year to stay in a small hotel owned by her friend's mother, Katie. Mom immediately hit it off with the Katie and couldn't wait to take the goddesses down there for a retreat. It is the perfect way for her to celebrate her birthday. I am happy she has so many wonderful friends who want to be there and support her through such a crazy time in her life.

XO, E

June 10, 2013

I feel so lucky to have all the amazing friends and the most supportive family I could ask for. Honestly, how did I get so lucky? Thank you to all of you who haven't given up on me. You know who you are. Love y'all.

-Hayz

June 15, 2013

Been struggling this past week. I have been letting others mess with my energy. I think my ex is going to tell Hayley to hit the road. She refuses help. She continues to use drugs, be dishonest, and manipulative with both of us. Of course we enable her, which isn't good, so I understand. I just don't know what to do at times. I don't know what to say to her. I feel I have lost my daughter. Her spirit seems to have disappeared. So much like a mental illness in many ways. I am better physically and have spent the past six months working on myself to stay strong and resilient as a cancer warrior.

Now there is time to go back here, and I am not sure how to proceed. I feel
pain, despair and sadness. Meditated this morning amongst the birds. I do
feel better. I need to start going to Alanon meetings again.

Namaste, Jude

June 20, 2013

The summer of 2013 is already full of wedding planning and house
hunting. Our wedding date is September 1st, so we only have a few
months to get everything taken care of. We are also trying to find a house
which has made our life a bit more stressful. When Mike drove past one
of the homes we put an offer on a couple months ago, he noticed a lot of
construction going on, almost like it is being flipped. He spoke to the
contractor who also happens to be the realtor, and he said they were
planning on selling after they remodel. Apparently, it needed A LOT of
work. Mike told him we were interested in purchasing the home when
they were finished, and he said we would be the first people to put an
offer on it. I am excited because it is the house we like the most out of all
of the houses we saw. It is also close to mom, so if she needs anything we
would only be a couple blocks away.

We love to go to concerts all year, but during the summer we usually see
at least 1 or 2 concerts a week! My love of music came from my parents.
They would go to concerts a lot and take me with them when they could.
They accompanied me to my first concert, The Rolling Stones. When
people ask me what my first concert was a look of surprise comes to their
face when I tell them. They go on to say how lucky I am to have such cool
parents. I still remember the first time I was awed by the lights, the
crowd, and the feeling I got from hearing my favorite songs. To watch
musicians get lost in the music, and to allow them to take you with them
is a feeling like no other. I was instantly hooked. Last night we saw the
legendary Jackson Browne with dad, and we saw Tony Bennett tonight. I

feel so grateful to have such cool parents who introduced me to music at such a young age.

XO, E

July 4, 2013

Today is Hayley's b-day. We picked her up and took her to dinner. She is again trying to detox and live a different life. I spent last night with her, just the two of us. There is such a fine line between caring and enabling. I gave her money to score some suboxone last night to prevent withdrawal symptoms. She is then entering an outpatient facility next week. I know we have been through this before, but what's a parent to do? She has a lot of anxiety and is depressed.

Namaste, Jude

July 4, 2013

The 4th of July is Hayley's birthday. Mom calls Hayley her little firecracker. I still remember the night when my dad woke me up to tell me mom was in labor. It was 2AM, but I was so excited I didn't care how late it was. I hopped right out of bed, and rushed to get ready. I couldn't wait to be a big sister! I sat on Aunt Marcia's lap as I watched Hayley push her way into the world. I knew at that moment that my one of my job's as her big sister is to be her protector, and it breaks my heart knowing I haven't been able to save her from the drug that is destroying her life. I try, but she won't open up to me. She tells me she is fine even though I know she's not. I tell her I am her for her, but it's all up to her.

Because I am 9 ½ years older I feel like her parent much of the time, but I have really tried to be more of a sister than a mom. I let her borrow my clothes, I would take her to the mall, and took her to her first concert, The Backstreet Boys. We have had a great relationship, until recently. She isn't the little sister I once knew. She is distant and defensive. We haven't ever fought before the drug inhabited her body. Now I feel like that's all she wants to do.

She isn't around much, but she makes sure to come home for her birthday. She seems okay, but I can tell she is struggling. None of us understand or know how to help her get better.

XO, E

July 12, 2013

Mom has her 3 month appointment with Dr. Wilson today. I couldn't sleep at all last night because when I measured her for her Mother of the Bride dress the other day she said it felt like the fluid was back in her stomach. I'm very anxious for today's appointment.

Other than my Mom's cancer things are going pretty well I suppose. Last week was my 23rd birthday, and it was probably my worst birthday ever. There were no significant events to make it that way. I just seem to have lost my spirit, and I feel an extreme disconnect with everyone and everything around me. Most days I feel lonely, lost, and depressed. I wish I didn't feel so miserable every day.

I need love, honest love. I need someone to talk to me about something else other than my addiction or treatment or finding a job. I need a friend. I need help.

-Hayz

July 16, 2013

I have been feeling very lonely, extremely misunderstood and out of place. I have never been so lost in my life. I keep procrastinating sobriety, and I don't quite understand why I continue to follow down this path of self destruction. I have been so out of touch, and high that I've been ignoring major events in the recent years. I think it is a big part as to why I keep self medicating the emotional pain.

Well, today I had a realization. I was talking to some friends about Grant, and after every story I told them about how he treated me they would both gasp. The more and more we got to talking, the more real the flashbacks became. Then, out of nowhere I started thinking about the abortion I had a couple years ago and the sexual abuse I experienced as a child. I continued to tell them about what had happened and how traumatic it was for me. I then realized this was the first time I had thought about let alone talk to someone about the hardest times of my life. No wonder I continue to run from the real world, real feeling, and real pain. I have been suppressing so many emotions that I finally understand why I feel the way I do every day. Subconsciously, I have been blocking out the abuse from Grant, the abortion and all of the pain I've endured. I have been so hard on myself because I have lacked motivation and I didn't understand why I wasn't able to want sobriety for myself. Now I realize I need to face my pain head on. I can't keep running from reality. Stop downplaying what happened to you. You are allowed to feel like a victim.

A lot of the times, I don't want people to feel bad for me, or I don't want people to think that I'm telling them these things so they will pity me or for the attention. I hold so much in that I constantly have tightness in my chest. I know that I am a victim of abuse, but why do I feel guilty? Why am I the one who has to suffer? I'm sick of putting on this front and fake-ass smile like I'm okay when really I am in so much pain.

Now that I look back, I realize I don't remember a time where I actually was doing something for myself. I was never confident with myself. In school, in sports, I was only doing it because that's what I was "supposed" to do. I have never truly wanted to do anything in life for ME! I don't know how to love myself.

I don't know how to be sure of myself. I'm always second guessing myself or thinking too much.

I feel trapped, not only by my addiction, but by my anxiety/self-image issues. I want to know what it feels like to actually love myself. To actually care and want what's best for me.

I need to learn how to make myself happy and to stop looking to others for acceptance. I feel so vulnerable right now. It seems like everything that people say about me whether it is constructive or not, I take it so personally. I've never been so sensitive, defensive, and closed off.

-Hayz

July 17, 2013

Just arrived home after a long, productive day at work. Stopped by the local market to buy dog treats, sushi and Dos Equis. The kitchen fan is whirring. Have shorts on, feet up on the chair in front of me. All is right with the world at this very moment. Bare legs, free feeling, full belly, refreshing taste of beer filling up my mouth, slowly going down to my innards. Listening to the quiet, gray clouds rolling in again like they have for the past several nights, rain? Trees stationery, no wind to move them, burn on my right arm stings from opening the autoclave too quickly, let it alone or tend to it? Looking at greenish gold toe nail polish that I have grown tired of on my toenails, what color next? Turquoise, orange, pinkish purple, tickles my toes when I paint them, dogs roll on the floor while smelling polish remover, wonder why. Another swig of beer, little burp, gentle smiling. Heart is full, bursting with star like bits of wonder and delight.

Namaste, Jude

July 17, 2013

Mike and I don't know where we were going to be married, but we do know we want to be married in the mountains. As we were driving past the McPolin farm in Park City, I immediately exclaimed, "Why don't we get married there?" Mike looked confused, so I pointed to the barn and said "There!" He didn't hesitate in turning the car around to find a place to park so we could explore the grounds. I drive past the barn every day I go to work, but I haven't ever taken the time to walk around. As we walked up to the large white structure I got the same feeling I did as when we walked into Wayfarer's Chapel. We aren't able to make Wayfarer's work and I didn't know if I was ever going to have that feeling again. I was relieved when I felt that same wave of electricity I felt only a few months ago. There is a large split tree with an opening in the middle that resembles a heart in the back of the barn. I could picture us saying our vows under the green canopy with our friends and family standing nearby. It is perfect!

XO, E

July 19, 2013

Today, I realized how negative and sensitive I've become. I instantly think people are criticizing or misjudging me when they are just trying to give me advice. I've always been a pretty positive person, so coming to this realization is a big deal for me. Not only have I been unaware to how much I've changed, but I seem to have turned into a complete opposite of my old self. I used to be able to see the good in everything. I used to love being around people, I loved summer, shopping, and boys.

I can't believe I've allowed myself to turn into such a miserable person. Grateful for the realization, but definitely have a lot to work on.

-Hayz

July 21, 2013

Erin's wedding shower is today. Hayley is home and seems to be finding herself this time. I will have both my girls around me today as well as my friends and Erin's too. Life is good.

Namaste, Jude

July 21, 2013

I asked Lexi to be my maid of honor. I always dreamt of Hayley being my maid of honor, but she isn't in a place where she can be the support I need. Lexi is one of my dearest friends, and was honored to take on the roll. She offered to throw me a bridal shower at her house, and it was beautiful. I walked into a backyard full of flowers and friends from throughout my life. I hardly get to spend time with my girlfriends because we have gotten so busy with our own lives. Being a care giver can be lonely at times, but seeing them support me during such special moment in my life was a reminder that I have some amazing women to help me when I need it the most. Hayley even made it! It meant so much to have her and mom there with my closest friends. It was a day full of love.

XO, E

July 24, 2013

My life has been pretty amazing lately.

Spent all of last Friday helping mom paint her kitchen, then went shopping for Erin's bridal shower.

Spent most of Saturday with friends and went on a late night stroll around the neighborhood with Celine (just like old times).

Sunday was Erin's bridal shower!!! Which couldn't have been a better turnout! Many of her friend's from elementary/ high school were able to come, and I hadn't seen most of them in over 10 years.

I honestly don't know what I did or I how I got so lucky to have SO many amazing people in my life.

-Hayz

July 28, 2013

Got some terrific news from my oncologist last week. My tumor markers are way down from six months ago, which means current treatment has been *effective keeping cancer a bay. Guess I need to start saving for retirement again.*

I am doing well apart from a bit of sadness that seems to ebb and flow day to day. Spoke with my therapist about it. She thought it may be the meds I am taking, but according to my oncologist not so. I think it is because of the losses I have experienced the past year. Just have to be easy on myself and not listen to the critic in my head. Today has been better mood wise. I try to remember that the mind weaves stories that we believe, but they are pure fantasy. Or, maybe they are flashbacks from acid and mescaline trips?

Hayley is okay, although I hesitate to look more than one day ahead. We went to dinner last night and to a movie.

Namaste, Jude

July 28, 2013

I feel like birthday celebrations have lost a lot of purpose. Recently, I was at a funeral, and I couldn't stop wishing that the person, whose life we were celebrating was still alive to witness all the love that people have for him. THEN, I realized that every birthday is celebrating another year that all of us are alive AND that we should make a bigger deal out of people's birthdays because you never know when they won't be there to celebrate their life with you.

Personally, I would much rather celebrate somebody's life with them, rather than wishing they were here.

Just a thought.

-Hayz

August 21, 2013

Hayley is 11 days sober. I went to a Heroin Anonymous meeting with her last week. Most of the people there were young men. Their stories and struggles were heartbreaking. With invisible tears I prayed for these lost boys. I remember thinking of heroin addicts when I was young? They were men and women strung out on the dirty streets of NYC. They weren't our children...

Namaste, Jude

August 21, 2013

I had my final fitting for my dress today. The skirt is so big it took over the tiny dressing room where it was waiting for me. The woman who designed my dress, Mary had sent me pictures, but I hadn't seen it in person until now. The dress is a sweetheart neckline ball gown in white with lace trim at the bottom. Mary sewed vines and handmade, organza flowers all over the bust and onto the top of the skirt. I couldn't wait to put it on.

As I lifted the heavy gown over my body I started to tremble with excitement. When I walked out of the fitting room, she and the owner of the store gasped! Tears came to my eyes as I turned around to look at myself in the mirror. Seeing myself in a big white gown made it all so real. I felt like a princess. It's hard to believe we are getting married in a couple weeks!

XO, E

August 25, 2013

Hayley has left again. Mom and dad have been going to meetings with her, but she isn't ready to get better. We can't force her to do something she doesn't want to do.

We were planning on closing on the house at the end of this month, but again things have gotten pushed back. I really want to get into our home, but I am happy we aren't adding the stress of buying a house a few days before we get married. I am not too worried about the wedding. It's funny; I haven't been bridezilla at all. Mike has been pickier than I have, so he likes to call himself groomzilla. I have really appreciated how hands he has been and make sure to tell him. Only a few more days away! I really hope Hayley will be there.

XO, E

August 25, 2013

I am back at the trailer park. I loved being with my family, but it was getting to be too much. I needed an escape from reality. It is hard for me to face myself, which has made me very depressed. I don't think anyone understands except for Grant. I know I should be happy, but a little voice in my head continues to tell me I am not good enough. Heroin is the only thing that makes me feel better. It is the only life I know.

-Hayz

August 28, 2013

Hayley has relapsed again. She also has a staph or some kind of bacterial infection on her face. She is living with her boyfriend who is a user as well. Sigh.

Namaste, Jude

August 31, 2013

Since we wanted to have our love for live music be a part of our wedding weekend I came up with the idea of going to a rehearsal concert instead of hosting a big dinner. Luckily, One Republic was having a concert at a local ski resort the night before our wedding. They allow food and drinks, so dad made a large picnic consisting of sandwiches, salads and cookies for everyone. Mike and I brought lots of wine.

The grassy hill where the audience sits was very wet and muddy due to the rainstorm we had that day. People were sliding down the soggy grass.

At one point Mike was jumping around with his friends, slipped and fell into a large patch of mud. His pants were ruined! We started laughing as he almost pulled me down with him when I helped him up. We weren't going to let a little mud ruin our night.

Our parents, bridesmaids, groomsmen, family from out of town, and even Mike's 85 year old grandma came. It brought a smile to my face to see her dancing with her grandchildren. Dancing is a form of expression that no matter how old you get you can still express yourself. None of us cared about our age or how silly we may have looked. We were too busy having fun and isn't that what's life is about? Living and having a great time doing it.

XO, E

September 1, 2013

Today is the big day! Many people have told me they were nervous on their wedding day, but when I opened my eyes and did a big stretch I was surprised I didn't feel any nerves. I was eager to wake up to start the day.

I asked my bridal party to go on a hike with me before we started to get ready. The crisp fall weather and the trees showing off their new colors excited me for the changes that lie just around the corner. It's incredible to watch the tree's get ready to show us just how beautiful it is to let things go and move forward. I stopped to let everyone walk in front of me. I needed a moment to myself before the busy day ahead. I closed my eyes and felt the sunshine on my face. I was happy. A feeling that was a little foreign to me because I hadn't felt it in a while. Thinking of all of the adventures I have ahead of me made me feel at ease. Getting married was one of the many things I have to look forward to. My little meditation was interrupted by the vibration of my phone in my pocket. It was mom calling to tell me that she can't get a hold of Hayley. She was supposed to pick her up to come get ready with everyone, but she wouldn't answer her texts or calls. She was crying, but more angry than anything. I asked her to come without her and we will figure it out.

Mom walked in the door looking very stressed. I immediately knew it was about Hayley. She said she called Carol on her way up the canyon and dropped off Hayley's dress. Carol promised she would get Hayley to the wedding on time. To calm her down I gave mom a glass of champagne. After a few sips the bubbles went straight to her head, and she was finally able to relax.

At one point our photographer, Heidi asked for me to help her put my wedding dress in a tree. I am all for being outside, but the tree she asked me to climb was a little high, so my bridesman, Lafe offered to help. He effortlessly hopped up onto the lowest limb and climbed the tree to place it in the perfect place. Everyone needs a bridesman!

It was time for me to put on my dress. Lexi held my hand as I stepped into the large gown. Ali and Kristin helped slide it up and Heidi laced up the corset. A local jewelry store lent me beautiful diamond earrings that matched my engagement ring for my something borrowed. My something blue was blue stitching of our wedding date inside my wedding dress, and the something old was an old six pence mom put in my shoe for good luck. The sixpence tradition began in late 17th century England as a part of the dowry gift to the groom. As time went on, the coin became more of a good luck charm worn in the left shoe of the bride on her wedding day. Since mom is from England, it was important to us to incorporate some of our British heritage. Everyone started to cry as we did one group hug.

We made our way to the limo to take us to the barn. During the short 5 minute drive mom called Carol to get filled in on what was going on. Carol said she was on her way to pick Hayley up with her dress in the car. For some reason I wasn't very stressed out. Everything was going to happen the way it needed to happen. Hayley's addiction is bigger than any of us, and I have learned the best thing to do is to not get too upset when she isn't around.

Mike and I didn't want to be at the altar when we first saw each other on our wedding day, so when we arrived to the barn I stood at the front while my friends went to get Mike. As he peeked around the corner of the barn a huge grin came to his face. He ran up to me like he hadn't seen me in weeks and gave me a big hug. Our friends cheered as he kissed me. Our bridal party has been with us for so many important moments in our life it was special to be able to share this moment with only them.

Mike took my hand and led me to the back of a little house near the tree where the bridal party was waiting. The ceremony was scheduled to start at 4 and when 4:05 rolled around Hayley still wasn't there. Mom called Carol, but she didn't answer. Everyone was frantic, but for some reason I stayed calm. Of course I wanted Hayley there, but we couldn't control the situation at that point. I asked if we could wait a few more minutes, but big gray clouds were rolling in. We needed to get the show on the road if we didn't want to be standing in a rain storm. At 4:15 I turned around to see mom giving Hayley a big hug. We were so relieved she made it. Carol and her daughter, Angela drove to the trailer park to pick her up, made her change into her dress and do her makeup in the car. Mom and I were so grateful for Carol to take over like she did. All of us wanted Hayley there, but I think mom was happier to see her than anyone.

The groomsmen and Mike made their way to the tree. My bridesmaids and bridesman walked one by one to meet them there. Lafe carried the black robe dad wore when he was a court commissioner instead of flowers. As I watched Hayley walk away I took a deep breath and held onto my dad's arm. I still wasn't nervous about marrying Mike. The only thing I was afraid of was not being daddy's little girl anymore. This was the last walk we were going to take together before I became someone's wife. We walked slowly behind the flower girls, Cosette and Giselle. As

Cosette would throw the petals Giselle would stop to pick them up. Because she kept stopping to pick them up my dad and I passed her by. Everyone laughed as she stepped on the train of my dress, trying to get the petals underneath. She stole the show and it was just what I wanted.

Dad took his position while Lafe helped him put on his robe. He has officiated many weddings while being a court commissioner. I always knew I wanted him to officiate ours and I am grateful that Mike agreed. The ceremony he wrote for us was beautiful. He included our love for the outdoors and it being the reason why we decided to be married in the mountains. He spoke about marriage being the intimate sharing of our lives, yet not letting this sharing diminish our individual selves.

He also included a quote by Albert Camus:

> *"Don't walk in front of me;*
> *I may not follow;*
> *Don't walk behind me;*
> *I may not lead;*
> *Just walk beside me and be my friend."*

Dad started to choke up as he asked me to say my vows. When I looked up at the strong man I always knew I was surprised to see tears coming to his light blue eyes. I had never seen him cry or hear him get choked up like that. Mike started to cry a bit too. Surprisingly enough, I was able to hold it in, but was touched to see the two men in my life get teary eyed. One man was letting me go onto the next chapter in my life, while the other was excited for the new one to begin. I feel lucky to have two, amazing men who love me so much.

XO, E

September 2, 2013

Mike's mom got us a hotel room at The Grand America for our wedding night. It was a real treat to be able to stay there and have breakfast this morning before meeting family.

Much of our family who had traveled from out of town are still in Utah, so we planned an after wedding event for all of those who stayed. A local ski resort, Snowbird holds an annual Oktoberfest, and we haven't missed a year yet. We thought it was the perfect thing to do with our guests. When the band played a German wedding song, they asked Mike and I to have another first dance in front of the crowd. We then danced with our family and ate yummy German food. It was a nice way to spend time with family who we don't get to see often.

On the way home we stopped by the reception venue to grab a few things we left there. They were still cleaning, so Mike and I helped finish up. We gathered our things and went to dad's house to open gifts. Since he was unable to come to Snowbird it was really nice to be able to spend some time with him after the wedding.

We had a great wedding weekend and although Mike and I have been together for such a long time getting married gave us a crazy high. It was like we fell in love with each other all over again. I didn't think I would feel this way and I don't want the feeling to go away. I am so in love with my husband.

XO, E

September 2, 2013

I barely made it to my sister's wedding. I was supposed to drive to Park City with my mom in the morning, but didn't hear her calls or texts because I was sound asleep from being up all night. I woke up two hours before the wedding! I felt terrible after talking to mom. It was the most upset she has been in a while. I started crying because I didn't know how I was going to get there. I don't have a car and didn't want to disrespect my sister by being late, so I figured it was best I didn't go, until Carol called. She assured me that she would be able to get me there in time. She even had my dress! I quickly straightened my hair and got dressed in the car as we drove up the windy roads. She was driving so fast around the turns I had a hard time putting on my makeup. I am surprised I didn't have mascara marks across my face. Carol slammed on her breaks when we pulled up to the barn and told me to run. I took off my shoes and sprinted up the cement pathway to the back of the barn. Mom was in tears when she saw me. She rushed to give me a huge hug before I went to get in line. I missed the rehearsal, so I just followed the lead of my sister's best friend's who used to know me as Erin's naive little sister, not a drug addict who was late to her sister's wedding.

While I watched my dad walk my sister down the aisle I felt glad I didn't miss such a memorable day, but I couldn't help but feel the judgmental stares from loved ones. I felt them looking at my fresh picked marks on my face and pale skin. I am so sick of being viewed as the drug addict sister, even though I know I am. I had to get high in order to be at the wedding, but I don't think anyone knew. I am used to putting on an act at this point. I really wish I didn't need to be in my altered state for on such an important day, but if I don't feed my addiction every two hours I will be sick to my stomach. It's not that I want to be high; it's that I want to stay well.

All in all it was a great day. I got to see a lot good friends and it was a beautiful reception. There were even fireworks! The highlight of the night was being able to dance the night away with my two best friends, Lydia and Celine. I am lucky to have two amazing people in my life who will never give up on me.

I was filled with so much love and joy that when I got home I wrote on Facebook, "A HUGE congrats to my gorgeous sister and my newly official brother-in-law! After dating for 10 years, they finally got married! When things are meant to be, it's funny how everything just seems to fall into place. I couldn't have pictured a more perfect wedding for you two and hope the life you have ahead of you is just as magical. Love you guys."

-Hayz

September 3, 2013

We have been approved for a loan to purchase our home, but it is still not ready. Mike is in his apartment and even though, we are officially married I feel silly to move into his place for a few weeks, so I have continued to live with my dad until we can move into our new home. It sounds so weird to be married and not living with my husband, but it makes more sense this way. I love living with dad. He is my best friend, and we have been able to spend a lot of quality time together while being roommates. I am sad to move out, but ready to take on this next stage with my now husband.

XO, E

September 10, 2013

Mame and I took off for the desert just outside of Moab on Friday. I needed to be in the quiet and with spirit most desperately. Mame has a '98 Toyota 4 Runner. She knew of a place to camp where no one would join us on the road to Canyonlands. I talked her into sleeping without a tent under the stars. We smoked a little, drank a tequila cocktail, and then headed to bed. I felt like the stars were talking to me. One star in particular seemed to draw me upwards into the night's sky. Got up the next morning long before Mame, read, and enjoyed the sunrise. We planned to rent inner tubes to float the Colorado River for a few miles. There were no inner tubes for rent anywhere. That should have been our first clue. The only tire company in town rented us a couple of truck inner tubes. The toothless owner, Cecil smirked when we told him our plan. He told us the river had eaten about a half dozen people that summer. Not to be deterred, we went across the street to a raft company to rent life jackets. I found out life jackets are not tailored to full figured women. My boobs were flattened. I was very tempted to cut boob holes to free myself. A couple of local Moab friends drove us to the beginning of our planned river trip. We dropped Mame's vehicle about three miles down the river. About 500 ft down the river what seemed like mild rapids divided the river into two lanes. Mame freaked out while I remarkably told her we could just go around the rapids. One of the inner tubes was deformed on one side making it next to impossible to lay in it comfortably. I ended up going straight through the rapids without mishap. Mame was able to divert her tube by madly paddling her hands. We floated for about a 1/4 of a mile close to the bank not realizing that the bramble bushes grazing the river could prove to be a problem. My inner tube had a mesh bag of beer and water serving as an anchor of sorts. I hit the bramble bushes head on, fell out of the tube and started to bob down the river. Mame grabbed my life jacket and pulled me to shore. The tube was hung up in the bush partly because of the beer can anchor. She borrowed my water sandals to navigate the rocky river bottom. At one point she yelled to me, "I'm scared!" She let the river take her to the tube and finally got back to me. Crazy! From then on, the river alternated with mild rapids and a very slow current. Our upper arms were chafed from paddling. The good news is the river was warm and mostly shallow. I think about that day and smile. We went to dinner with our friends, drove home in the dark and saw lightening on the horizon. Put our tents up in the dark with rain flies. Slept great while I was there. Came home on Sunday.

The wedding was beautiful. My ex, Mike used to officiate over weddings when he was a judge. They were married behind an old barn under a split trunk tree. I thought I would cry but really didn't shed a tear. Carol, my friend physically picked up Hayley to be there as maid of honor. She made it in the nick of time. Relief doesn't begin to describe how I felt. I think I wasn't emotional because Erin and Mike have been a couple for almost 10 years. I have loved him for several years now. Still, everything worked out fine. The weather cooperated. The reception was fun and elegant at the same time. Mike and Erin had arranged for fireworks at the end. My brothers and their *wives stayed for a couple of days afterwards. It's funny, but I cried when they left.*

Haven't heard from Hayley since the wedding. Trying to detach.

Namaste, Jude

October 15, 2013

Hayley rarely calls us back or texts us, but she has been posting on Facebook. It's hard not knowing where she is living. Is she on the streets? Is she back at the trailer park, or living with friends? When I see news stories about a young woman who has been involved in a shooting or drug bust my heart skips a beat thinking it could be her. It's hard not knowing where she is. At least I know she is alive when I see her posts, but I wish she can find a way to make it home soon. I want to be able to share this exciting time of my life with her. I still consider her one of my best friends.

XO, E

October 15, 2013

What was supposed to be an early morning drug deal turned into a 3 month long stay in the Devil's playground.

Imagine you are stranded in a trailer park for the next three months. With only the clothes on your back, an overwhelming sense of guilt on your conscience and a hunger for opiates on your brain. Three mentally ill adults around you.

-Hayz

October 25, 2013

Today mom, Mike and I went to the Strides Against Breast Cancer walk. It's been a year since mom was diagnosed. Of course, we invited Hayley, but she is still too sick to come. A volunteer gave mom a sash that said survivor on it. She was eager to put the pink, satin ribbon on. As she slipped it over her head, the memory of the doctor telling us she only had three months to live a year ago came to my mind. I almost started to cry because it wasn't true. She is surviving and wants others to know it too.

It was a cold and rainy day and the route was 2 miles. Even though mom doesn't have much energy, she was determined to walk the entire route with us. As we walked we spoke to others about their stories. Many people had lost loved ones to breast cancer where others were survivors. One story I remember was about a young woman who learned she had breast cancer when she was only 22 years old. Her boyfriend (who was walking with her) felt a lump and asked her to get it checked out, so she did. It turned out to be stage 3 breast cancer, but she was able to beat it and is now cancer free. She is proof that self exams can save your life.

Being with people who have fought or fighting was comforting. Cancer and addiction are both terrifying, but it helps to go through the journey with others who are equally terrified and who are honest about it.

XO, E

October 30, 2013

Beautiful Fall morning here. Sun shining through the golden trees, frost melting on the nearby roofs, mountains like shadows in the distance. I am drinking my second cup of coffee still in robe and slippers. Slept eleven hours last night. Jet lag probably.

My trip to Cleveland was better than anticipated. I stayed with my eldest brother, John and his wife, Bonnie. They live in the country. Their marriage is a long one but not without so many of the bumps that occur in a long partnership. My father recognized me almost at once. I kissed and caressed him quite a bit. His long term memory is remarkable. His short term memory is gone. He was at times very depressed, worrying what happens next to him. We tried to reassure him. At times there was a spark in his eyes especially

when he talked of my mother and the past. All in all a good weekend spent
with family. I wrote a poem about my visit with him.

The Visit

I leave him like so many times before.
Will this be the last time?
I drink in his dad smell, kiss his balding head.
I try not to let him see my eyes tearing up.
When I walked into his room earlier,
head, awkwardly in his lap.
Bones, protruded in places I had never seen.
Skin hung down like wet washing on the line.
He looked up, with recognition.
I silently gave thanks.
They say that music helps the brain
To remember the old days.
I find a Pandora channel of old show tunes.
He began to sing, "With a little bit, with a little bit,
with a little bit of blooming luck."
This moment, a treasure.

I saw my doc today. Good news: Next cat scan in six months rather than
three. Keep with current drug regimen. Seems I am going to live longer than I
thought a year ago. My doc said he may write a journal article about my case.
Such an enigma. It's funny but I don't get nervous about the results anymore.
I am resigned to dealing with whatever the universe hands me. October 1
was my cancer diagnosis year anniversary. I feel a combination of grief and
gratitude. My life is forever changed. And yet I am here to celebrate life at
this very moment. Life is good and to be savored

Namaste, Jude

October 31, 2013

We are officially home owners! We met our realtor to close on our first home this morning. I could barely sign the papers because my hand was shaking out of excitement. We have been looking for our dream home for such a long time I didn't know it we were ever going to be able to find it.

We aren't ready to move our furniture in, but we wanted to spend the evening in our new house. Since it was Halloween, we passed out candy to trick or treaters while we ate sushi takeout on the floor. We talked about what we wanted to do to make our house a home. Thankfully there isn't much to do. Just paint and furniture for now, and if I can talk Mike into it, a dog door for a new puppy. It was a great way to spend the first night in our new home. I can't wait to make many more memories here.

XO, E

November 10, 2013

Looking out my window to the southwest. One lone robin perched on top of the willow tree closest to me. A few small birds accompany him. Ahh. Now there are two robins and no small birds. Maybe they are friends, or lovers, or companions on the journey.

Life is good this morning. The Cathedral of the Madeline is within walking distance to my home. The church bells ring every hour starting at 8AM. I can almost imagine I am in a little town in Europe when they peel. Dogs pleading with their eyes and spirits for a wee walk. Of course I will oblige.

Erin and Mike have moved two blocks from my home. I helped her paint her spare bedroom bright pink with a metallic gold accent wall. I kept thinking of the feminine energy around me as I was painting. I felt like I was welcoming a little girl spirit to their home. I also saw Hayley on Friday after not seeing her since Sept 1. She is staying with her boyfriend and his dad. They are both trying to get sober together. It was wonderful to see her. I feel like I am holding my breath thinking of her. Seeing her helped alleviate some of that stress. Yes. I am living in the breath.

Mame and I, along with a few friends walked a labyrinth at the Jordan Peace Gardens today. Four benches surrounded the labyrinth. They are decorated with mosaic pictures depicting various spiritual aspects as well as the ethnicities making up the community. It was a beautiful sunny, warm fall afternoon. Lovely way to spend a Sunday.

Namaste, Jude

November 28, 2013

My ex hosted his annual Thanksgiving dinner for 25 of us. Hayley has been over two weeks sober and was able to join. She is doing it on her own. Lots to be grateful for just this minute.

Namaste, Jude

November 29, 2013

For many people the day after Thanksgiving is a day to shop for good deals for the upcoming holidays. For mom and I it means going to the mall, not to shop, but to see the holiday decorations and to watch the city turn the holiday lights on. It is a tradition we started when I was young, and we have continued to go every year with Hayley, and now Mike.

This year Mike thought it would be fun to give each of us ladies $25 to spend on whatever we wanted, but we had to do it by 9pm, which was only an hour away. We rushed to our favorite stores, trying to find something we loved. Mom found a scarf in the first store we went in, but Hayley and I were being a little pickier. We were almost out of time when we got to our favorite jewelry store. It was packed, so we didn't know if we would be able to find something by the time the clock struck 9. After we told a saleswoman what we were doing she quickly helped us find the perfect thing. We bought a set of bracelets with otter charms on them. The meaning behind them is that we would be there for each other no matter what we endured. "Known to hold hands to secure themselves from drifting apart, otters are symbols of friendship and unity. Rafting side-by-side, otters are comforting creatures adaptable to change and transition."

Mike was so sweet to come up with such a fun idea. After our treasure hunt we walked around the downtown area to look at all of the beautiful lights. It was a night where mom felt well, Hayley was sober and we could all be together without talking about cancer or addiction.

XO, E

December 7, 2013

This morning mom and I attended a wreath making class at Red Butte Garden with her friend Peg and her daughters. They had such a great time last year; they asked if we would want to go together this year. It was our first time at the class, but the instructors were very helpful. They had lots of greenery to choose from, accents to add to the wreath, and they even had a woman tying big, beautiful bows. Mom loves to do anything that has to do with creating. Especially when she gets to make something out of materials found in nature. It is a great stress reliever for both of us.

Whether I am playing a song on the piano or she is writing poetry, making art gives us a chance to use our imagination, and detach from thinking of cancer or addiction. We don't have to talk nor do, we get to simply be in the moment. It is a beautiful form of therapy that allows us process our emotions outside the moments of loss and grief. We are given a chance to escape and meditate, and it's a way to create joy in our lives because goodness knows, we need a whole lot of it right now.

XO, E

December 29, 2013

I keep doing better health-wise, to the amazement of my doctors. Still taking estrogen blockers by injection and pill form. Not many side effects fortunately. I used to have cat scans every three months. I have now graduated to every six months. Yeah! Guess I am going to be around to create trouble a bit longer.

Hayley is another story. I thought things couldn't get any worse, but she is living with her boyfriend, and his mother in a trailer court. Apparently she is addicted to heroin now. I am writing this on a new laptop because my old one was stolen out of my house a few weeks ago. I suspect the person who stole it was Hayley's boyfriend, who is also a desperate heroin addict. I hold her accountable as well, but she denies being involved. No forced entry, and they left a bus schedule in my bathroom. Neither one of them drive. Stealing from loved ones is a symptom of addiction. I know this intellectually, but am having a difficult time not being angry, sad or hurt. Going to see my therapist tomorrow for a good session to talk, and hopefully make sense of it all.

I did declare a truce at Christmas. I gave her some essentials like food and a hair dryer. Tomorrow, I plan to see her to talk to her about the theft and consequences. I feel I need to put in place. All of this is breaking my heart to say the least. I go to Al Anon meetings, which is for families of addicts and alcoholics. They teach you to detach and work on yourself. So many layers to this disease.

Feeling vulnerable, floundering and searching for the sense of it all. Grateful not to be in the throes of chemo, grateful for family and the others holding me up. Coming up for air-gasping, spitting, clinging to what is familiar and what isn't. Longing for light, peace in whatever shape I can find it. Sitting with the pain and aloneness. Trying to make friends with the sorrow-like cancer but not. Cancer is concrete-no hidden agendas. Google cancer and you have the answers. Google daughter and drug addiction. There are no easy answers. Take care of yourself because you have no control over the disease of addiction and your daughter they say. My daughter is unknown to me. Her spirit dissipates before my eyes. Will she come out of this stronger or forever scarred? Like cancer, all I have is this very moment, this time in the present. All I can do is send her love and the magic of divine intervention. Seems simplistic at best but it is all I have left in my arsenal. Is it enough?

Questions that cannot be asked. Go with the flow. Do life. Smile, nod, and pretend everything is wonderful. Well, it isn't.

Namaste, Jude

2014

"There are fairies at the bottom of our garden."
Her whispers lull me back to sleep.
The fairies will protect me.
I am safe again.

January 1, 2014

Mike and I met at a New Year's Eve party when we were only 21. I was just getting over strep throat, so I wasn't planning on having a midnight kiss. After hearing I was sick, most of the boys at the party wouldn't talk to me, but Mike did. I thought he was so cute. We didn't exchange numbers because I was leaving to go to school at the Fashion Institute of Technology in NYC in a few weeks. We both liked each other, but didn't want to start something serious before I was going to be gone for so long. When I got in the car to go home I lamented as much to our mutual friend. She went inside, brought him out to the car so we could exchange numbers and the rest is history.

Since it is the anniversary of the night we met, we like to go out to dinner before meeting friends. We had dinner at one our favorite restaurants in Park City before driving to a friend's family cabin in the mountains to ring in the New Year. Great way to start 2014!

XO, E

January 4, 2014

I am doing well considering the cold and pollution in the valley, although it has cleared out with the snowfall this morning. I had a talk with Hayley last week, letting her know my boundaries. She cried. I cried. I feel like I can at least live my life with some degree of constancy. The roller coaster ride with her was bringing me down to the point where I wasn't able to focus on my work and other relationships. I gave her photos of us together in happier times. I need to detach with love in order to survive. She called me at midnight on New Years -woke me up.

I had to take Sophie to the vet today. She has been dragging her hind paws when we walk to such a degree that they bleed. Breaks my heart. The vet said small dogs often have neurological issues with their spines. He said she may improve or not. He recommended a dog stroller because I told him I walk Ossie regularly. To not take Sophie as well doesn't seem right. I never thought I would be that person with a small dog in a stroller. Ossie is doing better. We are all geriatric here. Looking forward to longer days.

Namaste, Jude

January 10, 2014

I recently spoke to the owner of a local television station about being a television host. He told me he would keep me in mind if anything came up. I was surprised to get a phone call asking me to audition for a hosting gig for the upcoming Sundance Film Festival. I was so nervous. I am not a TV host, but because of my experience in retail and being a natural conversationalist, the owner of the station thought it was worth me auditioning. A tall beautiful woman, Brittany, asked me to stand in front of a monitor and pretend I was interviewing one of my favorite celebrities. The first person that came to mind was Lake Bell. I saw her movie last year at Sundance and admire her for writing, directing, and starring in the film. After a couple takes Brittany told me they would call me if I got the job. I got the call today! They asked me to co-host a show called Festival After Dark with a local comedian. I am ecstatic!

XO, E

January 12, 2014

Erin and I have enjoyed going to the Sundance Film Festival for the several years. This year I volunteered again. Our main library has a venue just a few miles from my home. The only thing that intimidates me is using a radio headset to communicate with other crowd control people and ushers.

Terry Tempest Williams will be speaking at the Unitarian Church's annual auction fundraiser at the end of this month. The talk this morning was two people reciting her works of environmental activism and ecology. Brought me to tears at times. I love her because she is so gently persuasive. A true warrior.

I am leading my women's group on Tuesday. Everyone is to bring their favorite poem or song lyrics. We will discuss what was happening in our lives when we read the poem initially and why it resonates with us now. I would like to start writing again. So cathartic for me.

Namaste, Jude

January 28, 2014

The last 10 days were amazing! We filmed 10 episodes and had content for more. My co-host and I worked very well together. Between the two of us, we knew a lot about who we were interviewing and could help when the other needed it. Mike met up with us the second night of the festival. The guys liked Mike so much they asked him to come along to help. I am so happy he was able to part of it. I didn't want him to feel left out from all of the fun I was having. We went to private events, big concerts, and I interviewed film makers, actors, musicians and designers. I never knew I had a passion for hosting and quickly fell in love with a new hobby, which could maybe turn into a new career. My dad is my biggest fan. He has watched every episode, and has told friends and family to tune in. He told me how much he enjoys seeing me do something I love.

XO, E

February 1, 2014

I am supposed to meet Hayley today, although she hasn't called or texted me. In the past I would have gotten upset, but now I understand it's the drugs talking. Just like years ago, when I would ruminate, and my shrink told me it was the depression talking. It's all acceptance for what is, if you can just see it without all the junk.

Took the pups to the park today with Sophie tucked inside her stroller. She used to whine before we got to the park. She is so short she can't see out, so I was amazed how she knew. She doesn't anymore. I feel sad that she is sad. Ossie seems oblivious of her struggling to walk. Good thing probably. Sucks to grow old in many ways. I am still moved by the world in a good way. Poetry, films that leave me pondering, the sun/moon, music, family, friends, a good book I get lost in, the voice of someone I love. But then there is the sheer drudgery of it all.

Think I will light a fire, have a cup of tea and ruminate about how I want life to look and then with a big sigh try to accept what is.

Namaste, Jude

February 19, 2014

I learned late last night that my friend, Carol's father passed away unexpectedly. He leaves a huge hole here. When I was going through my chemo he insisted on donating $1000.00 to me to offset all my medical expenses, but did not want me to know it was him. That gesture was symbolic of his quiet, loving presence. I have known Carol since 1983 when we worked together in a dental office. We were continually getting into trouble then. I remember one time at a dental convention where we snuck in mini bottles of Kahlua to put in our coffee while in the meeting. Carol has seen me through the demise of my marriage, cancer, and Hayley's addiction. She is a constant in my life like no other. The sister I never had biologically. I am tearing up. True unconditional love.

My father fell several days ago at his memory care facility breaking the ball off of his humerus bone. He will need a shoulder replacement. My brothers and I decided yesterday that he not having the surgery would not lead to a quality life for him even though the surgery itself might kill him. He is in surgery now at this very minute in Cleveland. The good news is I was able to talk to him on the phone yesterday from the hospital. He knew it was me. I know he is 91, and if he goes today it will be a blessing.

Namaste, Jude

February 25, 2014

Feeling grateful. What a beautiful day!

-Hayz

March 14, 2014

Going to southern Utah to spend four days in a house near Zions next weekend. I really need the break from the mundane craziness around here. Hope to do a lot of reading, nothing, and hiking.

I am taking a poetry class at Huntsman starting next week. Very excited to dip my toe in and see if I want to go all the way. The class is for cancer patients similar to the one I took last year. Different teacher I think this time.

I spent the evening with Hayley, Erin and Mike last night celebrating E's b-day. It felt good to be with all of them. We did not mention anything negative. Big breath. I came home and wrote a new poem about Erin.

Beautiful Baby Girl Daughter

I am a daughter of a woman named Joan. She is the daughter of a woman named Rose. My daughter's name is Erin.

She arrived two weeks late on an early March Sunday evening. She slid into my waiting arms as the doctor cut the cord. Beautiful, bald, big blued eyed baby girl child.

When the doctor told me about the cancer Erin was sitting next to me. The doctor gave us an expiration date which we ignored. She was 32 years old. I was 60. Erin, fierce cancer advocate warrior.

Erin's long blonde hair has never been cut short. Her golden crown turned heads. Little by little her hair started to fall out, get thinner. Stress, the doctor said.

Chemotherapy included wearing an infusion pack at home for several days. The infusion pump backpack was black, stiff, unyielding. Erin gifted me with a soft, hand sewn fleece, turquoise pack to protect me from the ugliness.

Erin married her love last year. They moved into a new, old house a few blocks from my own. I live to see her have babies, tend flowers in her yard. My daughter, my love, my warrior.

Namaste, Jude

March 18, 2014

Mike and I have wanted to adopt a dog for a very long time. We thought about rescuing one when he lived in his apartment, but didn't feel like it was fair to have a dog in such a small place. We decided it was best to wait until we had a home with a yard for it to play in. Now we have our own house, we feel like it is the perfect time to add a furbaby to our little household. Growing up, my family was never without a dog. My parents would take us to the local shelter to pick out a puppy who was in need of a home. Since my parents taught me how important it is to rescue I am adamant about adopting. We feel like when we meet or see the dog we will know. We told a close friend, who volunteers at a shelter in Denver what we are looking for and she said she is going to keep a look out for us.

Mike received a text with a picture of two puppies, one black and one golden who were being rescued from a high kill shelter in New Mexico. The shelter found them next to a dumpster in the middle of a rain storm, and they were close to being put down. I am not sure how they found them, but they did, and they were being transported to Denver this week! When Mike sent me the picture I immediately called him and said that's our girl (meaning the golden puppy named Harker Heights). We were told that there is another family interested in her, but they asked us to fill out the adoption application as soon as we could so we are the next in line. I filled it out ASAP.

XO, E

March 21, 2014

I saw my doctor today and all is well. The original cancer is still there but not going anywhere. Maybe cancer has found a home in my body. Has become a pacifist. No kill policy. I feel raw mentally. Poetry is opening me up to feelings and issues I have not yet dealt with since my diagnosis. A good thing I believe.

This Place

This place
where I can
recount stories
of times past.
This place
where I can
hide through
words not
spoken.
This place
where I can
be vulnerable,
open to feelings
I may have forgotten.
This place
where I can heal.

Namaste, Jude

March 22, 2014

We were accepted to adopt Harker Heights and I am beyond excited! Mike drove to Denver this weekend to pick her up and brought her home today. She was still a little tired from being fixed, so she slept most of the way. I was on pins and needles all day. I couldn't wait to meet her! Because she had a few accidents at our friend's house in Denver yesterday Mike thought it was best for her to meet me outside in the backyard. She looked a little scared as she peeked her head around the corner of the doorway. I knelt down and said, "come here sweetie, it's okay." Her ears perked up as she tilted her head. She ran to me with her tail wagging, and jumped into my arms before giving me kisses all over my face. I couldn't stop giggling while I cried happy tears. I felt like our family was complete at that moment. I was elated to finally be able to rescue a puppy of our own after all these years. I can't wait to spoil her with love and affection. Mike was surprised she was so excited to meet me. He said she had been so timid around everyone else. It was like she knew she was in her forever home. She found her parents, and we found her. I love her so much already.

XO, E

March 23, 2014

We set up a bed for Harker in a little kennel in the kitchen. She slept all night! When I woke up I sat straight up in bed to make sure our new furbaby was okay. I was worried because she hadn't made any noises. I smiled when I saw her poking her head out of the top opening of the kennel with her little pink tongue peeking out of her mouth. We were both so happy she was there. The image will forever be engrained in my mind.

Since I had the day off we were able to have a mommy daughter day. I couldn't wait to introduce her to dad and his dog, Lucy. Lucy can get very territorial, so we introduced them to each other at a nearby park. It was the first time I had taken Harker for a little walk. She lifted her head proudly as I attached her new pink leash to her matching collar. She was a little hesitant when I asked her to get out of the car, but after seeing a few other dogs playing nearby she jumped out enthusiastically. We made our way to where dad and Lucy were standing. Lucy wasn't aggressive with her at all. In fact, she and Harker played for a bit. Harker fell in love with dad and Lucy immediately and they with her. Dad even offered to take her while we are at work during the day. He is so good with animals, and everything I learned about owning a dog I learned from him. He is also retired, so he will take her on walks every day. She will learn how to be a great mountain dog because he goes on hikes in the mountains at least twice a week. I know she will be in great hands. It will be good practice for when he becomes a grandfather.

Mike and I have started to talk about trying to have a baby, and figured adopting a puppy would be good practice. I know a pup is not the same as a child, but it's a start. This is just the beginning of an exciting, new stage in our lives, and I am grateful mom and dad are here to be a part of it.

XO, E

April 17, 2014

I am so enjoying writing and reading poetry daily. My last class is next week. I love the validation of reading my poems to the class/teacher. I worry that I need that, validation I mean.

I saw Hayley a couple of days ago. Much is the same. I still loved being with her. Sobbed all the way home.

My goddess retreat is next weekend at my friend's place in Ivins, Utah. I am looking forward to being with my friends in a spiritual setting. Hope the desert flowers are blooming. I feel so lucky to have so many amazing women in my life I came home to write a poem about one of my oldest friends, who has seen me through everything, Carol.

A Walk Around the Park

My life can be measured not by years, births, deaths or marriages. Instead my life is measured by walks around the park with Carol. We met years ago in a dental office where we both worked. Finding instant connection, laughter and caring.

My life started to unravel after my daughter was born.

Postpartum depression they said. We started walking with dueling strollers. Daughters, just babies, separated by 6 months or so.

"Your walks are not exercise" said my husband. "You need to do more to lose weight." No, they are more than that. Our walks are a barometer of our lives and friendship.

I have laughed so hard listening to Carol that I had to stop to allow my belly to contract. I have howled with grief as we lamented Hayley's dissent into addiction. Two sisters, holding each other through happiness, grief and humor.

Most recently we have stopped walking for several months. Carol's father died unexpectedly last February. She was sidelined with grief. We are walking again around the park. Our friendship intact, while everything around us changes and evolves. The walk is the same.

Namaste, Jude

April 30, 2014

Grant and I are so deep into our addiction we can't hold a job, so we don't have a way to make money. Some friends told us that they get money by picking up an item at a store, and then immediately return it for store credit. They don't even leave the store! They sell the gift cards or exchange them for drugs. Grant and I are desperate, so we thought it was worth a try. We didn't see any other option. We both agreed that I be the guinea pig because I look more innocent and would be more likely to get away with it. Grant drove us to the store and waited for me while I went inside. I was terrified! I had a deep pit in my stomach and was starting to get a panic attack, but I knew I had to do it. I couldn't think of any other way to survive. I was told to get an expensive item, so I walked towards bedding to pick out a duvet. I remembered having a nice, luxurious comforter making me feel safe and cozy growing up. It is also a girly purchase, so I figured people wouldn't second guess me returning it. As I walked through the store I hugged the comforter like it was my life preserver and in a way it was. I found the returns and the woman who helped me was very sweet. She asked for my ID, and the reason why I was doing the return. I told her it was the wrong size for my bed. She asked me if I wanted to exchange it for the correct size, and I told her I already got something that works, but thank you. She smiled and told me because I don't have a receipt she can only give me store credit in the form of a gift card. I told her that was great. She handed me the gift card and said to have a nice day as I ran out of the store. It worked! Grant asked me how it went when I got into the car and when I told him how easy it was he decided to do it as well. Twenty minutes later he came back with another gift card we can sell or exchange for drugs. Wow! Who knew?

-Hayz

May 11, 2014

Woke up a little while ago after a restless night due to my bones aching. Side effects of the cancer drugs I take, or am I kidding myself and it really is this aging thing? Cloudy and cool here. I saw a Lazuli Bunting at my bird feeder yesterday. I stood still like a statue amazed at his blue hued head. Beautiful bird visitor.

Spent the morning OD'ing on a friend's poems. I love her response to mine. I have come to the sorry conclusion that my ego is stroked when people love my words. I almost seek that gift, which seems very self serving. Speaking of being vulnerable.

Mame and I were planning to go adventuring in the desert nest week. I pulled back because I am too hesitant about taking so much time off work. Responsibility sucks. We will take Friday off to go to the west desert.

Time to go outside and survey the property. (Pick weeds)

Namaste, Jude

May 15, 2014

We decided to name our new puppy, Bella. So far she has been very easy. She was already potty trained, and figured out the doggy door very fast. We take her on walks, but she was a little scared to leave the house at first. When we put her on leash she would quickly find shelter under parked cars. We figured this was how she hid from the dangers of living on the streets in Santa Fe, poor thing. The first few weeks, she would stop in the middle of the intersection and lie down when we would cross the street. And when we took hikes on nearby trails she would run back to the car once she was off leash. She was scared to go too far from the house. We think her previous owners abandoned her on the streets. I don't understand how someone could do that! Luckily, she is little enough we can pick her up and carry her until she feels comfortable to walk again. We quickly learned she wasn't going to chew on anything, so we don't feel the need to put her in a crate at night. She doesn't like to sleep on the bed or sofa, she prefers to army crawl under our bed and sleep there all night. There is about 1.5 feet between our bed and the ground, and somehow she fits just fine.

Since she is still a little shy we take her everywhere we can in hopes that it will help her become more social. We go to the new, dog friendly mall regularly. She has already figured out that most treats are hidden behind the cash wrap. If a salesperson gives her attention and heads to the cash register she is close behind, thinking she will get a treat. She loves going to the mall, just like her mom.

We took dad up on his offer to puppy sit while we are gone at work. He quickly became her favorite person and she adores Lucy. Lucy doesn't love her, but she puts up with her. I drop Bella off at dad's house every morning. It is so nice to be able to see him and catch up. Bella loves going there! Every time we pull up to his house, she wags her tail like crazy and starts whining because she is so excited. He takes her on walks and goes hiking in the mountains at least two or three times a week by himself or with his best friend Darrell and his dog Cooper. Bella sleeps under his desk in his office while he reads and under the dining room table while he makes dinner. Mike picks her up on his way home from work because he usually gets off work before I do. She is always happy to see Mike, but loves being at grandpa daddy's house. We are so grateful he takes her every day.

Dad, Lucy, Cooper, and Darrell have already shown her how to be a mountain dog. She leaps over logs with ease and has already learned how to swim. Lucy also taught her to hold her own. Yesterday, Mike was surprised to see Lucy dragging Bella down the hill by her ear. Bella was fine and when my dad noticed what was happening he just said, "what doesn't kill her makes her stronger." I am not worried about her there. I know my dad and Lucy are taking very good care of her. Dad loves her very much.

XO, E

June 8, 2014

Yesterday was mom's birthday. We took her out to a wonderful dinner to celebrate. Hayley even came! We continued the celebration by going to the Pride Parade today. Since the parade route passed by Unity, we camped out there. Shane and Jason took very good care of mom by finding her a great spot in the shade. After the parade, we took a drive up to the mountains for a picnic, and revisited where we were married. We hadn't taken Bella to the barn before today. When we got to the tree where the ceremony had been, we took her off leash, and she started to run around the area. She was so happy! It was almost like she knew it was someplace special. Uncle John is coming to town to spend some time with mom. We are all going to make a quick trip to Moab while he is here. It will be nice to get away for a bit.

XO, E

June 15, 2014

My brother left a couple of days ago. Erin and Mike joined us in Moab a week ago. The weather was just right, the scenery pristine. John and I took a raft trip on the Colorado. The wind made it difficult for our oarsman to navigate, but we managed. I haven't spent so much time with my brother in what seems like years. My heart softens a bit now when I think of him. Felt good to be surrounded by good times and laughter.

I met with the Huntsman Cancer poetry group yesterday for the first time since we ended class. Only one other patient showed up. There were four of us this time. We shared poems of our own and favorites. One of my poems is to be published in the Huntsman Newsletter! How about them apples? This is one isn't the poem going to be published, but it is one of my newest.

Summer Solstice

Hard to imagine
the dark nights of winter.
Today, daylight stretches
far into the evening.
Each year the sequence
remains the same.
Lending security to places
where there is none.
The ancient ones knew.
They created rituals,
to mark the changes.
Their people found comfort.
They had a sense of belonging
to something greater.
Not to worship but to honor
with respectful stewardship.
We are losing our grip
on what matters, sustains,
feeds our spirits.
The earth montage shifts.
Adrift among floating debris
we clamor to hold on to anything
that resembles what is seen
on the big and small screens.
No rescue is in store for the misguided.
Hope lies in going home to our roots,
ancestors, guides, the earth.
Spirit answers the door with a prayer.

Namaste, Jude

June 19, 2014

I got a call from Brittany a few days ago asking me to host a 30 minute show called "Make a Splash in Heber Valley." It showcases activities Heber Valley has to offer in the summer. The plan was for me to go fly fishing, scuba diving in a crater, boating and paddle boarding. I agreed to do it even though I am terrified of water due to a freak accident of getting caught in a wave in Hawaii a few years back. The first activity was fly-fishing. Although my Uncle Gary owned a fly fishing camp in MT for years, and my grandparents were avid fisher people, I had never been fly fishing before. I didn't catch anything, but loved being on the river so early in the morning. It was very peaceful. The next activity was scuba diving in a natural hot spring in a crater. The idea of being underwater for a long period of time petrifies me, so our tour guide, who is scuba certified took a camera down to the bottom to shoot some footage. Next was boating at one of the local reservoirs. We rode on the boat while the local kids went wake boarding behind.

The last activity was paddle boarding. Even though I was scared to be on a little board in the middle of a lake, I was determined to try it. My legs were quaking and my heart was pounding in my chest. I had a slight panic attack when a slight breeze moved across the water, making the red board I was clinging onto sway back and forth. I could barely keep my balance. To calm myself I started to think about how scared mom must have been at the beginning of her cancer journey. She has been able to conquer one of her biggest fears and so should I. This is small compared to what she has gone through. I closed my eyes, took a deep breath and slowly stood up. I didn't fall in! I was so proud of myself for doing something even though I was terrified. It was a reminder that I can do difficult things.

XO, E

June 28, 2014

I've been going to a singing circle monthly led by a voice coach/speech pathologist. I have discovered another voice! We sing rounds of world music, mostly from Africa and the Middle East. We start out with laughter yoga to warm up. I used to think I couldn't sing, but of course everyone can sing and should.

I don't look at my piece being published as validation I can write. I look at it as sharing the journey. Writing has done wonders for me. Here is one of my newest pieces.

"Another foggy morning. Getting to know myself is good. Making friends. Comfort of being alive. It's okay to be alone. It is okay to live a life of creative thought, not doing all of the time. Live within and without will make sense. Wisdom from within. Your teachers are here. Ready to help guide you. Peace awaits. Joy can be yours. There is a spark, a light, a flame waiting to burst faith and give you warmth. Love that they have never known. Healing is here. You can fuel it, know it. You know. Go in light, love, smiles."

Namaste, Jude

July 15, 2014

Tonight, we got to see one of our favorite hip hop groups, Jurassic 5! It meant a lot to see them together because when Mike and I were on our first date he asked me to play a CD from his collection. He must have had at least 100 to choose from, but I chose Quality Control by Jurassic 5. He was surprised I chose an album by a group that isn't as well known as others he had to choose from. He likes to say it was a test and one of the reasons why he asked me on a second date.

We were supposed to see Jurassic 5 a couple years later when they were in town, but I came down with shingles, so I was unable to go. We were both upset I couldn't be there, but when the band was doing a meet and greet after their show Mike asked one of the members, Chali 2na to wish me well over the phone. It was such a fun surprise! Chali 2na was my last interview of Sundance, and we told him both stories. He said it meant a lot to him that he and Jurassic 5 were a big part of our lives. The show was amazing! I am so happy Mike and I could finally see them perform together.

XO, E

July 23, 2014

My friend has been teaching me the art of mosaics. I have made two pieces. I have found that I love the process of creating, seeing the piece become an entity into itself and choosing colors that contrast, yet connect. Finding what pleases me.

Met with my poetry teacher last week. She has become my friend, as well as mentor. They want to place my fairy piece in the cancer garden for patients to read while they are gardening. I was moved by the legacy of my words. Brings me peace and joy to know this.

Going to find some coolness this weekend in the mountains. Mame and I have an ancient spring bar tent that we are taking. Hopefully, we can get off the beaten track to find solitude and quiet. No campgrounds for us. She drives a Toyota 4 Runner. We can go anywhere!

My doctor's have had me checking my blood pressure for the past month. It seems to be fine to me. I have been compliant.

Namaste, Jude

August 22, 2014

I have been feeling good. I met with the poetry group at Huntsman last week, probably for the last time for a while. I plan to take a Intro to Creative Writing class at the University of Utah, Tuesday evenings. I do have to obtain permission from the instructor to take the class since I am taking it for non credit. I plan to take a Tai Chi class Friday afternoons taught by a friend of a friend. There are some benefits to being an older adult.

I am going to take Hayley to dinner in a few minutes. She's talking rehab again. My therapist tells me not to get attached to the outcome. Very Buddhist, but sensible I think.

Namaste, Jude

September 19, 2014

Elton John is tonight! Since he is one of mom's favorite musicians, I made sure to get us tickets. Mom and I went to see Paul McCartney together a few years earlier, and I had invited Mike, but he opted out of going and regretted it ever since. He didn't want to miss Elton, too! We sung our favorite songs at the top of our lungs and when he played "Tiny Dancer" we put our arms around each other while we swayed to the music. It was a time where we were connected and bonded by the experience of singing together. I cherish moments like these. Moments that allow us to love our lives and be transported into a state of peace.

XO, E

September 20, 2014

My writing class turned out to be an undergraduate intro to creative writing. The big problem is that there are over thirty students, and I didn't like the instructor. Of course, I was the oldest person there which really doesn't bother me. I was pretty overwhelmed by the syllabus and the instructor's expectations. I slept on it and decided to drop the class. The Tai Chi class was wonderful and healing. It is taught by a gentleman a few years older than me.

Big sigh. I have been feeling a lot of sadness the past week or two. Usually, it only lasts a few days, but lately it has stayed with me longer. My therapist tells me I am grieving, not clinically depressed. The writing class proved to be too much to my vulnerable self at the moment. Maybe another semester will be better. I will continue to write, although, I think my writing is somewhat provincial, unsophisticated. The main reason I do it though is for my own enjoyment and healing

Namaste, Jude

September 22, 2014

Since most everyone thinks the origin of the cancer is from her breast, mom has been seeing an oncologist who specializes in breast cancer as well as her GI oncologist. Both doctors recently decided it was best for mom to start seeing one, instead of two doctors. Her cancer most likely originated in the breast, so they agreed for her to only see her breast cancer doc from now on. At the appointment we went to today we learned the hormone replacements are working, so she is going to stick with the regimen. There are a few different hormone replacements mom can take. When one stops working, they move onto the next until that one stops working, and then onto the next. With the type of cancer mom has, there are four hormone replacements she can take. Each one with different side effects, but mom says they are better than chemo, so she is happy. Just as the doctor was about to leave her nurse reminded her that the BRCA results had come in.

A few months ago Angela suggested mom get tested for a BRCA gene mutation. The National Breast Cancer Foundation describes it as, "the name "BRCA" is an abbreviation for "BReast CAncer gene." BRCA1 and BRCA2 are two different genes that have been found to impact a person's chances of developing breast cancer. Every human has both the BRCA1 and BRCA2 genes. Despite what their names might suggest, BRCA genes do not cause breast cancer. In fact, these genes normally play a big role in preventing breast cancer. They help repair DNA breaks that can lead to cancer and the uncontrolled growth of tumors. Because of this, the BRCA genes are known as tumor suppressor genes. However, in some people these tumor suppression genes do not work properly. When a gene becomes altered or broken, it doesn't function correctly. This is called a gene mutation. When a BRCA gene is mutated, it may no longer be effective at repairing broken DNA and helping to prevent breast cancer. Because of this, people with a BRCA gene mutation are more likely to develop breast cancer, and more likely to develop cancer at a younger age. The carrier of the mutated gene can also pass a gene mutation down to his or her offspring."

Mom grabbed my hand while the doctor slowly moved the mouse around her hot pink mouse pad. She squeezed it a little tighter when the doc exclaimed, "Aha! I found it!" Her eyes scrolled the screen quickly until she said, "you do not have the BRCA mutation gene." Mom let out a huge sigh of relief. I know she doesn't want my sister or I to go through what she has. Since both mom and grandma have had breast cancer there is a good possibility Hayley and/or I will, and if she had the BRCA gene mutation we would be at much greater risk of developing breast and possibly ovarian cancer in the future. We still need to take the right precautions, but knowing that mom doesn't have the mutation gives us comfort.

After hearing the great news mom's spirits seem to be up, but I am a little scared. The oncologist seems to know her stuff, but isn't as attentive as her other doctor. She is considered one of the best breast cancer doctors in the state, and I feel grateful mom can be seen by someone who is so accomplished, but I feel the doctor's ego gets in the way of really caring for mom. It's like she looks at mom as a number and not as a person. I miss the other doctor, and I think mom does too. I am sure she could go back to him, but we both know it's best to be seen by someone who specializes in the type of cancer where everything originated from. Hopefully the next appointment will be better, and we will have more comfort in knowing that she is doing the best thing for mom. The most important thing is that mom feels well, and the cancer isn't progressing, so if mom is okay with it then so am I. But, I will speak up if I feel like I need to. I need to make sure mom is getting the right care.

XO, E

October 8, 2014

Thought I would take advantage of the moon energy to write today. A blood moon no less! Tonight, I am meeting with the goddesses. We are meeting each month on the full moon to harness that energy. Powerful stuff. Tonight we will be walking a labyrinth by candlelight.

I leave Friday to go down south with my friends. This time there is no agenda besides getting together and savoring friendship.

Namaste, Jude

October 31, 2014

Today was Bella's first Halloween. We don't know her exact birthday, but the vet thinks it is in the fall, so we thought Halloween would be a good day to celebrate the day she was born. It was also the one year anniversary of buying our first house. Such a big day for us!

Park City has a big party every Halloween called Howloween. After the kids are done trick or treating at the local businesses there is a dog parade. I have always enjoyed watching the proud pups walk with their families in the past, but this year we had our own furbaby to march with. We dressed Bella up as a lion and strolled down the street with the other local dog parents. She was smiling and wagging her tail the entire way down. It was like she knew she was the center of attention.

After spending the day in Park City, we went home to hand out candy to the neighborhood kids. Dad, Lucy, and Mel also came over for a tiny bit to celebrate Bella's 1st birthday. They each brought a toy, and sang happy birthday. I am happy we can spoil her.

Since her life is so much shorter than ours I want to make it as good as I can. She deserves it.

XO, E

December 10, 2014

Hayley being gone has been very stressful. We don't know if she is alive because she doesn't respond to any of our texts. I have the habit of internalizing my stress, so the debilitating pain I experienced from the shingles I had years ago comes back when I am upset, and today it is on fire. On a positive note, my hair has started to grow back!

I received a text from our tenant, asking if we received the rent money he put in the mail slot. When I didn't see an envelope I started to get worried. I looked all over the house thinking Bella hid it somewhere, but it was nowhere to be found. My shingles started to burn when the idea of losing three months rent came to my mind. After looking all over the house I called Mike. Because Bella likes to take his shoes to the backyard he suggested I go outside. A cold gust of wind filled the house as I opened the door. It almost knocked me over because I was feeling so weak. Since I had my head down to protect my face from the cold snowflakes that had just started to fall I couldn't miss the green pieces of paper lying on the gray asphalt. It was money! As I rounded the corner I was surprised to see several bills scattered across the frozen grass. I quickly forgot about how sick I was feeling and started to frantically pick up all of the money. Luckily there were only a few bills that had been chewed up, but not bad enough the bank wouldn't take them. We won't make that mistake again. Silly Bella.

XO, E

December 20, 2014

Saw my oncologist yesterday. She seems to think everything is stable, although she wants to do blood work every three months instead of six. I did ask her why. My mind immediately went to the extreme. She said she wants to keep a closer eye on my tumor markers.

Namaste, Jude

December 21, 2014

Today was our annual baking day. Since it was a sunny day, Bella and I walked over to mom's with a bag of ingredients. The sidewalks were covered in a fresh blanket of snow. Bella looked so proud as she pranced through the white powder that turned into glitter as soon as it touched the cold air. One of my favorite Christmas songs, "Have Yourself A Merry Little Christmas" came on my ear bud. That combined with the snow instantly put me into the Christmas spirit.

Mom already had flour all over her hands and green apron when we arrived. She had been busy baking all day, but waited for us to make her famous press cookies. I recently found my grandma's red apron she wore when hosting parties and baking. I didn't get to know my maternal grandmother because she died of breast cancer when I was young. My mom says I remind her of grandma in a lot of ways. I wish I could have gotten to know her. So much so, that when someone asks me who I would like to have dinner with, living or dead I always say her. I slipped the satin, red apron out of my bag and tied it around my waist. Mom smiled, and tears came to her eyes when she saw what I was wearing. I am sure seeing it flooded her with happy memories of her baking cookies with her mom when she was younger. I didn't wear the cotton, red apron I wore every year before today. I had graduated to the more adult apron. It made me realize that I will soon be the one taking over the cookie making tradition. I will teach my children what mom taught me. I just hope she will be there as well.

XO, E

December 30, 2014

I am now the co facilitator for the Women's Sacred Moon Circle. Our Women's Sacred Circle has morphed into two groups: one that meets once a month on Tuesday evenings and the moon group that meets on the full moon monthly. We met on Thursday for the Beaver Moon. Cammi, the other facilitator is a former teacher. She is very structure oriented while I am a fly by the seat of your pants kind of gal. We work well together.

I also saw Hayley last week to have her teeth checked at the dentist I work for. She has been going there since she was 9 years old. I took x-rays a year ago, and she had a couple of cavities. This time she had 19 cavities and is starting to get some bone loss and gum inflammation indicative of the beginnings of periodontal disease. My boss will accept her father's insurance and not charge her. All of this didn't seem to faze her too much, or maybe she wasn't going to show me her real feelings. I was distraught because her teeth are a mirror for what is going on in her physical body, not to mention her spiritual self. I came home and wrote this poem.

Heroin

I am angry, wailing sad, helpless,
hopeless, alone, depressed, pissed
off in a major way.
I want to leave this world now.
I am tired of the pain, the what I
know to be future pain.
I am scared to see a daughter dying
right before my eyes.
Her teeth are becoming rotten.
Her mandible is diseased.
Her skin is pock marked.
All physical manifestations of
this horrific drug, disease, curse,
black plague,
Destroyer of lives, families, personalities,
souls, health, hope, future possibilities.
All dashed against the wall and splattered
in a million pieces.
The puzzle can't be put back together.
There is just too much missing.

Nothing will be the same.
World War I trenches had nothing on this demon.
Neither did a cancer diagnosis.
The horror continues with no end
in sight.
I mourn the loss of my baby girl.
Her health, future, our relationship, her sister relationship,
her joy in living a normal life with a career,
children, a house of her own, to dream of
what can't be seen or grasped.
Addicts have no dreams. They are entrenched in
the daily grind of the next fix.
That is all they live for.
When will this horror end?

Namaste, Jude

2015

Cancer is full of unknowns.
I am awake with eyes wide open.
Like a wild animal alert to danger.

January 1, 2015

I had a setback. Mame took me to the emergency room with stomach pain on Tuesday. They did a CT scan and admitted me to Huntsman for the night. I felt like I was having another bowel blockage again. The pain was the same. The docs said it was the beginning of one, and that it was good I came in before it became life threatening. On Wednesday, they did an endoscopic exam of my stomach. The attending doc thought my pain was coming from there. I will see my oncologist in two weeks to determine if a change in medication is necessary. She is being slow to react because I have done so well on the meds I am on now. She did say that the cancer is progressing a tiny bit in my colon which wouldn't be cause for alarm anywhere else in my body, but with my history of bowel blockages, the need for a med change may be now. I am so grateful for the care I receive there. The first thing my onco did was hug me sitting in my hospital bed. My therapist, Angela came in to see me as well. I was released from the hospital at about 6 PM New Year's Eve.

Namaste, Jude

January 2, 2015

We didn't feel like doing much for New Year's, so we went to dinner to celebrate our anniversary and ended the night at The Grand America for a glass of champagne before ringing in the New Year with Bella at home. It was just how I wanted it. There was no stress or expectations, and I was with my little family.

I started to feel like I was coming down with something near the end of the night, and this morning I woke up feeling terrible. I still went to work because it is the busiest time of the year, but when I got there my boss immediately asked me to go home. I looked so ill he could tell I was sick and didn't want me pass it on to anyone else. I am the sickest I have been for a while! Hopefully, I can take another couple days off to recover. I am no help to mom if I am sick. What a way to start the new year.

I hope it's not a preview to what this year has to bring.

XO, E

January 20, 2015

I see my oncologist today to determine whether I stay on the current medication regime or change it. Erin is going with me for moral support. I have been feeling pretty good, although I have had more pain and cramping in my abdomen lately.

Happiness vs. sadness. I am grateful for the joyful events. I am grateful for my energy pops because of the companionships and love. I feel grateful to have such a great support system. I am grateful for this security and shelter of my house. I am grateful I am still alive and feeling good. I am grateful for HCI and all of the wonderful people there. I am grateful for the people I work with. I am grateful that my spiritual foundation gives me refuge from the storm. It helps me to see clearly- The Divine is love. Keep Hayley safe in your arms. Protect her. Help her see the path she needs to take. Give her the tools she needs to improve her life.

Namaste, Jude

January 20, 2015

I am sitting here in the trailer with $10,000.00 in cash and more heroin and meth that I could ever want. I have become so paranoid I have also collected several cameras to keep an eye on things. Although, I am surrounded by several people all of the time, I still feel so alone and just want to die. I have all of these things I have ever wanted, but feel dead inside with no way out.

-Hayz

January 30, 2015

My father passed peacefully at around 4AM this morning. I was hoping he would stop by here to say good bye but he must have been anxious to get to the pub on the other side. I am emotionally spent, ready to sleep. To grieve is to honor the love that is left behind. I love him dearly. That will never end.

Namaste, Jude

January 30, 2015

Grandpa passed away today. He suffered from dementia the last few years, and it worsened as he grew older. When I heard of his passing, I didn't cry hard for some reason. I shed a few tears, but not an ugly cry like I did when grandma passed. Not because I don't love him of course, but he hasn't been himself for a while. He didn't even know who I was the last few times I visited him. Since I feel like he left us a few years ago, I have already mourned the person he once was. He lived in Cleveland, so we didn't get to spend as much time with him as we would have liked, but mom talked to him on the phone weekly and would visit him when she could. Most of the time he would remember her when she would visit him, but not always. The few times he didn't know who his only daughter was he would say, "Who is that? I really like her."

One of the many things he loved to do with us was go to the mall, so we thought shopping, and going to dinner at the Nordstrom café was the perfect thing to do to remember him by. As the elevator door opened we were startled by a Great Dane rushing past us to open the handicapped door by pressing his nose against the big blue button. He trotted proudly back to his trainer with his tail wagging, knowing he had just done something good. Seeing such a happy pup made us all smile and laugh. It was just what we needed on a tough day.

We shared several of our favorite memories of grandpa over a plate of our favorite sweet potato fries. We laughed about how he thought he was such a ladies' man and smiled at visions of him roller-skating around his local rink. We cried soft, happy years when we reminisced about the days we had feeding the ducks in Chagrin Falls and the many trips he took to

Utah. He was a true British gentleman I will never forget. Cheers Grandpa.

XO, E

February 1, 2015

Sundance is officially over. It was a lot of work, but so much fun! Mike was my co-host this year and Brandon was our camera man. Mike and I both produced the show and between the two of us, we had more than enough footage. Brandon actually said we had too much, so we stopped filming two days earlier than planned. It was a whirlwind to say the least. We were up until 2AM the first Friday doing interviews and started the next day with an interview and vodka tasting at 10AM (which was something I didn't think I would ever be doing) and we were on the go until 2AM again and then again on Sunday. We had a great time! We interviewed CEO's, local business owners, entrepreneurs, artists, and well known celebrities. We attended cast parties, saw concerts, films and rode a mechanical beaver (not a bull, a beaver!) It was a crazy Sundance but one of the best yet. We never know what Sundance will bring and every year is different, but so memorable. Now it's time to get some rest.

XO, E

February 4, 2015

I am trying to hold on to some degree of normalcy, while at the same time allowing sadness to flow through. Maybe by knowing grief so intensely, allows the life juices to sustain more readily. I know he is in a better place. Sounds trite, but oh so true. I have started a new breast cancer drug called Tamoxifin. My mother actually took it forty years ago while on her journey. So far the side effects have been minimal. I see my oncologist the end of March to see if it is keeping the cancer at bay. Feeling grateful that I feel good.

Namaste, Jude

February, 5, 2015

Mom's tumor markers are going up because the hormone replacements she has been taking have stopped working. Her oncologist decided to put her on a different regimen. I am worried because there are only a handful of hormones she can try before going back to chemo. This will be number two, so hopefully it will last just as long if not longer than the previous one. The hormone prior to this lasted a very long time, and mom didn't have terrible side effects. I didn't feel like mom was sick. She was able to live a life without thinking about cancer all of the time. Here's to hoping this new hormone will work just as well if not better.

XO, E

February, 5, 2015

We have gotten really good at our grab and go scheme. When I make a return the clerk inputs my ID number into the system. At most stores we can't make more than 3 returns in a year, so we are running out of places to go to. Grant had the great idea to scratch out the numbers on my ID and passport and write in new ones. This way I can still have an ID with my correct information and picture, just a different ID number each time. Now we can hit the same store more than once without any problem.

-Hayz

February 18, 2015

Mame and I are going to San Francisco April 22, 23, 24 and then off to Yosemite. We may hit Point Reyes on the way back depending. I am looking forward to the experience and getting away for a week or so.

I have hired a friend of mine who is laid off from her job to do some painting. She is in dire need of the money. When I went to pick out the color, I went right to a light periwinkle. Looks fabulous! Now for new kitchen vinyl and carpet in the living and bedrooms. My plan is to ask for top dollar for the *rental space. It will allow me to stay in my home if I retire, or need to cut back at work. I do love this house.*

Namaste, Jude

March 2, 2015

I am laying in bed just before sleep time. Ossie is laying along my side breathing regularly. He is starting to seem more frail and anxious. The cold bothers him. Makes him tremble at times. Sophie is at the foot of the bed guarding against night warriors.

I have been painting up a storm and thoroughly sick of it. Erin and Mike came over to help yesterday in exchange for me to feed them. A good exchange I think.

Namaste, Jude

March 18, 2015

I was asked to co-host the Morning Show! It was my first time hosting live television, and I was so nervous! I had a difficult time sleeping last night. Partly because I was nervous about hosting, and the other part was knowing I had to get up at 5 in order to be there by 6:45AM. I was asked do the weather, but since it is on a green screen I was terrified, so I opted out. They said I did a great job, and asked me to come back tomorrow. I promised myself I would try to do the weather. I really need to do things that get me out of my comfort zone. I was done by 9, and then went to work until 6. It made for a long day, but the natural high I got from hosting live television helped get me through.

XO, E

March 19, 2015

I am actually so grateful to still be here and feeling good. I currently take meds to block the estrogen my cancer feeds on. So far, so good. Not many side effects that I can tell anyway. If someone lived with me, they might say I am moody. Guess I should ask the dogs. They are geriatric as well. I am still grieving my dad passing away. He was 92 years old and lived a good, long life. We are having a celebration of his life at Fairport Harbor where he used to sail. We will drink his favorite beer, sing Frank Sinatra songs and generally party it up. A fitting closure for a lovely man, and father. It's tough knowing I am no one's "favorite" any longer. My dad always loved me best.

Hayley is still in the depths of addiction, living with her asshole boyfriend. I do see her periodically for lunch or an outing. I have gotten pretty good at letting the grief of all that go, although sometimes it reaches up and grabs me by the throat.

Erin and Mike are super busy with their lives, but I do see them once a week or so.

Namaste, Jude

March 20, 2015

Mom's tumor markers are up, which has me worried. The doctor doesn't seem too concerned, but said she will keep an eye on them. Since mom isn't having too many side effects with the new regimen, the doctor advised her to stick with it for now. Mom didn't seem very upset, but the original feelings I had about this doc popped up again. They hadn't fully gone away, but she had been more attentive and caring until recently. I am starting to feel like her ego is getting in the way. We are so lucky to have Huntsman so close to home, but right now I don't know if this doc aligns with us. I brought it up to mom, but she says she feels fine with how she is being treated and knows the doctor is one of the best in the state, if not the country when it comes to breast cancer, so she doesn't want to change at this moment. I feel like she is looking more at the doctor's reputation instead of how she is being treated. We will see how things go. I just want to make sure mom is getting the care she needs.

XO, E

March 25, 2015

Just got back from seeing a podiatrist. My right foot has been painful for several weeks. I suspected arthritis but turns out the major problem is my left leg is 2 cm shorter than my right. Apparently as a result of breaking my leg when I was 30 yrs old. The doc is recommending an orthotic as a conservative therapy initially. I am a bit worried because our Yosemite trip is about a month away. Ibuprofen helps to alleviate the pain. I really don't like taking any more meds than I have to.

The apartment downstairs is just about ready to rent. I have worked hard on it for a woman my age. I painted the Formica countertop to look like granite. The extra money will be nice, but I am not looking forward to having to share my space again. I do love the quiet.

Hayley seems to be doing the same. I have been successful not letting her situation get to me, although I wish she could see the way to the light. Erin and Mike seem happy.

I am still working about three days a week, which is just about right. My energy level seems to be declining a bit, but that may be my age.

Namaste, Jude

March 27, 2015

We don't have a car, so we asked a friend to drive us to commit our usual crime. Grant went into the store while I waited with our friend. About 15 minutes later, we saw Grant sprinting towards us with his arms full of merchandise. He stole it instead of returning it and security was right behind him. He jumped into the passenger seat as we sped out of the parking lot. I was panicking, and I could tell Grant's adrenaline was out of control by the eerily way he was laughing. We thought we were in the clear once we got home, until we heard a knock at the door. It was the police, and they were there to talk to us. The store's security guard was able to write down our friend's license plate, and when the police came to confront him he ratted us out. They arrested us, but we weren't booked into jail. There was no room. We were released and now back at the trailer. We need to be more careful next time.

-Hayz

April 12, 2015

It is a blustery Wednesday morning here. Life is starting to calm down. We are anticipating some much needed moisture. When I walk on my grass, it crunches. I still haven't turned on my water. It is tempting though. Ossie is sitting on my lap while I type this. Such a good canine friend. I found a tenant for the apartment last week. There is a glut of apartments for rent right now, and it is approaching the end of the school year at the university. I feel lucky to have found a quality tenant.

Mame and I leave for Yosemite soon. We got together last week to map out our itinerary. I will do most of the driving while Mame will navigate. We aren't renting a car until we leave San Francisco. The one thing I really want to do there is walk the labyrinths at Grace Cathedral. I am not counting on getting a tan while we are there.

I saw my doc a couple of weeks ago. Tumor markers are up, but she wants to wait until May and then do a cat scan and more blood work. The new med has very few side effects. My mood seems to have stabilized as well. I have been feeling so good, and for that I am grateful.

The Sacred Moon Circle met Saturday night for the full moon. It was a powerful night with so many convergences spiritually, and astrologically. I feel the power of the women who have gone before us at our circle gifting us with their wisdom and love. It is truly a sacred space.

Namaste, Jude

April 24, 2015

I received a call from mom, telling me she was coming home from San Francisco tonight. She fell and broke her ankle on a segway tour around the city. She thought about staying, but because the break is really bad she figured it would be best if she came home. She is understandably very upset. Mike and I picked her up from the airport, and helped around the house a bit before heading home. I feel so bad for her. She really needed a break from everything, just not this kind.

XO, E

April 26, 2015

I am supposed to be in Yosemite right now, but while in San Fransisco, I was taking a Segway tour of Golden Gate Park, fell off the Segway in a freak accident and broke my right leg where the fibula attaches to the my ankle. I tagged Mame with my wheel while trying to get situated for a photo that our guide wanted to take, and over I went. My right foot stayed in the Segway while I went down. They took me to the emergency room, and I was able to return home late Thursday night on the plane. My kids took me home and tomorrow I see an orthopedic surgeon to figure out what is next. Hopefully no surgery, but I am taking each day at a time and trying not to worry about what may be in the future. Sucks, huh? Mame stayed on in California, but is not happy being there without me. I've done my share of crying the past few days. I was really looking forward to the adventure. My friends are rallying around me bringing dinner and giving support. I am so blessed to have my tribe. Not sure how much time I will have to take off work. Will worry about that later.

Namaste, Jude

April 27, 2015

I went with Mom to meet with the doc about her foot today. The break is so bad she has to have surgery in order to lead a quality life. My heart broke when I heard the bad news. She has already been through so much the last few years. She inspires me daily as she faces the harsh side effects of chemo and hormone replacement therapies with extraordinary courage and strength. I have no doubt that she will able to get through this as well. She is the strongest person I know.

XO, E

April 30, 2015

I have been up for an hour or so. Ossie was impatient for me to get out of bed, telling me to celebrate a new day. I am laying on the couch in the living room facing southeast. The sun is hazy, mountain peaks still snow covered. Weather is beautiful here. Warm and sunny. I am having surgery on Tuesday for pins and a plate in my ankle. My friends from the Women's Sacred Circle are organizing help for me. One of them even mowed my lawn! I feel so blessed to have the friends I do. I will be off my foot for two months. Nice time of year to recuperate anyways. Taking it day by day, minute by minute. All in all I am coping well.

Namaste, Jude

May 1, 2015

The doctor I saw today explained the nature of my injury to me so that I could understand. I tore two ligaments as well as breaking my fibula. He said I can't put any weight onto my right foot for two months. I am taking a month off work to begin with. I am reaching deep inside to garner the strength I need to heal and make the best of things. My friend's daughter, who I hired to house and dog sit while I was in California, has stayed on. She sleeps in my spare room on the couch. My surgery will be outpatient same day. I feel less vulnerable having her here. I try not to think she should be Hayley. I still haven't seen her since I got home. Twice she planned to come, but something always comes up. I am getting good at realizing it is the drugs talking, not my daughter, but still.

Namaste, Jude

May 3, 2015

Mom is hosting the goddess group this month. I didn't know if she was going to act as hostess because she originally planned on doing a May Pole to celebrate May Day. Since she can't walk I didn't think it was possible, but she was determined to make it happen. Her fellow goddesses surprised her with a May Pole made with ribbons wrapped around her apricot tree in her backyard. Mom sent me pictures of her house, decorated to the nines. She had flowers in her hair and colorful streamers wrapped around her wheelchair. She looked so happy! I love that even though she is in pain she still finds happiness. She has shown me that even if you are going through a tough time, the best way to cope is to embrace it, not matter how hard it can be. She is a true inspiration.

XO, E

May 5, 2015

Today is Mom's surgery day. She didn't seem nervous at all. She has gone through so much the last few years that having a small surgery doesn't seem to faze her. After watching her get wheeled into the operating room, the feelings I had a couple years ago started to well back up. It was traumatizing to have to sit in another sterile room while mom was getting surgery, so I opted to do some retail therapy instead.

Since it was Tuesday afternoon the mall wasn't very busy. As I let my hands glide across the silky fabrics, the stress of mom slowly slid away. I have always found it funny that stepping into a clothing store relaxes me. Even if I don't buy anything I feel better. I figure it's because mom would take me to the mall when she was having a hard day, and her mom did the same with her. Shopping therapy was something I learned at a young age.

Mom was already out of surgery when I returned. She was awake from the anesthesia and eating red Jell-o. She was in great spirits for just having her leg cut open. We only had to wait another hour until she was discharged. She was there for a short while, but made friends with all of the nurses during that small window. They all made sure to say goodbye and wish her luck before she left.

Mom has a hard time using crutches because she doesn't have a lot of upper body strength, so when we got to her house dad was waiting to help walk her up the stairs. I tried to assist, but dad took over. He practically carried her up to her kitchen like he was Superman. Mom said he was the only person she trusted to do it. I find it so sweet that even though they are divorced, they are still there for one another.

Dad has been there for mom since day one. They met while dad was studying law at Cleveland State. While they were waiting in line to get in to a bar, she realized she had forgotten her ID. Dad overheard the bouncer giving her a hard time, so he stepped in and told him that he could vouch for her. They talked and danced all night, and the rest is history. Since dad wasn't especially fond of Cleveland he would drive his little fiat across the country to come back to Utah as often as he could. Mom joined him a couple times, and quickly fell in love with the west. They married when he graduated, and moved back to his home state. Living in Utah is great for them because of everything it has to offer. Most of their free time is spent outdoors, especially in the mountains or dessert. They both taught me that escaping to nature in the best thing we can do to feel at peace, and we all do so on a regular basis.

XO, E

May 9, 2015

I am down for a month or so. I am doing quite well for the most part. Erin took the day off yesterday to clean my house and do a couple loads of laundry. I am sleeping well, pain is manageable, and I use a knee scooter to get around. I can shower myself, microwave meals, and make coffee. Peggy will drive me to the doctor's in a couple of weeks and is willing to help me with stuff I need doing around the house. I feel lucky to have the friends I do.

Good times, bad times. All in a day's work. Take the good with the bad. Let it be. There will be an answer. Let it be. Motor on. Keep on trucking. One foot in front of the other. If it ain't broke don't try to fix it. Look and breathe. Remember to breathe. Breathe in love and let it go. Feel it in every fiber of your being.

Namaste, Jude

May 9, 2015

Mom has been healing well and is a wonderful patient. I have to go to work, but check on her as much as I can. She has more friends than anyone I know! They all love her and have been a big help. Being able to witness what good friends these ladies are to her is proof of what kind of friend she is to them. Even though she doesn't feel well because of the cancer, and now her ankle, she is still fun to be around. People rarely tire of her.

Mom has found the office chair to be the best mode of transportation to get her around the house. She lifts herself off the sofa or bed, sits in the chair, and then wheels herself around like a little kid. I smile when I hear her giggling as she glides along her wood floors as the pups try to move out of her way. She is a kid at heart.

XO, E

June 1, 2015

This morning Grant and I did another grab and go. Our ride wasn't there when we finished the return, so we waited at a nearby store. Little did I know, the loss prevention lady at the first store knew who I was and when she saw me on camera she called the police. I was casually reading a magazine when Grant came over to tell me he saw two undercover detectives walk in. I told him not to worry because they weren't there for us. He wasn't convinced, so he went to hide. I continued to flip through the pages of the magazine, trying not to look too inconspicuous. Next thing I knew the two detectives approached me and asked if I was Hayley Evans. I said "no," thinking about what my dad once told me. He said to never do two illegal things at one time, and don't ever disclose information to the police. The detectives then said, "Yes you are. We know who you are, and where is your boyfriend?" I said, "I don't have a boyfriend." They were starting to get impatient and arrested me on the spot. I was escorted outside where the loss prevention woman from the other store was waiting for me. She seemed way too excited to see me in handcuffs. She called me a junkie and told me I was her white buffalo. Apparently she had made it her goal to catch me and send me to jail. Meanwhile, Grant didn't know what was going on. He thought I had gotten away, so he came back to get me. The detectives knew what he looked like and put an all points bulletin out to find him. As he came out of the store, they arrested him. When they put us into the back of the police car I began to cry. One of the detectives asked why I was crying. In between sobs I told him, "My mom's birthday is in a few days, and she is sick with terminal cancer. I don't want to disappoint her." He paused before saying, "You shouldn't be doing this if it makes you so sad then." I felt hopeless.

As we were waiting to be booked the officers handcuffed us to a pole. They then proceeded to call Grant derogatory, racist names. Grant asked, "Are you really saying these things to me right now, while I am handcuffed to a pole?" Which just egged them on. They raised their voices and got in his face even more. It made me sad to see the officers taking advantage of their power like this.

It was my turn to be booked and when I saw the printout of my charges I died inside. It stated that I forged documents 5 times, which was a third degree felony. I had no idea what I had done was considered a felony. I am always going to remember this day as the day I became a felon.

The detectives called my parents, and they were extremely upset with me, especially dad. I don't think he ever thought one of his daughters would be in the situation I am in. Sitting in the pit gave me a lot of time to think, and I started to get scared about the idea of living in jail. A felony sounds serious, so I thought I could be here for a while. A few minutes later an officer came to tell me they were letting me go. They pretrialed me out because the jail was full. Apparently, the first of every summer month is the craziest for the jails, and they weren't taking anyone who committed nonviolent crimes. I was booked, and then released. Another close call!

-Hayz

June 6, 2015

One of my best friends, Ali is pregnant with her first baby, and today is her baby shower! Another friend, Kristin and I are co-hosting at our house. Ali asked for a book themed shower, where everyone brings their favorite childhood book growing up with another gift if they choose. She is the first of my best friends to be pregnant. I love being able to celebrate these monumental times in our lives with one another. As I watched Ali hold up the tiny onesies she had pulled from the colorful gift bags, I started to think Mike I should start talking about starting a family. Our life has been such a whirlwind lately; we haven't had much time to think of what our future holds. I know we both want kids, but mom has been my main concern the last couple years. Now she is doing better I think it is time to start talking babies again.

After everyone left I quickly cleaned up and rushed to the Pride Festival to meet Brandon. I interviewed the organizers of the festival, a few of the vendors and volunteers. The theme this year is "Pride is _____," so as we were finishing up I walked around to ask several attendees what Pride is to them. People said, community, courage, inclusiveness, equality, being myself and embracing that and having others embrace it as well. It is accepting people for who they are. It is life, living, loving, breathing, growing, inspiring, and being honest and open.

It brought tears to my eyes to see so many people, from all different walks of life there to unite, and support the LGBTQ community. I realize there are still a lot of people who don't understand, and there is still a lot of work to be done, but seeing the love I saw today gave me hope that there will be a day people won't be discriminated against because of their sexual orientation.

XO, E

June 12, 2015

Just got back from seeing my oncologist. I have been on an oral chemo for the past two weeks due to the cancer spreading a little more again. We have managed to keep it from going anywhere else for two years now. The chemo isn't working yet, but it is too soon to evaluate it. I will see her in another couple of weeks. She may need to up the dosage. The good news about this chemo is that the side effects aren't as bad as the other chemo I had to have an infusion for. I have actually been smoking for the nausea instead of the anti-nausea drugs that were prescribed. Too many side effects. All in all, my spirits are good. My philosophy is that we are all terminal. Every day, minute, second is a gift.

I still have my cast on, although I cannot put body weight on it, so no tennis for me. My friends have rallied around me since I broke my ankle. I think I have someone offering to drive, come by to do the laundry, groceries every day. I will see the orthopedic surgeon to hopefully get a boot that I can take on and off. I won't be able to be fully weight bearing until mid July.

My birthday was quietly spent in the mountains with Erin and our dogs. We came back later on. Hayley joined us while Mike grilled turkey burgers on the deck.

I am going to see Willie Nelson! I had to change our seats to handicapped seating because I will still be rolling around on the scooter. Looking forward to some live music.

We are making plans to go to Cleveland to celebrate my dad's long life. Erin and Mike will be traveling with me, but Hayley is not stable enough to go I don't think. She is still struggling with her addiction.

Namaste, Jude

June 12, 2015

Hayley, Mom, and I went to see mom's doctor together. I love when Hayley can be there and I know mom does too. She needs all of the support she can get. The doctor said that the cancer is still spreading, but she wants to keep mom on the oral chemo she is on. I was confused. If the cancer is spreading, then why not try something else? I was about to ask the doc the reasoning behind her decision, but she walked out the door before I could say anything. I will keep going with what mom wants, but I may need to have a more serious talk with her soon if I continue to feel like this doc isn't doing what she can to prolong mom's life.

XO, E

June 21, 2015

Today is the first day of summer, and also Father's Day! Hayley actually came to dad's house to spend the day with us. We were all very surprised because she hasn't spent time with dad on Fathers' Day or his birthday the last few years. Dad never let it show that he was upset when she didn't come around or contact him on his special days, but I knew it bothered him. He has been her biggest support system, and is doing everything he can to help her. He doesn't deserve to be treated like that. I guess it's the price we pay for loving someone so much. Sometimes we get hurt because we don't get the same love and respect in return. When she does make an effort I can definitely notice a difference in his mood. He was all smiles today. Both of his girls were there to celebrate the amazing dad he is.

XO, E

June 22, 2015

Willie did not disappoint, even for a 80 year old man. My hot pink cast was a hit with everyone around us. Carol helped me write "I HEART WILLIE" in big black letters. I don't remember the last time I got so much attention. Many people wanted to sign it.

I see my leg doc today and will hopefully get the cast off! One perk through all this is a handicapped parking permit. When I am riding with a friend somewhere and we find a handicapped spot, I feel like we have won a prize or something.

Sad life I live, huh?

Namaste, Jude

June 23, 2015

I am writing a bit with so much time on my hands, although I have to be in the mood. We are planning to go to Cleveland to celebrate my dad's life. I may still not be fully weight bearing by then. I am sure there will be plenty of physical therapy visits in my future. I will start working three days a week mid July.

My mental state vacillates from gratitude, to anxiety, and back again. I feel like a prisoner in my own home at times, but that depends on my perspective. I hope to begin driving soon. After being independent for so long, I go crazy when I can't manage on my own. Ossie took off a couple of nights ago for two or three hours. He's never been gone that long. He is 13 now and can't see or hear well. A neighbor heard me calling him, and offered to walk the neighborhood to find him. He finally came strolling in after midnight. I am trying to be more vigilant about knowing where he is.

Mame is taking me to the doctor tomorrow. She is still contemplating moving to Montana. Her daughter is going to grad school there.

Namaste, Jude

June 30, 2015

Since I have been posting my hosting gigs on social media, my friends have started to ask me to cover different events. Last week, a close friend of mine asked me to interview key note speakers and attendees at a tech conference in Deer Valley. And this week a childhood friend, Lance Allred asked me to come to his basketball clinic for kids with hearing loss.

Lance is the first legally deaf player in the NBA and played for the Cleveland Cavaliers in 2008. To give back to the community he started a basketball camp for deaf children. He asked me to come to the camp to get some footage and conduct interviews. Brandon thought it was a great idea to make it into a package, so I interviewed Lance this evening at the basketball courts he played at as a child. As Brandon was setting up the camera he looked confused. I asked him if everything was okay and he nodded yes while looking around. He then grabbed a large camera case, brought it over to me and asked me to stand on it. I stared at him in bewilderment. No one has asked me to grow taller; they usually ask me to crouch down. Brandon said that even though I am tall, Lance is still over a foot taller! He was having a difficult time getting a good camera angle. I shrugged my shoulders, took off my shoes and proudly stood on the box. We all got a big laugh, which was a great way to start.

My conversation with Lance flowed naturally. We talked like two old friends. It was like Brandon wasn't even there! When he spoke about his time in elementary school I thought about when we would play at the playground together. I remembered him as a friend who excelled at shooting hoops, not as the student who was hard of hearing. He hasn't let it hold him back or define who he is. He is someone many people can look up to, in more ways than one.

XO, E

July 1, 2015

I felt so lucky to be at the basketball clinic for kids with hearing loss today. I talked to a couple of the parents who said their children went to the camp last year and couldn't wait to come again this year. They are so grateful for Lance, and what he has done for the community. While I was waiting to talk to the coaches I was able to watch the kids in action. They were smiling, laughing and having so much fun. I am thankful I could witness what Lance has been able to accomplish, and conduct interviews so others can see it too. Whether it's a bruise, a scar or an inner struggle, we all have things we attempt to cover up, but if we choose to tell our stories instead of hiding them they can help bring us together by showing others they are not alone. Our stories can be medicine if we allow them to be, and we can help people by sharing what we have learned along our journeys. I feel like the camp is doing just that. It is very special.

XO, E

July 3, 2015

Sixty Minutes recently aired a segment on the exorbitant cost of cancer drugs. The term financial toxicity was coined by one of the experts to describe the horrendous financial burden placed on this vulnerable population. Many patients must choose between life and death depending on their financial situation.

What is more shocking is that citizens of other developed countries pay 50 to 80% less for the same drugs. That sounds impossible until realizing that their government agencies negotiate directly with the drug manufacturers. In fact, they're getting a discount for buying in volume. That's economics 101, and just plain common sense. This is something we Americans have been noted for, but unfortunately not our elected officials.

President Obama has begun pushing for congress to use some common sense and allow Medicare to negotiate prices on the same basis that other countries do. Unfortunately, that doesn't stand a snowball's chance in hell because congress is bought off by special interests including the drug company lobby.

I am a terminal cancer patient. What it comes down to, is corporate money is more important than my life or the quality of life I have left to live.

Namaste, Jude

July 4, 2015

As we were cleaning up after the annual 4th of July party I received a call from mom saying she had to put her beloved dog, Ossie down. She took him to the ER for pets, where they told her that he had a fast moving, incurable cancer. As much as it pained her, she decided it was best to let him go over the rainbow bridge. She didn't want him to suffer any longer. Hayley rushed to meet her to say goodbye before he went to his forever sleep. Mom has her other dog, Sophie, but she and Ossie have a special bond. I have heard stories where a pet develops a similar disease as their owner to try to take some of the pain way, or to feel what their human is feeling. I believe that he did take on some of her pain, and it could be the reason she has been feeling better. But now she is experiencing a different kind of pain. A pain he can't help her with, grief.

That night we met family at the usual dinner spot, The Dodo. Since they were super busy we got it to go and ate dinner on mom's deck. We got a late start on the birthday festivities, so Mike and I couldn't make it to the other parties we were invited to. I felt very bad because I know Mike really wanted to attend. But, boy am I grateful for his help at work and for him celebrating with my family. After dinner I noticed dad sitting alone outside, so I walked out to spend some time with him. Since Mom's deck has a great view of the valley we were able to marvel at the fireworks going off all over the city. It felt like people were putting on a firework show just for us. Growing up I would watch fireworks and lightning storms brighten up the sky with dad. It was a time where we would talk about life, and I felt safe. For just a few minutes I had no worries in the world. It was just dad and I, and the fireworks.

XO, E

July 14, 2015

Just got back from visiting my family in Cleveland. It was a bittersweet visit, but an enjoyable trip. We spread my dad's ashes at the spot where we used to launch our sailboat. Being there brought back so many wonderful memories I have of my father. He and I shared a close bond, just like my daughters do with their father. I shed a few tears, mostly because of dad passing, but partly because Hayley wasn't there. She and Erin were his two favorite grandchildren. I wish she could have been there to celebrate his life. I hope she doesn't regret it when she can put this addiction past her.

I loved spending time with my niece Donna, and of course my other niece and nephew, Kalie and Kevin and their son, Nate. I think I fell in love with little Nate. John and Bonnie took such great care of me while I stayed with them. I truly felt loved and cared for. It really meant a lot to me.

I start chemo today and have a physical therapy appt this afternoon. Keeping my fingers crossed that the anti nausea drug will work.

Namaste, Jude

July 14, 2015

Since most of Mike's extended family also live in Ohio, our time there can be rushed because we want to make sure to see everyone. I really enjoyed being able to visit with Mike's Grandma Leibsla. She and I have formed a special bond throughout the years. She treats me as if I was her own grandchild, which means a lot because all of my grandparents have passed. After a nice afternoon with her, Mike and I met my family at Fairport Harbor for grandpa's celebration of life.

Mom, Mike and I decided to take a walk around the little town of Fairport before the ceremony. The Main Street only has a few shops and restaurants to explore. We came across two sailboat ornaments made out of wood in a small boutique. Since grandpa loved sailing, and we were there to celebrate him, mom and I both bought one to remember the day.

We found everyone waiting for us at the beach. Uncle John asked us to form a circle and close our eyes while he said a prayer. When he said, "amen" a gust of wind went through my hair. Mom must have felt it too because she grasped my hand. It was grandpa saying hello. I whispered I love you to the wind while slowly pouring a few of his ashes into the blue water he loved so much.

XO, E

July 23, 2015

Tomorrow is Pioneer Day. It is the day Brigham Young pointed at the Salt Lake valley, and said "This is the Place." It is actually a bigger deal than the 4th of July in Salt Lake. There is a large parade, parties, and a big fireworks show at night. I rarely went to the parade growing up, but my dad started the tradition of driving the parade route the night before. Spectators want a good view of the brightly colored floats, so the city has allowed people to camp out overnight. The parade route is over two miles long and there are people camped out in every inch of those two miles. I have driven the route every year with my dad. When Mike and I started dating I told him about it. Even though he has lived in Utah most of his life he had no idea people camped out overnight. He now drives the parade route with me ever year. This year Mike drove my dad, Bella, Lucy, and I in Mike's Jeep. Bella was afraid of the loud noises, so she hid in the back by my dad's feet with Lucy. She really trusts him, and Lucy has become her best friend. She feels safe with them. It didn't hurt my feelings that she went to them instead of me. I feel safest with dad as well.

XO, E

August 3, 2015

I saw my surgeon today for my ankle. He has given me the go ahead to give my boot the boot in three days. I was hesitant to tell him that I wasn't wearing it while at home anyway. Trying to be compliant. He was very pleased with the healing and joint flexibility.

I had to put my beloved Ossie down on the 4th of July. We were or are soul mates. He knew before I did. Sophie is reveling in being the only dog in the house.

Namaste, Jude

August 14, 2015

I am housebound today while my car is having all its fluids replaced. It's got 60,000 miles on it. According to the manual, I need to do this. I want to keep this car running till it can no longer. My friend, Adrienne just left after a chat and coffee. She brought me some magic oatmeal raisin cookies. She put lots of love in them, not the green stuff. I am back to work which wears me out but in a good way. My patients and coworkers seem happy to have me back and the paycheck is nice. I am only working three days a week. Perfect, really.

Mike's (my ex)'s brother performed with his partner of 30 years a couple of weeks ago. Mike's brother is 75 years old. He tap danced for three of the dances! Amazing really and so talented! We went out to dinner afterwards. It warmed my heart to see his partner, Don and to know they are so accepted by the family and society at large. Love prevails.

I saw my doc yesterday. I am refusing to take the oral chemo she has had me taking, primarily because I feel so poorly while taking it. I am thinking that I may forgo any more chemo to live a quality life while I am here on this earth. I will do a cat scan next week to determine what the status of the cancer is. I need more information to make a decision. I am feeling quite overwhelmed with all of this.

On a positive note, I am walking on two legs without any contraptions at all. I see a physical therapist every week. She scolded me yesterday for wearing Birkenstocks instead of sensible shoes with a back. Feels so good to be driving and be mobile again.

Brother John had a wonderful time in Hull with our cousin and his best friend from the old days. Donna, his daughter had a good time as well visiting London, Whitby and Scarborough. John spread dad's ashes in Hornsea where we always went on holiday while living in Hull.

Namaste, Jude

September 7, 2015

I had a great time with Carol in Fort Collins visiting her kids who are going to school there. Before I left, one of her daughters kind of chastised me for not being more assertive about my care. (In a loving way, of course). I was pretty miserable when I saw her. I called my onco's nurse that day and she got me in the next day to drain 3 liters of fluid out of my belly. I have what is called ascites due to the cancer in my abdomen. The fluid has no place to go. Anyway, I feel tons better and ready to have some fun.

Namaste, Jude

September 12, 2015

I co-hosted the Mountain Morning Show a couple days ago. They needed guests, so I took it upon myself to find someone to interview. I reached out to the owner of my favorite local fitness clothing brand, and she was excited to do it. Since they are holding a fitness retreat at a resort in Park City I thought she would be a great fit. The interview went so well she invited me and the other two women who work at the station to come to the media event at the retreat and today is the day!

The two women who work at the station with me backed out, but I decided to go anyways. I was a little nervous because I didn't know anyone there. When I signed in, I was able to choose two pieces of clothing from a rack. I chose a pink hoodie and gray leggings. The first class I took was a high cardio dance class outside on the main deck. The views were gorgeous! It was a great way to start the day. After the tough cardio class I thought it would be a good time to listen to a speaker talk about something I have always been interested in, nutrition. They served us lunch, and then I went to sit by the pool to relax for a bit before heading to an aerial flow yoga class.

I hadn't been to an aerial flow yoga class before, and it was amazing! I have done yoga in the past, but nothing like this. In aerial yoga, you let the hammock support you while you do different poses and shapes. It felt good to have the support from something other than a person. I love my friends and family, but they can't always be there when I need them. It was like the hammock was there to help me work through the feelings I have deep inside out of me. I was able to relax because I had something dependable to keep me from falling. When the instructor asked us to wrap up into the silky fabric, I felt like I was in my own little cocoon. I was a caterpillar about to transform. I have learned so much about myself, and who I want to be these past few years I am ready to break out into a changed person. The beautiful butterfly I know I can be.

XO, E

September 14, 2015

I went an all expenses paid retreat for breast cancer patients last weekend. It is with the same organization Erin told me about last year, Image Reborn. They provide no-cost healing retreats to women diagnosed with breast cancer, and assist them in living rich and fulfilling lives. They offer weekend long retreats held in the mountains. Survivors may attend at any time during their cancer journey, and are invited to attend up to once per calendar year. We stayed at a lovely old resort with hot springs and all the amenities. There were fourteen of us, mostly not advanced cancers. We still all go through the same fears and experiences. The group took us fly fishing on the

Provo River Sunday morning. I managed not to fall in or catch a fish! They took excellent care of us.

I had a colonoscopy last week. The doc was unable to navigate past the lower part of my colon because of the cancer that was there from three years ago. I don't know anything about the other malignancy the radiologist saw on the cat scan. My oncologist recommended doing chemo again, which I will start on Thursday. It is a low dose chemo as they say. It will mean staying in the hospital for three hours while they infuse me with it. I will have one week off. That means three weeks on for once a week and one week off. Not sure for how long. They are going to do a new test with the biopsied specimens they took last week to determine what chemo is most effective against my cancer cells. I won't have the results of that for three weeks though. I am feeling stronger these days. I am hoping the side effects from the chemo will allow me to enjoy life. That is what I am promised. I will not do it if I can't have fun on earth while I am here. I still have a lot of trouble to get into yet.

No new news regarding Hayley. Communication with her seems more difficult these days. I can't remember the last time I saw her. Might have been August.

Namaste, Jude

September 15, 2015

Hayley text me last night to tell me she wants to stay overnight Wednesday, so she can go with me on Thursday. I can't rely on her, so Cherie may need to come too. I don't know what I would do without my friends. Every one of them is filled with so much divine feminine love that when given, heals my heart, and dries my tears. I love them all so much.

I became very depressed after Ossie died in July. The past six months have been filled with losses. Some I can explain, but others leave me sad and wondering, but all in all, I am in good spirits.

Namaste, Jude

September 17, 2015

I am feeling great! They have given me Decadron in my IV. Which is a steroid to help with nausea and joint pain. I feel like I am on speed! Euphoric and boundless energy. I just talked to my nurse at Huntsman, and she said enjoy it while it lasts. Tomorrow the side effects kick in. Erin spent the morning with me, and then went to lunch at The Point with my friend, Cherie. Beautiful panoramic view of the valley! Today was the best initial chemo appt I have ever had.

Namaste, Jude

September 17, 2015

I took mom to Hotel Huntsman this morning. We are so lucky to have such an amazing place for her to heal. She told me she would like to be able to share her story, but also find a way to keep loved ones up to date on what she is going through. I suggested we take short videos every time we go to chemo. Once mom was hooked up, I sat next to her on the armrest of the large, leather recliner to film a quick video about her first day back in the chemo chair. Mom isn't used to being on camera, so she would make funny faces until I asked her if she was camera ready while giggling. She smiled and said "Am I camera ready? Yes, I am" while fixing her hair and laughing her infectious laugh. I then asked her what we are doing today. She explains the process of the nurses cleaning and accessing her port so they don't have to use an IV every time. She says she is feeling good about the treatment called, Taxol. It is a more natural chemo derived from the yew tree in California. Before we end she fluffs up her hair and says "Take a look at it now because it might be gone in a few weeks," but she is in good spirits. I love the video! We are our goofy selves, but get the information across as needed. I look forward to taking more videos with her. I am sad we didn't take any in the beginning, but at least we can start now.

XO, E

September 18, 2015

I am happy mom is doing well, but the new chemo treatment is scaring me. Since her symptoms are starting to worsen she is not able to take hormone replacements. I started to talk to Mike about my concerns, but I stopped when I realized he wasn't paying attention. I am sure hearing about cancer gets old. I know I have grown tired of talking about it all of the time.

I must have really needed to talk to someone, because when I dropped Bella off I couldn't help the emotions that burst out of me. Dad is my rock, and I know he is there if I need anything. He gave me the biggest hug, and just let me weep in his arms while listening to my concerns about mom. He gives the best hugs, and his healing hands make me feel safe. No matter how old I get I will always need my dad.

XO, E

September 21, 2015

Doing well with this chemo. No nausea or vomiting. Yeah! Today is a day to remember. You are loved by yourself, the others, your girls, friends, patients, bosses, dogs, flowers, plants and every atom in your body loves you. Yes, even the cancer. Love it all. Surround, infuse it all with love, peace, harmony. We all work in sync with the other. We are inter dependent. Not dependent, but inter dependent. You know there is a difference. Remember to breathe. Stay open to ideas. Fundamentals that visit you from time to time. The future is now. Hold the now. It is precious. So precious. You are beautiful, full of life, hope. All will be well. You will see. All will be well. Now breath my love. Breathe in my love. Breathe it out for others to heal, and to find peace.

Namaste, Jude

September 22, 2015

Dad has been sick with terrible heartburn for about a week. He can't understand why he can't eat anything without feeling sick. He has tried several home remedies like over the counter medication and apple cider vinegar, but nothing is helping. Just two weeks ago, he took a long back packing trip, and just got back from helping his girlfriend move to Colorado. He was doing fine. He doesn't like seeing the doctor, so I knew it was bad when he made an appointment to go to the ER. He declined my offer to join him. I didn't want to intrude, but when I text him at 10:30PM to see how he was and didn't get a response I started to worry. I asked Mike if he thought I should go to the ER and he said I should. I quickly changed, but I was in such a hurry I forgot to wear my lucky evil eye bracelet. I rarely leave the house without it. I realized I didn't have it on when I was half way to the hospital, but didn't think I needed to turn back for it. Dad was going to be fine. I didn't need luck on my side.

The ER was empty when I arrived. A nice nurse walked me back to a room where dad was curled up in a fetal position. He looked vulnerable, and in so much pain. I said, "hi dad" very quietly, not wanting to startle him. He looked over his shoulder, surprised to see me, but happy I came. A few minutes later an older man hesitantly walked into the room. He smiled at me, but I could tell he had bad news. He handed dad a cup of water and asked how he was doing. Dad said terrible. The doctor sat down and told us the reason behind the terrible heartburn is liver cancer. Dad and I were speechless! My legs started to shake so badly I would have fallen to the cold laminate floor if there wasn't a table for me to grab onto. The doctor said he would like dad to stay overnight because he wanted to run more tests to see if he can find out where the cancer originated from. He also wanted to keep a close eye on him to make sure he was going to be okay. When he left the room dad said, "Well, this sucks." I immediately told him we will figure it out. We will get more answers, and a second opinion in the next couple days. Everything will be okay. But both of us knew everything wasn't going to be okay. He was too sick. I stayed calm for dad, but all I wanted to do was to cry while he held me in one of his big bear hugs, assuring me everything was going to be alright. He is my best friend. I can't lose him.

At 12:30AM, he was transferred to hospital room where he was going to be living the next few days. I was right behind him. I wasn't going anywhere until I knew he was safe. He asked me to go home to get some sleep after the nurses got him situated. I told him I loved him, and I would stop by on my way to work in the morning. I gave him a big hug and raced to my car. I couldn't get to the parking garage fast enough. I felt like I was in a dream, or in this case, another nightmare. I needed to get out of the hospital as fast as I could. When I sat down in my car I stared at the gray cement wall in front of me, still in shock. I began to cry a soft cry, which quickly turned into full on convulsions of snot and tears, my breath not able to catch up with my own sadness. I felt so alone and afraid. I was surprised I was able to hold it together this long, but I had been through similar news before. I needed to be strong for dad. I tried to put my key into the ignition, but I was shaking and crying so hard all I could do was sit there and feel what I needed to feel. Two parents who have terminal cancer and a sister in a deep heroin addiction. What was my world coming to? After a few minutes, I began to think that our family has been given these struggles because we are able to handle them. Mom is inspiring people with her strength, her courage, her fight and her will. Why can't dad do the same? Why have no hope and instantly go to the negative? It won't help anything or anyone. This realization halted the flowing of tears and my body came to a still, making it so I could finally drive home.

I rushed up the stairs to my little red brick house. I wanted to get be in my bubble as soon as I could. A bubble where cancer doesn't live and Mike and Bella are waiting for me. As I stepped onto the hardwood floors I let out a familiar sigh I experienced just a couple years ago. I was relieved to be at home. I went to slip off my lucky bracelet I wear every time I leave the house, but it wasn't wrapped around my tiny wrist. I forgot that I had left it on its porcelain tray. After hearing the news I just received I decided to never leave home without it. I tip toed to bed, trying not to wake Mike, but when I slid underneath the puffy cloud of down I started to cry again. I really didn't want to wake him, but I was sobbing so loud I couldn't help it. He rolled over, whispered that everything was going to be okay and held me until I went to sleep.

XO, E

September 23, 2015

I woke up to the birds chirping outside. I couldn't help but think that everything that had happened last night was a bad dream, but when I saw the texts from mom asking if dad was okay I started to cry all over again. It was real. Bella must have heard me sobbing because she walked in the room, and placed her head on my lap. It was like she was giving me a hug, and reminding me that a walk with her is the best medicine. I took a deep breath, wiped my tears away, and laughed as I told her I would take her. She lifted her head as she started to wag her tail in excitement.

It was a beautiful, fall morning. The sun began to rise over a nearby ridge, spilling a gold light across the valley. It took it's time a first, but then started to spread faster and faster, melting the frost that had formed overnight. The few red and orange leaves on the trees were a reminder that death can be beautiful, but I am not ready for the green leaves or dad to go just yet.

As I watched Bella trot along the grass, I thought about how much I love seeing her enjoy the simple pleasures in life. Whether it's feeling the wind in her hair as she cruises in the car, taking the time to process all of the scents on our strolls or cuddling with us on the sofa she seems so happy. I can learn so much from her if I allow myself to be more present, and grateful for everything that happens to me, the good and the bad. I am going to try to learn to be happier, like Bella.

I went to the hospital to visit dad on the way to work. The hospital he chose to go to was the hospital where I was born. As I walked through the hallways I thought that my parents may have walked through these same hallways anxiously waiting for a new life to begin and here I am, walking through them, nervously waiting to hear if my dad's life was going to end.

When I arrived to dad's room his best friend, Darrell was already there. They are so close many people mistake them for brothers. I like to think of him as part of our family. He said he was going to take care of Lucy for the next few days, so I didn't need to worry about her. Dad already seemed to be in better spirits. He despises hospitals and having to rely on people to take care of him, so he is more than ready leave, but because the doctors are still running tests he is not going anywhere soon. I didn't want to leave dad, but Darrell assured me he was going to stay with him most of the day. It is very comforting to know he can be there with I can't.

After seeing him in better spirits I felt a sense of hope. We know he has liver cancer, but we don't know how bad it is yet. On my drive up the canyon I saw an eagle flying over me. I have once heard that eagles are prayer carriers. I am not a religious person, but I figured a prayer couldn't hurt, so I prayed for dad to be okay, hoping that the eagle would carry it to where it needed to go to be heard.

XO, E

September 25, 2015

When Dad was released from the hospital he was instructed to see a cancer specialist. I am still adamant about getting him to Hunstman, but since the doctors at the hospital recommended this particular oncologist, dad thought it was best to go. We were greeted by a young receptionist who asked dad to fill out some paperwork. He is still so weak, mentally and physically he asked me to fill it out for him. We were discussing what we wanted to ask the doctor when a nurse called his name. I helped him up, and we walked slowly to an examination room. Whether we are taking a hike or walking through a store, I have always had a hard time keeping up with dad. To see him try to catch up with the slow pace of the nurse made my heart sink. She didn't seem to notice we were lagging behind when she walked us through hallways full with people being injected with chemo. This facility wasn't like Huntsman at all. It was very depressing, and I didn't get a feeling of hope being there. It is definitely not the right place for dad. I have to get him to Huntsman, ASAP!

We sat in the room for about 15 minutes until the doctor arrived. He was an older man who didn't have much of a bedside manner. Another one? I thought to myself. He didn't ask dad many questions. He dove in head first to tell us dad has stage 4 small cell lung cancer, and didn't show any remorse when he told us he only has a few months to live, even if he does chemo. The sinking feeling I had just a couple years ago came back. I was scared, but more than that I was furious! I wasn't going to take this as an answer. I started to get very upset with how the doctor was delivering the bad news. I kept thinking I had to get out of the office so I could make an appointment with a different oncologist before the end of the day. I told the doc I needed to make a phone call, but he asked me to stay so I could hear what the next steps are. I knew I needed to be there, but I felt like he had taken me hostage when he slowly moved in front of the only way out of the sterile room. Dad didn't cry or get angry. He stayed silent, listening to what the doctor had to say. He could tell I was upset and asked me to calm down, but after about 15 minutes of hearing the doctor talk in circles, I practically forced my way out and went to the waiting room to catch a doctor at Huntsman before it was too late.

It was 4:55 on a Friday, so no one was answering the phones, therefore I couldn't make an appt. I felt defeated and hopeless. I wanted to cry, but again I needed to be strong. Shortly after I hung up the phone dad met me in the waiting room. I calmed down when I saw him because he was already upset enough, he didn't need my angry energy to bring him down even more. On our drive home, we talked about what the doctor said and the options available. The doc has scheduled dad to start chemo next week. I suggested that we keep the appointment, but I would still really like him to get another opinion. He needs to be somewhere comfortable.

I dropped him off so he could get some rest and went home to give Mike and Bella the bad news.

XO, E

September 26, 2015

I couldn't stop thinking about dad and his diagnosis while I was at work today. I am so scared. One of my biggest fears is losing my parents and it is slowly coming true. I want to spend as much time as I can with him, so when I got off work Mike and I went to his house to watch the Utah football game. We all love Utah football. My love for the sport came from watching it with dad and going to games with him when I was little. I remember being so excited when he bought me my first red and white pom poms so I could cheer on the team like the cheer leaders. I still have the pom poms and keep them in a chest my grandmother gave me. I like to tease Mike by telling him I am a bigger Utah football fan than he is. Because the Utes recently joined the Pac12 conference they are playing harder teams than ever before. Tonight they played against Oregon in Oregon, and they are tough team, especially on their home field. Dad got comfortable on the sofa while Mike and I sat on the floor with Lucy and Bella. We all cheered on the Utes as they rose to victory! Dad was so happy. It was good to see him smile and be able to forget about how terrible he is feeling, even if it was for just of couple hours.

XO, E

September 26, 2015

Mom called me today to let me know dad had been in the hospital, and I needed to come home to talk to him. I asked her why he was in the hospital, but she wouldn't tell me. She said he wanted to talk to me about what was going on in person. I was very confused. Dad is so healthy and strong. I walked in to find dad sitting at the dining room table watching college football and eating yogurt. My heart dropped when I saw him. I knew something was very wrong because I had never seen him look so weak before. I gave him a hug and sat next to him. He told me he had been feeling sick for the last few weeks and finally went to the ER where the doctors told him he has cancer. My body tensed up as tears started welling up in my eyes. He continued to say the oncologist says it's lung cancer, and he doesn't have long to live. The tears that were welling up started to roll down my cheeks and became black from the mascara on my long eyelashes. I hugged him as my black tears fell onto his shoulder, staining his white shirt. He held me, and then told me his only wish is for me to get my life straightened out, and for me to be sober. I really want to get sober, and maybe having both of my parents so sick will be a reason for me to do it. I grabbed a yogurt out of the fridge, and sat with him, promising myself that I would get better. My family needs me.

-Hayz

September 27, 2015

It has been quite a week. The weather has been unseasonably warm. I've even had the air conditioner on at night. The colors are changing in the mountains, and starting to in the valley. I do love this time of year.

Mike was diagnosed with advanced lung cancer that has spread to his liver on Friday. We are all in shock, naturally; I am very concerned about Erin. She is a strong young woman though, and does have her husband to lean on. Mike is very ill. He can't eat much of anything due to the liver enlargement that is pressing on other organs. The doc wants to do chemo ASAP to help alleviate his symptoms. Liver metastasis is not a good thing. Trying to be hopeful. After all, I have lived for three years more than the docs predicted.

On a good note, the chemo I am doing has proven to be pretty easy to bear. Day three is my worst day, but at least I know which days I can be active. I am still working three days a week. I love working because I can forget I have cancer, and feel I am making a difference, and doing something worthwhile.

I most likely will be losing my hair. My friend, Mame is my hairdresser. We are planning a head shaving party in a couple of weeks. Mame is going to invite our friends to attend. Everyone is invited to bring a fun head cover in preparation for my baldness. I am feeling pretty good mentally. Mike's illness has shocked us all.

Namaste, Jude

September 27, 2015

Mike and I stayed with dad most of the day. While he slept, we cleaned the house, took Lucy for a walk, and ran errands. Dad can't eat much, but asked for soup and yogurt because they are easiest on his stomach. We thought he was getting better, but as the day went on, he began to feel terribly sick again. He is declining at a rapid rate, which worries me. It's heart breaking to witness someone I have always seen as superhuman act like a mortal. I am taking him to his MRI tomorrow morning, and while I am waiting, I am going to make sure I get him an appointment with a different doctor. I am not taking the original diagnosis for an answer. I just hope it's not too late.

All my life friends would tell me I don't have a normal dad; I have a cool, adventurous dad. He spends as much time outside as he can. So much so, he was certified to take groups cross country skiing to a yurt in the winter with only a pack on his back filled with supplies. During the summer he backpacks to remote areas to camp and explore the area in every way possible. He knows the local mountain range so well he has helped search and rescue teams find lost hikers and takes a walk around the neighborhood every day.

He is a never miss a piano recital or soccer game type of dad. My girls can do anything type of dad. He is a, "you got this; don't let them get to you" type of dad. Family before anything type of dad. He is one of a kind. He is a smart, loyal family man who taught me to act with love and accept people for who they are. People would tell me he was intimidating because of his height and the way he carried himself, but I never saw him that way. He is a gentle giant I only know as my dad.

XO, E

September 28, 2015

I drove dad to get his MRI this morning. He is so weak he couldn't even get out of the car without assistance. I rushed to get a wheelchair before pushing him to the appointment. I have heard MRI's can be pretty scary, but dad didn't seem anxious at all. I think he is too sick to think about anything other than how terrible he feels. I filled out his paperwork while he sat in the chair with his eyes closed and his head resting on his hand. I had never seen him so fragile. I felt like he would fall out of the chair if someone gently tapped on his shoulder. While he was getting his MRI, I called Huntsman to make an appointment with an oncologist tomorrow. I wish it was today, but I am grateful they can get him in on such short notice.

When we got home he was sicker than I had seen him for a while. I think the MRI took a lot out of him. He couldn't make it up the stairs, so he collapsed into the sofa in the basement to take a nap. I thought it was best if Bella and I hung out at his house in case he needed anything, but he didn't need anything except for a lot of sleep. Aunt Marcia and Uncle Kent came over to say hi and to bring soup in the afternoon. They knew he was sick, but hadn't seen him in person after he got the diagnosis. He had made it to the upstairs sofa at this point, but was still so weak he could barely talk to them when they arrived. He loves seeing family, especially his only sister, so it was very unlike him to not be the gracious host they have always known him as. They pulled me aside to express their worries and insisted I take him to the ER again. Dad must have heard us talking because when I walked into the living room he had used the little energy he had to sit up and ask that I take him.

Uncle Kent and I put his arms around our shoulders while we slowly lifted him off the sofa. I don't know how, but we practically carried my 6'4" dad to the car. I asked them to meet us at the University of Utah hospital, knowing he could be admitted to Hunstman if the doctors felt like he needed to.

On our way to the hospital I told dad the plan as he nodded his head in agreeance. The kind woman at the front desk asked me what his symptoms were, but didn't seem too worried until she peeked over her desk to see his jaundiced skin. She asked an attendee to quickly escort him to another room to take his vitals. His liver enzymes were off the charts! Even though the ER was busy and there were several people in front of him they were able to find us a room right away.

Aunt Marcia and Uncle Kent followed us to a room in the back of the ER. It was a lot busier than the last hospital we were in, but I am glad we were there. A very nice, young doctor came in to check on dad. He turned out to be the son of the doctor who first told us dad had cancer at the other hospital. He called his father a couple times to ask questions about dad's symptoms a week ago to see how much he had worsened. Everyone was very caring, and dad and I were comfortable there. I trust the doctors at the U. I know they have just about every resource he might need.

To pass the time, Dad and I watched Dancing with the Stars, reruns of Friends, Modern Family, and Seinfeld. I loved spending the evening with dad. Since he had arrived to the hospital he was himself and we were able to have a daddy daughter night like we used to. We talked about the people on DWTS, my upcoming trips, his camping adventures, Utah football and how worried we are about Hayley. It was just the two of us with only a small tv to distract us.

We were in such a rush to leave the house I didn't bring a book with me. I was tired of looking at my phone, so after dad went to sleep I worked out in the room and went to get dinner. The cafeteria had closed, but the gift shop was open, so I had gummy bears and baked lays. Since mom has been diagnosed with cancer and now dad, little things like not having a great dinner one night doesn't matter to me anymore. There are much bigger things to worry about, and right now the most important thing to do was make sure dad was okay. When the clock struck 12 the doctor came in to let us know a room was available at Hunstman. A wave of relief went through my body. He was finally going to be where he needed to be this entire time.

The rooms at Huntsman were just like I remember them. They feel more like hotel rooms than ordinary hospital rooms. Dark planks of laminate cover the floors, a large wood shelving unit is home to a TV and you can see gorgeous views of the city or the famous Wasatch Mountains through the big windows. Dad has a view of the mountains, which is very fitting for my mountain man of a father. I gave dad a kiss on the forehead, told him I loved him and left once I saw he was comfortable. I walked slowly to my car. I didn't feel like I had to run to get to away. I had more of a sense of hope than a week ago. I drove home knowing he is in good hands.

XO, E

September 29, 2015

Bella and I stepped out of the house when the sun was about to rise. In the middle of our walk we stopped to watch the blazing ball of fire make its appearance over the horizon. I couldn't help but think it was a symbol of new beginning. I instantly went into a state of gratitude, setting myself up for positive energy to motivate my day.

I made sure to visit dad on my way to work. He was the best I had seen him in weeks! His spirits were high and he said he felt good being where he was. Nurses came in and out while I was there, so I didn't get to have much one on one time, but I was able to tell him I love him and that I would come back to visit after work. He told me "I love you too sweetie" as I walked out the door. Since we had a normal conversation I left thinking he was on the upswing. He would probably be released tomorrow.

I was in the middle of writing an email when I received a call from dad. I asked him if everything was okay, but he didn't answer my question. Instead, he asked me what we were doing for lunch and was very, very out of it. I was so confused. What had changed in a couple hours? After I finished talking to him my aunt came onto the phone. I asked her if I should come down and she said yes, right away. I was in a panic. I didn't know what was going on! When I called my boss to tell him what had happened he told me I could leave, so I locked the door, put up a sign saying we were closed for the day, and rushed to the hospital. As I drove to the hospital I thought about how many people have had to make this drive. Driving into an unknown. I knew something was bad, but had no idea how bad it was. My feelings of hope were dwindled as my body grew numb, and I went into autopilot mode.

Mom, Darrell, Aunt Linda, Uncle Gary, Aunt Marcia, and Uncle Kent seemed very worried when I arrived. It was great to see everyone, but I rushed by them to talk to dad. He still wasn't making sense and kept asking for his girlfriend. I held is hand as he drifted off to a deep sleep. The doctors said they could give him a dose of chemo which could either help or make things worse. One of them pulled me aside to let me know that he made both Darrell and I his power of attorneys. Dad never talked to me about taking on that responsibility. I understood why he would appoint me, and I was flattered that he did, but I was so scared. He was the person I went to for advice if I ever needed to make a difficult decision. I was terrified knowing I had to make a decision that will change both of our lives forever without him. How was I supposed to do that?! Darrell and I thought it would be best to speak with Aunt Marcia, Hayley, and Mom before we did anything. This was an important decision that needed to be discussed with family. We talked it over, and unanimously decided to let the doctors go ahead with the chemo. At this point we didn't see him getting better if he didn't get it. We called Uncle Bill to tell him what was going on, and he is trying to catch the earliest flight to UT. We also called his girlfriend, hoping she would perk up his spirits. She lives in Colorado now and was a little hesitant in coming, but we pleaded for her to make the trip since she was the only person he was asking for.

Since I refused to leave dad's side, Mike brought me a change of clothes, food, makeup, etc. Most everyone had left by the time he arrived. I practically jumped in his arms when I saw him. I didn't even let him put anything down until I gave him one of the biggest hugs I have ever given him. The hospital usually doesn't allow two people to stay in the room overnight, but made an exception for us. We slept on a sofa that was more like a bench because it was so small. I didn't sleep much, not only because the sleeping arrangements weren't the most comfortable, but because I wanted to be awake when dad woke from his long nap. I would stare at him sleeping from across the room. He had so many tubes and wires coming out from underneath the blue blankets keeping him warm. I still didn't feel like it was real. I thought dad would live until he was at least 95. I never thought he would be lying in a hospital bed, with machines keeping him alive. To get my mind off of things I looked up at the stars lighting up the big black sky. When a shooting star shot across the sky I closed my eyes and wished for dad to open his eyes. I then tip toed to his bed, held his hand and told him I was there, hoping my wish would come true.

XO, E

September 29, 2015

Mom and Erin were calling and texting me all morning. I am going through withdrawals, so I am very sick, and have been in a deep sleep. When I called mom back, she told me dad was at the hospital, and I need to get there right away. I don't have a car, but I found a friend who was able to drive me. When I got to Hunstman, dad was really out of it. He knew who I was, and the first thing he said was, "What are you doing here? They don't have yogurt here." The last thing I had eaten at dads was one of his yogurts, and he was giving me a hard time about it. I smiled because he still had his sense of humor, even though he was so sick. I sat with him for a bit, and then went outside to smoke a cigarette and make a quick Facebook post. "My dad is really sick. We need a miracle. Please send all the positive vibes our way. We need all the love we can get." I stayed at the hospital with the family all day. Many people came and went, but my sister and I didn't leave. Dad had fallen asleep and the doctors didn't think he would wake up anytime soon, so once the sun went down, mom and I went to get some food, and I am sleeping on her couch. I really hope dad wakes up. I don't know what I will do if he doesn't.

-Hayz

September 30, 2015

I woke up to the sounds of high pitched beeps coming from the machines keeping dad alive. It was a new day. Hopefully a day where I can talk to him again. I slowly climbed over Mike, hoping not to wake him, and made my way to dad's bed. He slept through the night and there were no changes. I told him good morning as the nurse came walking in. She asked how we all were before checking on his vitals. I told her we were fine, just worried. While she was there I decided it was a good time to try Uncle Bill and his good friend from college, Marc, but no such luck. I know Uncle Bill is trying to get a flight out here, but the short notice has made it difficult.

Family began to arrive around 10. They each took turns coming into the room to find out if there was anything new to report. When Hayley arrived with mom they asked me to go home. They saw how tired I was and said I would be no good to anyone if I didn't get a break. I didn't want to leave dad's side, but I knew they were right. I needed a shower, and to change. Mike agreed and followed me home.

When I got into my car I didn't know how to feel. I wanted to cry, but nothing would come out. I was still numb to everything. I have taken the drive from Huntsman to home so many times I can probably do it with my eyes closed, which was good because even though they were open I didn't have any sense of reality at that moment. I was still in autopilot mode. When I pulled up to the house I was surprised to see Ali and Kristin waiting for me with flowers. A large knot immediately formed in my stomach and slowly moved into my throat. "Here they come" I thought to myself. My bottom lip started to quiver and the knot came undone as tears came pouring out of my eyes. I didn't have to be the strong one in front of them like I did in front of my family. They began to cry as well. Ali lost her dad when we were in high school, so she knows what it is like to lose a parent. Kristin is like another daughter to my dad. We were best friends when we were younger, so she spent a lot of time at our house growing up. I wanted to cry with them for hours, but I needed to get in the shower so I could get back to the hospital.

I couldn't wait to get a hot shower. I am able to collect my thoughts when I am there. It is a place with no distractions, where I can be alone. I closed my eyes and let the hot water run down my face and into my mouth. I wanted it to wash away all of the stress I was feeling. It didn't take long for the clean water to be mixed with the salty taste of my tears. It felt good to be able to cry alone. No one was watching me, or had any expectations. I could just let my emotions out without any judgment. My tears came to a halt when Mike rushed into the bathroom to tell me the doctor called. She said they don't know how much time dad has left and we needed to get to the hospital as soon as possible. My time to be vulnerable was over. I had to go back into super hero mode. I quickly got out of the shower, got dressed and we sped to Hunstman.

Mike almost hit one of the young valet's as we pulled up. I hopped out while the car was still moving and ran in. I felt like we were in a movie where I was the stunt double jumping out of a speeding vehicle. Mike threw his keys to one of the valet's and followed close behind. The valet drivers looked confused, so Mike said her dad is dying we need to get inside. We were panicking because the doctor made it sound dire. The ride in the elevator felt like hours. I was so anxious I wanted to pry open the elevator doors with my hands when we finally arrived to the 5th floor. As the doors opened I squeezed out and ran to the main waiting room to meet loved ones.

Hayley was the first person to tell me I still had time. I was relieved I was able to make it, but I felt terrible knowing that this could be the last time I would be able to talk to dad. He isn't awake, but at least he is still breathing. The doctor who was attending to dad was also there. She waited until I arrived to tell the whole family that dad's cancer spread faster than any cancer she had seen. She didn't know how much time he had left and advised everyone to say their goodbyes. No one said anything. We didn't know what to say at that point. It had all happened so fast. None of us thought this day would come so quickly. He is only 64! He still has so much to live for. Everyone started to take their turns and agreed that I be last.

Having loved ones around was a great distraction. People came and went to talk to dad and each time they came back their eyes were swollen from crying. He made such an impact on all of our lives. The sun setting over the valley was the sign that it was going to be my turn soon. Even though I had all afternoon to think about what I was going to tell him, I still had no idea what to say when my time came. How am I supposed to say goodbye to my dad? The first man I ever loved and, who has ever loved me. He is my problem solver, my protector, my biggest cheerleader, my therapist, my walking partner and my best friend. Mike held my hand as we walked down the long cold hallway. I felt like I was holding onto him for dear life. I asked him if he would come inside with me because I didn't want to face it alone. He smiled, shook his head no, gave me a hug and opened the door for me to go inside the room I had just spent the night in. It felt so different than before. It was filled with hope, but now it was filled with despair.

The setting sun filled his room with a soft orange light. I took a deep breath, held his hand, and told him how much I loved him. I shared a few of my fondest memories, and said "thank you for giving me confidence, and showing me that I deserve everything I work for. I always knew he had my back and prepared me for the challenges that lie ahead. I am lucky to have a dad who allowed me to be myself, and because of that I will continue to live courageously. I will miss him dearly and I am not ready for him to disappear from my life."

About 15 minutes later Hayley walked in. She sat across from me and we each took a hold of one of dad's, cold, lifeless hands. We grasped each other's fingers across the light blue blanket covering his still body. It was quiet except for our soft cries. When the time between his breaths started to get longer we knew he was going to be gone soon. Hayley and I squeezed each other's hand as he let out one last breath. My heart felt like it shattered into a million pieces of glass and the shards were moving throughout my body. I never felt a pain like this before. It forced my heaving body to collapse into his lap while my lungs gasped for air between my deep cries. I really don't know what I am going to do without him.

XO, E

September 30, 2015

We went straight to the hospital this morning. Erin was still there and looked exhausted. She had been up most of the night. Mom and I told her she should go home to take a break, but she didn't want to. She wasn't going to leave dad's side. We told her we were there, and we would call if anything happened. She would be no good to any of us if she didn't take care of herself. Mike said the same thing and followed her home. I didn't leave dad's room because if he woke up I wanted to be there. Family members made quick appearances to see if there were any changes, but he slept all day. His doctor came in to check on him and said she is going to call Erin. She needed to come back so she could talk to her about dad's condition.

Erin came running out of the elevator, looking scared. I ran up to her, gave her a big hug and told her she still had time. The doctor arrived shortly after to let us know she didn't know how much time dad had left and we need to begin to say our goodbyes. Family and friends started to take their turns to say goodbye. I stayed in the waiting room with everyone else. I started to think about what I was going to say to dad. I wasn't ready to say goodbye. I can always count on him. I don't know what I am going to do without him in my life. Mom walked me to the room, gave me a big hug, and I slowly walked inside. I tip toed to his bed like I was a little kid trying not to wake him. I grabbed his hand, told him I was sorry, and that I will always love him. Erin and Mike were waiting for me outside the door. I gave them both a big hug and stood outside the door while Erin went inside. After Erin was done the doctor went in to check on dad and told us it was close. Erin and I sat across from one another and held each other's hand. We didn't say anything. We just waited. We felt him take one last breath, and he was gone. I fell into his lap and lost it. Dad has been there for me through everything. He was my biggest supporter. What am I going to do without my daddy?

-Hayz

October 1, 2015

Mike and I met the family at dad's house to try to figure out what to do next. I had no clue how to plan a funeral, and I wasn't in the state of mind to make so many important decisions on my own. Dad and I didn't have a chance to talk about what he wanted, so it was really nice to have family there to help. I asked Uncle Bill if he would write the obituary. Dad and Uncle Bill were close, and I have always admired my Uncle's talent for writing. Aunt Marcia and Uncle Kent told us they went with dad to the cemetery to check on the plots grandma bought them a couple months earlier. They said he didn't mention that he wanted anything different, and the fact that he was looking at his plot made all of us think that it is where he wanted to be laid to rest. Mike helped me make calls to different funeral homes and the cemetery.

I excused myself and went upstairs to dad's office when it started to get too overwhelming. It was his safe place, and I needed it to be mine, even if it was just for a few minutes. I sat in his big, brown, leather chair looking at all of the pictures and memorabilia he collected over the years. I felt close to him without him being there. I started to think about how I was going to pay for everything. I had no idea funeral's cost so much, but I have enough money saved to be able to cover most of the expenses. I find it ironic that I was able to save money because I lived with dad instead of renting, and I am now using the money I saved to pay for his funeral.

I started to process the events from last night. When I left dad I was surprised to not see anyone waiting for us near the door. They were all in a smaller waiting room. The first person I saw was his good friend, Marc Welch, who is like an Uncle to me. I remember getting so excited when he would take me for a ride in his Jeep Wrangler when I was a little girl. He gave me a huge bear hug when I saw him last night, a hug like my dad used to give.

Uncle Bill wasn't there yet, but he was on his way. It broke my heart knowing that he wasn't able to say goodbye, but dying isn't something we can postpone. It won't go away if we try to forget about it. Whether we are prepared or not, it's going to happen. My dad leaving without warning has left me with a broken heart, but there's no way he would have wanted us to watch him suffer. Nor is he one to want to feel like a burden on his friends or family. It helps knowing his last days were spent doing the things he loved. Traveling, hiking, camping, cheering on the Utes, and spending time with the people he cared for the most. It would have been difficult for him to be able to do all of those things if he had to spend hours in the chemo chair. His life wouldn't have been a quality one and I can't imagine he would have been very happy. At least he died before having to suffer any longer than he already had and I didn't have to watch him turn into a stranger. I can't fathom my life without him, but I am glad he didn't have to be hurt for a long period of time. I think that's what anyone would want. He died the father I always knew him as. Strong, caring and the best dad I could ever ask for.

XO, E

October 1, 2015

I have received so much support and love from my friends. My dad will forever be my hero and will be forever missed. I am going to make sure to remember to tell my loved ones I love them every day because life can change in an instant. Rest in peace, pops.

-Hayz

October 2, 2015

Uncle Bill went with mom, Hayley, Mike, and I to make the final arrangements. First stop was the funeral parlor. I almost drove past it because it doesn't look like a typical funeral home. It is an old, stone house the owners turned into a place to grieve. Gardens surround the property and when we walked in it was like we were walking into a friend's home. It was very comfortable. The funeral director met us at the front door before showing us around. After hearing our story he asked Hayley and I to pick out a casket. I really didn't want to follow him up the steep flight of stairs. I never thought I would be planning my father's funeral so soon. A showroom of caskets was waiting for us when we reached the top. Since dad was so tall we had to get an XL casket. I was kinda happy that there weren't too many options for the larger size because I wanted to get out of there as soon as possible. We quickly chose the one that reminded us of dad the most, a natural walnut with a light blue liner. The liner will look nice with dad's favorite navy blue suit we brought. I am so happy Hayley was there to help with the decision. It really helped knowing I wasn't the only person having to do everything.

Mom and Hayley needed to run some errands, so Mike and I and Uncle Bill went to the University of Utah to meet our friend to talk about dad's celebration of life. We had gone back and forth on the idea of holding a celebration of life, but many people who were part of the law community knew and respected dad. He had been director of legal aid, a court commissioner for over 20 years, chaired or was a member of several committees and created the Divorce Education for Children program. We thought it was important to have a celebration for those who didn't want to attend his viewing or funeral.

The venue has a gorgeous view that looks over the Salt Lake Valley on one side and the football stadium on the other. It was a perfect place because dad loved Utah sports and looking at the city lights from his deck. While Uncle Bill was getting a tour I stood at the large windows looking over the valley, thinking how much dad enjoyed living in Utah. He took advantage of the beautiful landscape by hiking and camping weekly. He supported the local arts by attending concerts and giving donations. He made a difference, both professionally and socially. A knot started to form in my stomach. It was a warning sign that tears were going to start flowing down my face, like a river escaping a dam. As it started to make its way to my throat I swallowed a big gulp, hoping it would help hold it all in. Crying wasn't on my list of things to do at the moment. I needed to hold it together.

XO, E

October 2, 2015

I woke up this morning sweating, and feeling terribly anxious. I am sure the anxiety has to do with dad passing just a couple days earlier, but I can't help but think it is the beginning of withdrawals. I am scared to tell mom how I am feeling, but even more frightened to tell her why.

She doesn't know how deep I am into my addiction. I don't want to disappoint her more than I already have. I walked slowly into the living room where she was sitting on her floral sofa. She looked so cozy in her blue robe and pink, handmade beanie. She smiled when she saw me walk in and asked how I was doing. I immediately started to cry. I don't want to be an addict, especially now, but the fact is that I am, and if I want to feel well I need to get high. I told her that I need to get more drugs in order to go to dad's funeral. If I don't I would be sick to my stomach for days. She started to cry as well, but understood. She promised we would figure something out. She doesn't want me to miss such a crucial time in my life.

The main plan today was meeting family at the funeral parlor. I needed to be there for Erin, even though I really didn't want to go. The funeral director was very sweet. He didn't seem to judge me for the dark circles under my eyes or the scabs on my face. He only was there to help us. The funeral home was understated, but also had a lot of character, it reminded me a lot of dad. I am glad I could bet there to help Erin with such difficult decisions.

As we were pulling out of the parking lot a light pink Land Cruiser drove past with a pink U sticker on the back. A wave of excitement went through my body. It was dad showing me he was here. He loved driving his old Land Cruiser and knew my favorite color was pink. Whenever I see an old Land Cruiser I will think of dad. It will be his way of showing me everything is going to be okay.

-Hayz

October 3, 2015

We were asked to deliver a few things that would remind people of dad to the funeral home for the viewing tomorrow. We found a few items around the house, but most everything was in his office. I felt like we were trespassing when we walked inside the once secret room. It was known as, "dad's room" growing up and we hardly ever went inside unless we needed him for any reason. I really didn't want to invade his privacy by rummaging through his things without asking, but I couldn't think about that now. I had to do it. While I was flipping through his wallet I found a picture of him, Hayley and me on one of the many vacations we took as a family. The worn corners and the crinkle of the paper showed me he had kept it with him for years. I saw a couple other copies of the same picture on his desk. Mike ran in from the other room when he heard my loud shriek of excitement. I didn't know what I wanted to put in his casket until now. The picture from his wallet is perfect, and now Hayley and I can each carry one of the copies wherever we go. It is a way for all of us to be together when we can't be.

We found pictures, records, paintings, and books; lots and lots of books. I wonder what people will remember dad by the most. Will it be his successful career as a court commissioner, a mountain man, a wonderful father, family member and friend, or all of the above? Mike and I thought it was important to find several pieces that really showed who dad was and what he loved to do, so we took a lot of things to the funeral home, hoping they would find a place for it all. I think it was better to have too much than too little and the funeral director didn't seem overwhelmed by the amount of boxes we delivered.

After the funeral home we stopped by Nordstrom to find me a dress for the weekend. Even though I have been to Nordstrom several times I felt lost looking through the few dark blue dresses they offered in my size. Dad didn't wear black often, so I felt like dark blue was more appropriate. A nice young saleswoman must have seen the look of hopelessness in my eyes because she approached me with a sense of caution, and practically whispered in my ear when she asked me if I needed help. I opened my mouth to speak, but nothing came out. I couldn't believe I was looking for a dress for my father's funeral! I looked at Mike for help, hoping he would answer for me and he kindly told her what we were looking for. She didn't flinch when she led me to a rack of dresses she thought would work before taking me to the dressing room to try a few on. Mike was very patient and sat in the waiting room with Bella. Every time I stepped out of the fitting room to get their opinion Bella would get would wag her tail and run up to me like she hadn't seen me for hours. I love that we can bring her to the mall. She truly is my therapy dog. After I found the perfect dress, we walked around the mall to help get our minds off of things. The next couple days are going to be a lot. It was nice to feel some sort of normalcy.

XO, E

October 3, 2015

My best friend who lives in Hawaii called me today to let me know she has booked a flight to Utah. She knows how close my dad and I were, and she is like another daughter to him. He actually took us on a backpacking trip to Havasupai falls when we were 12. I am so grateful for her. We have been friends since elementary school and have been there for each other through the good and bad. It will be really nice to have her here with me.

-Hayz

October 4, 2015

I woke to my phone vibrating on my bedside table. Friends had been texting me all night, sending their condolences. It was nice to hear from people, but after a while I felt like I needed to put everyone on silent. A gentle cry has become part of my morning routine. When Mike saw me rub the tears I have cried every morning since dad passed from my eyes he asked me to take a walk with him before the day started. I slowly nodded my head yes, knowing today was going to be hard. It was the first of the three events we were hosting in remembrance of dad.

Birds greeted us with their poetic chirps from the electric wires above. I was so distracted by the gorgeous music, Bella's leash slipped through my fingers as she chased a squirrel until it went up the highest branch squeaking at her "na, na, na, na, you can't catch me." Robins followed us down the tree lined streets, creating a theme song for just us.

I dreaded the walk back home. We had such a wonderful morning; I didn't want to face the reality to what I had to do that day. When I looked into the mirror, wearing the dress I had just bought the day before a huge pit grew in my stomach, and it didn't move until I saw my cousin Dewey standing over dad's casket. I knew he was gone, but at that moment it hit me like a ton of bricks. To see my dad lying in a casket was heart wrenching. The knot had suddenly turned into tears without any warning. They streamed down my face like a waterfall with no sign of stopping. I took a moment to step outside, with Mike close behind. He rubbed my back until I was able to gather myself.

As I walked through the door for the second time I took the time to really see the space, and was taken back at how beautiful everything looked. All of the items we brought were strategically placed, and there were several bouquets of flowers loved ones had sent. It was wonderful to have so many items around to remind people of dad. The night was a whirlwind! I was talking to so many guests I didn't cry again the remainder of the evening. I actually felt like I had to console a few people instead of them consoling me. Lots of friends, family, and colleagues came to show their respects. Dad made a huge impact on a lot of people, so I wasn't surprised the viewing was busy from beginning to end.

When the last guest walked out the door I made my way to dad's casket. It was the first time I had really gotten close to him, lying in the big brown box. He didn't look like himself. The heavy makeup that was caked onto his pale face made him look unreal. I whispered "I love you" one last time as I gently placed the picture I had found in his wallet on the blue satin lining his body.

XO, E

October 4, 2015

Since my withdrawals were starting to worsen, I had to ask mom to drive me to the trailer park to get some heroin. Today is dad's viewing; I am not going to miss it because of withdrawals. Dad hated that I was an addict, but I am sure he would want me at his funeral, even if I have to be high in order to show up. Mom was reading the paper at her kitchen table when I woke. Me being an addict has already hurt her so much, I didn't want her to have to be the one to enable me to possibly hurt her again. She could tell how distraught I was when I walked into the sun filled kitchen. She already knew what I was going to ask her, so instead of me having to say anything she said she would get her keys and take me. Mom and I have always been able to read each other's mind. I think she chooses not to read mine because it breaks her heart, but she knew what we needed to do in order for me to be able to be there for our family.

We were mostly silent on the drive to the trailer park. I felt too sick to talk. I really hate that I can't act normally without poison coursing through my body. It doesn't make sense to me. As we pulled up the trailer I started to feel even more anxious. I wasn't ready to see Grant right now. He never did understand how good my family is. He always made them out to be the bad guys, especially dad. He repeatedly said dad didn't protect me from being sexually abused when I was a child, but that couldn't be further than the truth. Dad did everything he knew possible to help me. He had no idea I was being abused until I told him after it had happened a few times. Erin and I like to say that Dad is like Liam Nesson in *Taken*. He would do whatever he could to save us from danger and when he found out he couldn't save me from this he was heartbroken. I was so young I was afraid to tell anyone. When I finally did, mom and dad took all the right steps to try to help me from the trauma, but it didn't work. I am still trying to work through the terrible experience that helped form me into the addict I am today. It is still deep down inside of me.

Grant met me at the front door and didn't say much. He was surprisingly pretty nice. He gave me a big hug, said he was sorry and handed me what I needed. I told him thank you as I ran down the stairs to jump back into mom's little blue Suzuki. Mom's eyes were filled with tears when I got back into the car. She didn't want to help me get high, but she also knew it was the only way.

Lydia and Celine were a huge support at the viewing. They didn't leave my side when people would come to talk to me. They are my rocks and have been there for me throughout my addiction. Sometimes I don't feel like I deserve to have such great friends because I haven't been a great friend to them lately. I couldn't walk up to the open casket to look at dad. From what I could tell he didn't look like himself. I didn't want to remember him as a corpse with makeup on. My sister and I planned to put a couple items in the casket when we said our goodbyes, but because I wouldn't let myself get too close, Lydia and Celine did it for me. Dad would always bring me home a rock from his adventures, so I chose to include a rock from one of his favorite places, Southern Utah.

-Hayz

October 5, 2015

My own sobs woke me this morning. I didn't even know I could cry in my sleep. Mike rolled over to give me a big hug once he heard my blubbering sounds of despair. Bella put her head on the bed and looked up at me with her big brown, humanlike eyes. She was giving me permission to pet her soft, furry head. I cried so hard my chest was heaving and tears soaked my pillowcase. Mike squeezed me harder, as if he was trying to get all of the tears out of my body. I think it worked because shortly after the tears stopped flowing. I started to think that today was Monday, which is usually daddy daughter day. I should be getting ready to meet dad at his house for a walk with the dogs, not at the cemetery for his funeral.

As I zipped up the dress I had worn just hours earlier I felt different than the first time I put it on. My new dress gave me confidence. A new found confidence that I could take on whatever was going to be thrown at me that day. It was my navy blue, suit of armor.

Other than dad, we were the first ones to arrive. I placed my hand on the beautiful casket and closed my eyes hoping I would get the tears out before everyone came, but nothing happened. I had become numb again. Uncle Bill gave a beautiful eulogy before Darrell and Marc both spoke about their time with one of their best friends. Hayley and I were the last to speak. We wrote out what we wanted to say, but when we stood in front of our close family and friends I put our notes to the side. I didn't need a piece of paper to help me. I started with, "My dad is one of my very best friends. He is my hero and I strive to be more like him every day. I am a true "daddy's girl" and will miss our daily phone calls, Monday walks with the dogs, cheering on the Utes together and so much more. He is one of the kindest, selfless, generous people I know. He did a lot to help the local community and strived to make the world a better place. He loved to read and hike in the mountains with his best friend and dogs. Family and friends were two of the most important things to him. Whether it was a birthday, wedding or a weekly get together he rarely missed family gatherings and cherished the time he spent with everyone. He supported every decision I made and was my biggest fan. I couldn't ask for a better dad and I am grateful for the relationship we had." I held Hayley's hand the entire time, she was understandably upset. We planned on each taking turns speaking, but when it was her turn she looked at me with her big hazel eyes, telling me that she couldn't do it. I gave her hand a quick squeeze as a signal that everything was okay. I was happy to do it. I am the big sister, her protector. She asked me how I got through it without crying when we were done. I told her I have no idea. I am in fight or flight mode. I just knew I needed to do it.

I am glad to have all of this behind me, but I am afraid to step into a "new normal." No more Monday walks with dad and the pups, no more daily chats, no more morning drop offs, no more daddy daughter dates, and worst of all, no more dad.

XO, E

October 5, 2015

Today was the day I was dreading. It was dad's funeral. Mom and I pulled up to the service to find family and loved ones waiting for us. Everyone was so happy to see me, but I knew they were judging me on the inside. I already felt so terrible with the way I left things with dad. I didn't need other people criticizing me for it. When I stood up to talk my knees almost buckled under, but Erin caught me before I fell to the soft ground. She held my hand to lead me to where our dad lied in brown case of wood. All I could do was look down at the green blades of grass. I didn't want to see all of the eyes staring at me, judging me for not being the daughter I know I should have been. I froze when it was my turn to talk. Erin squeezed my hand gently, telling me everything was okay. She was happy to take over. I truly don't know how she did it. We were both experiencing the biggest loss of our lifetime, how is she handling it with such grace? She has been so strong through all of this.

I was happy the funeral was over, but we still had the celebration of life to get through. It was a little easier, but the man who sexually abused me when I was a child was there. My heart sank when I saw him. I was already uncomfortable as it was. I didn't need him to make it worse. I know dad was a big part of his life, but why does he feel like it's okay to make my day harder by making an appearance. Luckily, Celine and Lydia stuck by my side like velcro the entire night. I don't think I could have made it through this without them.

The only way I know how to cope is to numb my feelings with drugs, but this is something that can't be numbed. Not even the heroin can take away the feelings I have. I feel a sadness I have never felt before, and regretted how I left things with dad. I didn't see him much during his last years of life, which destroyed our relationship. I know he loved me no matter what, but I hate the way I treated him. I didn't mean to hurt him. It was hard for me to realize I would never be able to tell him I am sorry. I can tell nothing good is going to come from the overflow of emotions I am feeling. I want to get sober for my family, and in memory of my dad, but I don't know if I can.

-Hayz

October 6, 2015

My boss allowed me to take another few days off to get things sorted out. There is a lot to do, and I am the only one to get it done. I am grateful I can, but wish I had more help from Hayley. I made calls all day to let utility companies know of dad's death, cancelled credit cards, the newspaper, etc. Most people I have spoken to have been very nice, and understanding, but when I called the newspaper the woman on the phone didn't believe me when I told her dad had passed. Dad recently made a payment a few days before he went to the hospital, so I had to explain to her that his death was unexpected, and we had no time to prepare. It was hard to be in such a vulnerable state and have to explain myself when I did nothing wrong.

After I hung up the phone with her I decided it was a good time to stop. I needed to take some time to myself, so I took Bella for a walk to dad's house. I didn't realize how much I needed it until I walked outside. I closed my eyes to feel the wind brush past my face, and the warmth of the sun. I was holding so much tension in my body I had a hard time breathing. It was like my body forgot how. How can something so natural become so hard? My bottom eyelids felt heavy from the tears welling up, and the air that was trapped in my lungs started to ache. I needed to release all of the stress I had inside me, but how? When I looked at the steep hills ahead of me I decided that running up them would force me to breathe heavily, allowing everything to escape. Bella anxiously pulled me up the steep hill. It felt so good to feel my heart pounding, and my lungs gasping for air when we got to the top. All of a sudden my lungs were filled with the natural medicine of the fresh fall air instead of the stale air from before. I was breathing!

When I opened the door to dad's house, Bella squeezed past me to go upstairs to his office. She stood on her hind legs with her paws on the door and started to whine. After she scratched at the door a few times, she looked at me with a confused expression on her face. She couldn't fathom why he wasn't answering. I told her dad wasn't home, and everything was okay. I knew she didn't understand me, but I think it was my way of trying to tell myself everything was okay, even though I know it's not. I sat next to her, cried, and gave her a big hug while my tears wet her golden hair.

I felt weird being in his home. We hadn't moved or changed much, and the house felt empty without him or Lucy there. Being alone in his house, with no distractions made me realize how hard this is going to be. I am going to hurt like I never have before. At that moment I promised myself I would not turn to something harmful to cover the pain. Whether they are good or bad, all feelings are for feeling, and I need to feel what I need to feel in order to get through this. I am going to limit my alcohol and sugar intake and especially hold back on retail therapy. They aren't going to do me any good. Instead, I will spend more time outside with Bella, do fun things with mom and Mike and concentrate on loving myself more by working out and meditation. I cleaned up a bit, and then walked back home to continue closing the estate. I really hope I can come through on the promises I just made to myself.

XO, E

October 6, 2015

I am having a hard time sleeping because I am still feeling lost with dad. I want to stay with mom as long as I can, but I need to get back to the trailer park. I am not ready to be sober yet and that is where the drugs are. While I was trying to plan my escape I heard a light tap on the window. It was Lydia and Celine! They had snuck into the backyard to make sure I was okay. I really wasn't in the mood to talk to anyone, but they aren't just anyone, they are my best friends. We talked and laughed under the stars for hours! I was able to forget about cancer and my cravings. It was just what I needed in that moment.

-Hayz

October 8, 2015

The past week has been a whirlwind of shock and grief. Mike, my former husband, passed away suddenly of cancer after only being ill for two weeks. He was backpacking in the mountains just a month ago. The cancer had spread to his liver leaving little hope for survival. My girls are stunned as am I. We were fortunate to have stayed friends after our divorce. I will miss his support and friendship. We shared the love of our girls and the hope that Hayley can resume a normal life free from addiction and pain.

I am losing my hair with this chemo. At first, the thought of it depressed me greatly. In light of everything else, I have accepted the fact. I will really present an authentic face to the world now. No hiding. Mame is giving me a head shaving party tomorrow. My friends are coming to surround me with love and healing. We will make a good party out of the occasion.

Namaste, Jude

October 9, 2015

One of the side effects from mom's new chemo is hair loss. To help make her hair falling out a little less traumatic, Mame and the goddesses planned a hair cutting ceremony. Mom said, "instead of mourning she would like to embrace the transformation and celebrate with friends," which I couldn't agree with more. Many of her friends brought her hair coverings they had knitted, or that were on her registry at a local wig store. As each woman cut a strand of mom's hair, they would say an affirmation and a blessing. Losing hair from chemo is often viewed as something terrible, but she and her friends were able to make it into something beautiful.

I am grateful Hayley and I were able to witness the strong female bond they all have, and be reminded of the strength in the warrior we get to call our mom, but I am still in a fog from dad's passing. I am having a difficult time knowing how to feel, and don't want to be put into a situation where I have to fake happiness. Everyone at the party was very sweet, but they continued to tell me how sorry they were about dad's sudden passing. They would mention how impressed they were with how I was handling everything, and said I was doing it with grace. I took it as a compliment, but I am handling things the only way I know how. I don't want dad's death and mom's cancer diagnosis to define me. I would like to be a story of strength, not victimhood.

XO, E

October 11, 2015

My friends made me feel like a true goddess last night. The affirmations they said while they cut my hair took me back to when I was first diagnosed with cancer. I was camping with Mame just realizing the battle I had ahead of me. I came home and wrote a poem about that weekend. I was living in an unknown. The doctors tried to predict how much time I had, but in reality no one knew what to expect. They didn't know how strong I can be. I am woman!

Bra-less in the Wind Rivers

I have large, pendulous, breasts.
They have suckled two babies,
aroused young lovers and
most recently, been invaded
by cancer spreading toxic cells
throughout my body.
Difficult to imagine.
The tumor was never
detected, not even
by an MRI.
But today none of that matters.
I am a wild woman camping in the
Wind River Mountains.
No one is around for what seems
like miles, unless you count
chipmunks and hummingbirds.
I decide to go without my bra, whose
straps leave indentations in my shoulders
like memories of restraint.
The under-wire holds my breasts high,
but at what price?
I unhook my red, lacy bra.
My breasts leave their cage with delight.

I haven't known such freedom
since my breasts were just
a handful, perky,
and ready
to take on
the world.

Namaste, Jude

October 13, 2015

Still waiting for someone to pinch me and wake me up from this nightmare. I miss you so much already, pops, I still don't believe it. I am so grateful for all of the amazing memories we share. Although, I only knew you for 25 years, you taught me so much in that short time. I will be forever grateful for every moment.

I love you.

-Hayz

October 14, 2015

Darrell and Corey are officially Lucy's new dog parents. It was a hard decision, but Mike, Hayley, and I felt like it was for the best. We know they are going to take great care of her, and Darrell is retired, so he can take her on all of the hikes she is accustomed to. Darrell called me today to let me know he took Lucy to the vet to try to figure out what the big bump on her leg is. I told him dad had already had a doctor tell him it wasn't cancerous, but they wanted to get another opinion. I am glad they did because it turns out it is cancer. When I hung up the phone tears started rushing out of my eyes. Even though Lucy wasn't living with us she is still our family dog and an extension of dad. I have already lost dad I don't want to lose her so soon. The vet doesn't know how much longer Lucy has to live, but they do know the tumor will grow, making it harder for her to walk. It's crazy to think that both she and dad had cancer at the same time and neither one of them knew. Again, it's like she wanted to take the pain away from dad. Similar to what Ossie did with mom. I hope she can live a quality life for a long while. She is such a great dog.

XO, E

October 17, 2015

Mike and I took some time to drive around the Alpine Loop. We have each grown up taking this drive with our families and love to be able to continue the tradition. The scenery is gorgeous all year long, but it is extra special when the colors in the trees have changed into their yellows and reds. Since dad is buried near the canyon we made sure to stop to give him a pumpkin on the way.

The drive was as beautiful as I remembered. I was able to take it all in since the top of the Jeep was down. I heard the wind whispering through the trees, smelled the crisp autumn leaves and felt the heat of the sun shining down on us. As we were driving down the canyon a gust of warm wind came up. Golden leaves began to fall and circle around us. I got goose dimples all over my body and started to sob. It was dad saying hello. I was so happy to receive a sign showing me he was there, but it also made me miss him terribly. I believe he is around, just not in person. He will send me signs showing me is here. Today was the first of many.

XO, E

October 18, 2015

I asked Hayley to walk around the city cemetery with me today to get ideas for dad's headstone. We didn't get to talk to dad about what he wanted, so we were clueless as to what to do when it came to his marker. As were looking at different styles we stumbled across Porter Rockwell's grave. He was a figure of the Wild West period of American history, as well as a Mormon, and a law man in the Utah Territory. Dad read several books about him and was fascinated with his life. He and I drove around the cemetery one day to find the headstone and did, but then I couldn't find it again. Hayley and I felt like dad led us there.

We ventured across the street to a headstone company. I remembered playing hide and seek behind the giant slabs of rock when I was a child. I saw them as playthings back then, but now I see them as a reminder that my father is gone. As we walked around the showroom we noticed the perfect red rock. It looked like it came straight out of Southern Utah, one of dad's favorite places. The owner said someone found it at a rock quarry. I immediately called an artist who I know frequents rock quarries to find bases for his bronze sculptures. He recommended me go to American Stone, so I made my way out there to check out what they have.

I took the two hour drive to the quarry alone. Hayley blamed her being tired for the reason why she wasn't able to take the long drive with me, but I am positive it was because she was high. I thought of dad while I drove through the tree lined roadways. He shared his passion for the outdoors with me ever since I was young. He taught me to fish, camp, ski, and respect the land. Whether he was hiking on a dirt trail or taking a long drive he made sure to take in the breathtaking views all over Utah. Instead of treating this as an errand, I thought of it as some time alone with dad. Time to listen to my favorite music, and enjoy nature just like he taught me to do.

XO, E

October 19, 2015

Bella and I take a walk to dad's house every morning. Even though it's been a few weeks, she hasn't given up on the idea that he will be there to greet us. She continues to run up and down the stairs looking everywhere for dad and Lucy. When she can't find them, she begins to whine and jumps on his office door in hopes he will open it with a smile. I don't cry about it every day, but it breaks my heart every time I hear her sobbing. He was her favorite person, and I know he loved her as well. When I was going through paper work, I found some of his passwords. A lone tear went down my cheek when I saw one of his most recent passwords was Bella1. He was a great dog grandpa. Before he passed, Mike and I were talking about starting a family. I know dad would have been the best grandpa to our child. He would have shown his grandchild his love for the outdoors, Utah sports, animals, and taught them so much we couldn't. Now he is gone I don't know if I want to have a child. I can't imagine our child not knowing one of the most important people in my life, and me not having him here to watch them grow. I have so much on my plate right now, I am not really sure how or what to feel, especially when it comes to starting family. I do know it is something we need to talk about again soon. I am not getting any younger.

XO, E

October 22, 2015

Just got home after spending the morning at the Huntsman Infusion Center. The chemo I am getting is derived from the bark of the California yew tree. It is a natural chemo. Aside from baldness, a little neuropathy and fatigue, this one is fairly tolerable. Since Mike's passing, I have renewed sense of purpose to stay alive. Mostly, to be here for Erin and Hayley. Hayley seems to be more motivated to change her life. She will inherit some money from Mike's estate which she can use for treatment. We are putting it in a trust with Erin as the executor. I hope this arrangement will work for them in the future. I saw an attorney yesterday to piggy back my trust with Mike's. For an attorney, he was a very nice man.

I have not been writing at all. Not sure why. Jigsaw puzzles and watching Netflix seems to take up my downtime. Walking Sophie some days. Going for a massage this afternoon. The steroids they give me with the chemo makes me wired for a day or so afterwards. I hope I can relax enough to enjoy it.

Namaste, Jude

November 7, 2015

Mike and I originally had plans to get together with friends to watch the Utah football game, but they fell through. I was relieved because I didn't really feel like seeing anyone after a long day at work. I asked Mike if he wouldn't mind just watching the game at home with me. I am so tired (physically and mentally) from crying every day, working on the estate, trying to figure out what to do with the houses, being back at work, etc. so a nice, relaxing Saturday night at home sounded perfect to me. Mike agreed, but changed his mind last minute and invited a bunch of our friends over to watch the game. When I heard the new plans, I didn't want to go home. I couldn't understand why he would do this. It was like he didn't hear me and went ahead with what he wanted without thinking of my feelings.

I needed some time to myself before walking into a house full of people, so I told him I was going to grab dinner to go from somewhere. I was upset, but the idea one of getting one my favorite meals, lifted my spirits a bit. I thought about going to dad's house to eat dinner alone, but that seemed too depressing, so I went to the mall for some retail therapy. Right as I walked off the elevator I saw a good friend. We had a nice talk while doing some window shopping. Even though I didn't buy anything, I felt much better after having some girl time at the mall. I arrived home to a house full of guys. Usually I am fine with spending time with them because they are my friends as well, but tonight I really wanted to chill. I put on a smile and just went along with it, but really felt like I shouldn't have had to be put into that situation. I need Mike to listen to my needs. I feel unheard and unseen, which is a terrible way to feel on top of everything else.

XO, E

November 15, 2015

Mom loves Dancing with the Stars. Since she hasn't been to a live taping of a show before I thought it would be fun to take her to see DWTS live! I reached out to the ticket office, and was surprised when we got tickets. I was so excited I couldn't wait to tell my friend, Lafe, I was coming to visit. He is a television producer and told me the tickets I got were for the waitlist, so I probably wouldn't get in, but he might have a way to get us tickets and he did!

Mom and I flew into Long Beach this morning where we rented a car I could drive while we were there. This was my first time driving in the infamous LA traffic, and I was terrified! But because Mike and I have been to CA several times I was able to get a hang of it. Mike wanted us to have a nice time, so he took it upon himself to make reservations for a nice brunch in Huntington Beach. We giggled about the celebrities we were going to see the next day over mimosas, eggs and toast. Mom asked to take a walk on the boardwalk before we left to meet her friend Mary Ann. Not very many people were out due to it being a cold, windy day. We slowly strolled along the wood planks suspended over the crashing waves, taking the time to relish our surroundings. When we made it to the end I closed my eyes and smelled the fresh ocean air. I felt grateful I could be here with mom. I snapped out of my trance when I heard mom squeal from inside a small museum. I ran in, worried that something was wrong, but it was her getting excited over a large set of shark teeth. I smiled and shook my head endearingly as mom walked around it oohing and aahing. She has been a dental hygienist for years, so to see a set of teeth that large, in perfect condition was quite the treat for her. After a few pictures we decided it was best to start our drive.

It took us about an hour to get to Mary Ann's house where we were greeted with a fresh batch of homemade veggie soup. I wanted to give Mary Ann and mom some time to talk, so I met Lafe at the Hotel Roosevelt for a drink and fries. I love when I can get time with Lafe. He and I understand each other like no one else, and I am lucky to be able to call him one of my best friends.

XO, E

November 16, 2015

I slept so well at Mary Ann's. I didn't I realize how much I needed a night with no distractions. It was nice to be taken care of instead of me having to take care of things for a night. Since the hotel we were staying at was only a block away from Grauman's Chinese Theater I took mom to see the signatures and handprints. She was so excited when she saw Hugh Jackman's handprints. She jumped at the chance of putting her hands where his once were. He is her Hollywood crush.

The emails I received about the show didn't give us very good directions on how to get to there. We were very confused as to where it was, and ended up walking a lot further than expected. We decided it was best if I ran ahead while mom and Mary Ann waited for me to find the entrance. Mom was weak from chemo, and her new shoes she bought for the trip were killing her feet. I probably looked hilarious, running around Hollywood in a long, bright blue dress, but I wasn't going to miss the show. I didn't care what I looked like at that point. After running about ½ a mile I finally found the entrance, which was closer than we thought. I just took the scenic route. Mary Ann helped mom find her way to me before we said our goodbyes. It was so wonderful to see her. I love that she and Mom have kept in touch throughout the years. She has been another great friend to mom, especially through her cancer journey.

Before the show, the audience is encouraged to dance on the dance floor. Mom's feet were very swollen from all the walking we had done, so she was a little unsure, but the hype man helped get her moving. She and I giggled as we did the twist and joined the conga line with the other guests. Our seats were in the second tier right above the stage. We had a great view of everything. At one point, mom yelled to one of her favorite dancers, "Go Nick!" It made her night when he looked up at her and waved. Mom was smiling, dancing and singing the entire show. She reminded me of a young girl seeing her favorite band. She was having so much fun she told me she forgot about how badly her feet ached and cancer.

With everything going on, it was nice to get out of town with her for a couple days, show her around one of my favorite cities and see one of my best friends. I am grateful I was able to make it happen. It is a weekend I will never forget.

XO, E

November 18, 2015

I was in LA a couple of days over for a very short time with Erin, last weekend. We managed to get to the beach, and see MaryAnn in Valencia. Erin drove in LA like a pro with the help of MapQuest. We were amused to see people walking around with winter parkas even though the temperature was in the low 60's.

Back to winter here. Snow just in the mountains so far. I have two more infusions to go, another CT scan, and then we will see from there. The good news is I feel pretty good generally, and my tumor markers have gone down 30 points. I quite like my hairless scalp, although I am growing a five o'clock shadow. I am wondering whether I will have white curls or gray wisps when it comes back in. In the meantime, my head gets cold even inside. I wear fleece or wool hats to bed in an effort to preserve body heat. Now I know why Scrooge wore nightcaps most of the time.

Hayley is living with me, seeing a therapist, and will be doing detox and rehab soon. She is trying to navigate Obamacare to help defray rehab costs. Or Cobra which is exorbitant, but may be the most expedient way to go.

Erin went to probate today. She said it took all of 30 seconds. She is intent on assuming the mortgage of Mike's home. I hope she can withstand the stress of it all.

Namaste, Jude

November 18, 2015

Dad hadn't updated his will for over 15 years! Right now, if anything happened to him, Aunt Marcia was the person in charge. She declined the responsibility when I asked her if she wanted to take care of everything, and said it would be best if I took on the role as executor. In order for me to be in charge I needed to get a petition for probate, and my court date was today. I would visit dad a lot at his work throughout his career, but this was the first time I had been inside the courthouse since he had passed. I really wasn't ready. I have tried to pretend everything was okay and live a "normal" life the past couple weeks, but there are things that shock me into reality, and pulling into that parking garage of the courthouse was one of them.

The familiar gut feeling I get when I am about to cry appeared. I knew I was going to be emotional being there, but didn't think it was going to hit me this hard. I thought about the times I played Barbie's in his empty court room when I was young. If I was lucky one of his large, uniformed bailiff's would join with me. As I got older I would do homework in his chambers while he read over future cases. When his clerk would see me hard at work she would ask if she could take me to the cafeteria for a quick candy break. After I graduated I would meet dad for daddy daughter lunch dates. I remember walking down the hallway, peeking my head into the other commissioner's offices to say hi and high fiving bailiff's on my way to meet him. I used to love going to see dad at work, but today I was scared. The courthouse was a safe place for me, but even though I wasn't going to court because I was in trouble I was still nervous. Being there without dad was a reminder that he was gone.

I was comforted by the warmth of the sun shining through the large glass dome in the lobby, but the pit started to move up the back of my throat when I didn't see any familiar faces at the metal detectors. Dad has been retired for about three years, so there was no reason for me to see someone I used to take candy breaks or play Barbie's with, but I was still disappointed. I swiftly walked to the courtroom, hoping that if I got there fast enough I could get out of there and go home. The knot continued to creep up my throat. I was about to let it all out, but I couldn't quite yet. This wasn't the place or time. About 5 minutes later, I looked up and saw my attorney walking towards me. It was nice to see him, but I was still on the verge of tears. The hearing was fast. I didn't even have to say anything! My attorney answered the few questions the judge had, and we were done.

Once the hearing was over, the mango sized pit from earlier had shrunk into a cherry sized pit. Since I was feeling a little better I thought I should go say hi to dad's co-commissioners. When I told the receptionist I was Mike Evans daughter and wanted to say hi to his colleagues she smiled as she touched the button to buzz me in. The walk down the hallway of commissioner's chambers brought back memories of walking through the same corridor, holding my dad's hand when I was a little girl. He was so proud of me, and I of him. The pit started to grow when I got closer to dad's old office. I tried to hold back the tears, but when I saw his friend, Julie I couldn't stop them from coming. It was so hard to be there without him. She gave me a big hug, rubbed my back and talked with me until I was able to gather myself. Being in the courthouse and going to court, even when I wasn't in trouble was stressful, but being there and not having dad there made it worse. It's crazy how grief can overcome you. I want to find a way to navigate this a little more smoothly if I can. I know people understand, but I hate losing control like I did.

XO, E

November 20, 2015

Uncle Bill emailed us a few weeks ago about coming into town to see the new piece he choreographed. The local dance company, RDT, is honoring three former board members, including dad, during all three nights of their coming performance run. Uncle Bill said he has dedicated his new work to dad because he was able to watch the dancers rehearse it when he was in town last summer. The dance is Uncle Bill's take on Utah history, and since dad was able to understand it he felt like it was only right to dedicate it to him. I absolutely love the piece! It is my new favorite of Uncle Bill's dances, and the dancers performed it beautifully. The piece is called *Crippled Up Blues and Other Desert Tales*. I wish dad was here to see it live. He would have really enjoyed seeing in performed on stage to the American Desert Music band, 3HATTRIO. Uncle Bill reminds me so much of dad in a lot of ways. I feel like we have gotten closer since dad has passed. It was really nice to have him in town.

XO, E

November 21, 2015

Mike and I really want to move into dad's house, but in order to do so we would have to buy Hayley out. We were told that if we were able to rent out the home we live in now we should be able to make it happen. We bought our home with the intention of buying something larger and renting it out in the future, we just didn't know it was going to be so soon. Whether we are moving in or have to sell it we need to start moving a few of dad's belongings out. Mike and I had been there several times since dad has been gone, but today was different. We stood in the kitchen in bewilderment. Neither of us wanted to start getting rid of dad's things. It made his death way too real. We held each other as we broke down in tears at the exact same time. We knew this was going to be a hard day, we just didn't know how tough until we got there. We found old dishes from the café my grandparents owned in Lehi, hand crocheted oven mitts from loved ones, his turkey platter he used when he hosted Thanksgiving and so many other treasures.

It was hard to give too many things away because I felt like they were a piece of dad. I know they are just inanimate objects, but I have already lost him, I am not ready to say goodbye to items that bring back so many wonderful memories. We decided to put much of it in bins we could store until I was more prepared to give things to charity or family members. Hayley and mom were only there for about an hour to pick out items they found sentimental to them. I would have really liked to have had them there most of the day, but have learned not to count on Hayley right now. She can't be the sister I need or want her to be. I am trying not to judge her because everyone grieves differently, but it would be really nice if she helped out a little more. I am so overwhelmed with everything it would feel good to be able to talk with her about how I am feeling. She is the only one that knows what it feels like to lose our dad.

XO, E

November 26, 2015

Sitting at the kitchen table looking out over Salt Lake Valley this Thanksgiving morning. Sophie just went out for her morning pee. She's a little shaky on her hind legs, but seems to get the job done. Sometimes, she goes out, turns around without doing anything, and still expects a treat which of, course I give her. My right butt cheek has been hurting, making me a bit grumpy, and not wanting to stand for long periods of time. I think it is sciatica. A reminder that I need to stretch and get more exercise.

The girls and I are going to my niece's house for Thanksgiving this afternoon. She is Mike's brother's daughter. She is married, has a married daughter who has three daughters ranging in age from 5mos-6 years old. They are delightful little girls. Mike, my former husband always did Thanksgiving in the past at his house. Hard not to be there this year, but thankful to have family to celebrate with.

Namaste, Jude

November 26, 2015

As I opened my eyes this morning I started to cry. This is the first Thanksgiving I am not rushing to dad's to help him prepare for the big day. He loved hosting our extended family for Thanksgiving, and made the best turkey. His friend Marc told me that he and dad experimented with a few turkeys to find the perfect time and temperature based on its weight when they were in their early 20's. It took a few tries, but they were able to figure it out! I actually found the paper they used in grandma's old recipe book. I hope to be able to use it when we have the chance to take over his Thanksgiving hosting duties.

My wonderful cousin, Tandi and her husband Troy invited us to their home for dinner. They have been a huge support to us through everything. Tandi checks in on us regularly and brought lunch for the family the day after dad passed. Troy took the time to make videos with different pictures of dad for the viewing and funeral. It is hard to be grateful with dad gone today, but I am thankful for our wonderful family. They invited everyone, even Barb and Mel. It was beautiful, but I couldn't help but think that dad should be the one carving the turkey. It is another new normal that we have to get used to, whether we like it or not.

XO, E

November 26, 2015

Thanksgiving was today. Another day I have been dreading. Dad was the best host when it came to Thanksgiving dinner. I missed a few holidays due to my addiction, but I made sure to never miss a Thanksgiving at dad's house. It is one of my favorite days because I get to eat a lot of food while spending time with the people I love the most. My cousins were nice enough to invite us to their house this year. They haven't judged me for being an addict, and have always welcomed me with open arms. I felt comfortable being there, but it wasn't like being at dad's. When Troy mentioned dad in his blessing a tear rolled down my cheek. Mom could tell I was upset and put her hand on my leg to let me know it was okay to be sad.

I kept nodding out on the drive home. I blamed it on the turkey, but it was definitely because of the drugs. I didn't have the heart to tell my family the truth. Today hurt way too much and I can't be who I am around my family. I need to go back to the trailer park. I am not ready to face the pain from the grief I am experiencing.

-Hayz

December 5, 2015

We were approved to buy dad's house and today is demo day. We have been anxious to start on renovations, but didn't want to make any drastic changes until we knew for sure it was ours. Mike and his friends started demoing the kitchen, the living room, and upstairs. I had a really hard time watching them tear up the home I grew up in. It needed to be done, but I became nauseous when I watched them start tearing up the floor and cupboards I knew for so long. I didn't want to make so many changes, but it has been hard to be in dad's house the way he left it. We needed to make changes in order to live there comfortably and make it our own. I decided it was best for me to get a few things done upstairs while the guys were having fun destroying downstairs.

As I was folding up dad's collection of tee shirts, tears slowly streamed down my cheeks. When I traveled I would always bring him a tee shirt as a souvenir. Seeing the cotton mementoes brought back memories of him wearing them. I came across the tee shirt with my alma matter printed on it. I remember the day he asked me to get him one from the college bookstore. I was surprised because I didn't think my manly dad would be excited to wear a shirt with the Fashion Institute of Technology on it, but he wore it proudly. I missed home terribly while I was in New York, and now I miss the city after being at home. If I chose to stay in NYC, I couldn't have been the support system I am for my family. I am beyond grateful that I can be the glue that holds everyone together, but there are times I think about how different my life would have been if I had stayed.

Mom stopped by to see how everything was going. When she noticed the destruction that was happening on the middle floor she quickly made her way upstairs to help me pack away his clothes. While we were in his closet a brown hat fell down onto mom's head. She giggled, but when she pulled it off her head her sweet giggles turned into a soft cry. I was so confused because I had never seen it before. Between her sobs she told me it was his favorite hat when they were dating. She remembered him wearing it on their road trips to Utah from Ohio. One of her fondest memories was cruising down the highway with the windows down listening to "Take It Easy" by The Eagles while my dad's shoulder length hair blew in the wind. I wish I knew more about my parents when they were younger. They remind me so much of Mike and I. Camping, seeing live music, being with friends. They have always been fun parents, but I would enjoy hearing more about what they did before they had kids.

After a few hours of packing dad's things I thought I was ready to see what the guys had done, but I don't think anything would have prepared me for what I walked into. The majority of the carpet had been pulled up throughout the house, the kitchen sink was gone as well as the dishwasher, and the drywall was removed from one of the major walls. The kitchen was unrecognizable except for the magnets on the refrigerator. I had a mix of emotions when Mike walked me through the destruction that used to be my family home. I felt incredibly sad that it was torn up, but knew it was time for a new beginning.

XO, E

December 12, 2015

I am laying on the couch in the living room, knit cap on my head, faux fur blanket over my legs, listening to old Beatle songs. I have been home today resting after a chemo visit Thursday. My doc wants me to do three months of this particular chemo. The CT scan didn't show any progression, but no improvement either. I bargained with her to take two weeks off over Christmas. She agreed to it on the condition I start again Dec. 31st. I am considering getting a second opinion with another oncologist. I don't feel supported by my doc, and I feel she has too many patients. She seems rushed and distracted at my appointments. I feel unsupported. I am actually going to see a younger doc.

The holidays are upon us. There will be a full moon on December 25th The last one was in 1977. Time for a celebration! I will be gathering with my crone friends on the 23rd to celebrate.

All in all, I am doing well except for a few aches and pains and GI issues. I am content to stay home most of the time, reading and watching movies. I haven't been writing much, although I have been doing some mosaics with my friend. She is a good teacher. The time just flies when I work with her.

Mame and I still get together at least once every couple of weeks or so. Her new passion is painting Christmas cards for everyone. She is quite good I think although she is somewhat bashful about her art.

My bed is calling me. I seem to go to bed earlier and earlier these days. I am grateful sleep comes easily most nights.

Namaste, Jude

December 12, 2015

The holiday season has been hard this year. It is the last Christmas in our first home and the first Christmas without dad. Everyday finds a way to make me think about dad. Like today when we were picking out our Christmas tree. I have fond memories of going to the tree farm and him tapping the trees on the ground to see if they lose their needles. We would search and search until we found a tree we could all agree on. I kept up the traditions I have with mom, but I really miss not going to dad's house to trim his tree, helping him make chocolates, and being his personal shopper when it came to Christmas gifts. I have had a lot of distractions, which has made it easier, but the holidays aren't the same without him. I am going to try to smile because I am sick of crying, but it's really difficult this time of year. Dad loved to celebrate every holiday and made each one so much fun. People say it gets easier as time goes on, but I don't want time to take away the memories we have shared throughout the years.

XO, E

December 19, 2015

Went to visit my Dad and bring him an Xmas present. We're still waiting on a headstone, and I definitely forgot about the snow. Guess we'll just wait for spring! He has the best view of the mountains.

-Hayz

December 20, 2015

Mom and dad taught me the importance of giving to charities every year, especially during the holiday season. The last year dad was alive, he told Hayley and I about the 10 charities he likes to donate to every year for the holidays. Since he had retired, he wasn't able to give to all of them, so he asked us to each pick out one to give to, and he would give to three that year. On top of sending money to his favorite charities, he would take us to go shopping for people in need. Sometimes we would choose an Angel from the Angel tree, and other years, we would go shopping for presents at a local charity, The Candy Cane Corner. At the CCC, parents visit the store with their case manager and select gifts for their family. For many of the families, it has been a very long time since they were last able to shop for new clothes or toys, and the CCC makes is possible. One year Hayley and I had the opportunity to volunteer at the store. We were given a list of items a family needed and got to shop for them. Seeing the family's faces when we brought them a shopping cart full of gifts felt amazing. I would cry happy tears with the families as they hugged us and repeatedly told us thank you.

Mike and I started donating to Candy Cane Corner on our own the last few years. Today, we went shopping for gifts and took Bella with us.

When we walked in with bags of clothes, the women volunteering were elated, and Bella was icing on the cake. I love when we can make people happy just by bringing Bella. She isn't just our therapy dog; she is a therapy dog for everyone she gets to meet.

Bella was prancing down the sidewalk on our way back to the car. I grabbed Mike's hand, stopped and we smiled at each other. We were all happy knowing we had just helped a few families and it was even better that we could do it together.

XO, E

December 28, 2015

Our loan went through, which means dad's house is now ours, and Mike can go ahead with the purchase of a small business. Mike recently heard about an opportunity to buy a local shipping store in Park City. He has been working in the shipping industry the past few years, and has always wanted to own his own business. Buying a business will be another huge challenge on top of everything else, but I know Mike really wants out of his job. This is the first time I have seen him so excited about a new job opportunity. He is ready to make a change. I really hope he is much happier with being a business owner. He has a lot of great ideas, and his new venture has a lot of potential. I can't wait to see what he does with it all. What would one more stressor do at this point?

Since we bought dad's home, we had to buy Hayley out. In dads will, Hayley and I got half of everything he owned, so it was only right. Since she is very deep into her addiction, none of us, including her, felt like it was a good idea to allow her to have control of her money. I spoke to my attorney, and he wrote up a contract for her to sign saying I had legal control over her finances, which she signed. I put her money away in a savings account until I am ready to talk to someone about what would be the best option for her in the long run. Having the money when she becomes sober will really help her take the next step into becoming a responsible adult. Being executor has been hard, but I am grateful that I am able to take care of it all and Hayley can trust me.

XO, E

December 31, 2015

I can honestly say that 2015 was one of the most challenging years I think I have experienced. Many thanks to my friends and family who helped me through the rough times. On a good note, the chemo I am doing seems to be working. I saw my oncologist today. He asked me what I wanted from him, and I said to be treated like Jimmie Carter or a rock star. He gave me the gift of hope for the New Year. Bring it on 2016.

Namaste, Jude

December 31, 2015

2015 has definitely been one of the hardest years I have experienced yet. The last few months proved to me how strong I am and showed me I can get through a hell of a lot. Bob Marley once said, "you don't never know how strong you are until being strong is the only choice you have." I definitely have to agree. I used to be one to sweat the small stuff, but after mom being diagnosed with cancer, dad passing, and Hayley's addiction, I don't get upset over the smallest things anymore, which I am grateful for. I don't like to think all of this happened to me for a reason, but I do like to think that I can come out of it as a better version of myself.

To celebrate the last day of 2015 and our 12 years of knowing one another Mike, and I went to one of our favorite restaurants for a romantic meal. We met with friends for a champagne toast at midnight. I don't like to put a lot of pressure on the New Year. I am not one to make resolutions nor do I treat it as something "new." I prefer to reflect more in the spring and treat it as a new beginning, but this year I don't feel like waiting. I am ready and hopeful for a great year ahead.

XO, E

2016

"Mum," I call into the darkness.
She has been gone for many years.
Our cancers are the same.
She visited me once at my father's house.

January 3, 2016

Now that the holidays are over, and the January doldrums are setting in, I find myself floundering on this roller coaster of cancer treatment. My spirits ebb and flow. I have many friends to support me, but they can only do so much.

Namaste, Jude

January 4, 2016

Hayley promised us she would go into detox, but she has been so sick with an unknown illness the detox center won't allow her to be there until she gets better. She is starting to get strange scabs all over, especially on her face. Mom took her to the doctor, but the doc didn't know what would cause the scabbing. I personally think it is a side of effect of the heroin. It's making her body deteriorate. Hayley seems to care about it, but not enough to stop using. She used to freak out about getting a small pimple, so I would think that having unsightly lesions on her face would make her want to try to stop what is causing her body to react the way it is, but the drug is in charge right now. Things will only change when she is ready to take control of her body and mind again. I just hope it's sooner rather than later. It's hard to watch her slowly kill herself.

While I have been mourning the loss of my father, I realized I am also mourning the loss of the people my sister and mother once were, and trying to accept who they have become. As many of my friends are starting their families I am losing mine. Mom has been so sick I have been more of a caregiver than a daughter. She still tries to be the light I have always known her to be, but our roles have changed. I am thankful that I can be there for her, but it's different. Hayley is not psychologically the person she once was. She is someone I do not recognize, and it has gotten worse as time goes on. I try to help her, but I don't fully understand what she has been going through. I feel helpless when it comes to her.

XO, E

January 5, 2016

We are officially moved out of our first house. Dad's house is a huge, organized mess! I feel like we are in an episode of hoarders. The majority of our belongings are in the living room, including a new stove, washer, and dryer. The other rooms in the house are full of boxes, or they are unusable because they haven't been remodeled yet. Thankfully we were able to get the flooring done on the main floor, so we have somewhere to put everything. We can't use the stove because the kitchen is in the middle of being remodeled. We have a microwave and dad's old fridge is in the garage for the time being, so we are not at a huge loss. It just means that we will need to get creative with our cooking. On a positive note, there is new tile in the bathroom, so we can put the washer and dryer in this weekend. We also have our bed setup in the master and the other bathrooms are tiled. It could be a lot worse. Our new fridge is on backorder, which is probably a good thing because I have no idea where we would put it! We are planning on working on the house every free moment we have. Living in a mess is good motivation. Between dad's passing, mom's new chemo, Hayley's addiction, Mike starting a new business, renting our home, and renovating another home, our marriage is going to be tested. I hope we can make it out of this intact.

XO, E

January 9, 2016

Mike asked me to go to dinner with a few friends who are in town for a conference. I have been experiencing small slumps almost daily because I have really been missing dad, but I figured seeing friends would help. On my drive home from work I asked for dad to show me a sign he was around. I immediately heard a loud bang as a ball of fire rose from the ground and burst into a shape of a heart. Tears came to my eyes while I watched the fireworks dad and I loved so much light up the dark sky. As the last speck of fire fell, the new song by X Ambassadors, "Unsteady" came onto the radio. My ears perked up as the melody began. It was the first time I had heard it and the notes immediately put me in a trance. The lyrics coming from the speakers hit me like a ton of bricks. They made me stop and stare at the radio like it had just sent me a cryptic message only I could understand. I held onto the steering wheel tightly as I wept crocodile tears. I cried because I was happy dad was able to send me a sign, but also because I miss him terribly. I took a few deep breaths before I told myself, "this too will pass" hoping it would help. I didn't say this to take away the pain. The pain I feel is real and valid. I did it because it is one of the most honest statements I have ever heard. I need to feel what I need to feel in order to try to grieve.

XO, E

January 10, 2016

My boss called me to let me know my first patient cancelled. My first reaction was, damn, less money in my paycheck. Then I started to think of the extra time I had to meditate, write, and think. All of a sudden, the gift appeared. The church bells that ring at 8AM. Reminding me of the beautiful community I reside in. The bells remind me of my British heritage. They welcome the day to me. I am grateful for this time to reflect. For the bells. For my community. Smiles.

Namaste, Jude

January 10, 2016

Because dad was happiest in the mountains, Hayley and I decided to put mountains on his headstone. But which mountain range? We couldn't just use any mountain range; we wanted to include somewhere that meant something to him. I looked through pictures on his phone to see which ones showed up the most. Darrell went to the mountains with him regularly, so we asked him to help us decide. We unanimously agreed on a particular mountain peak in the Uinta Mountains. Dad grew up going to the Uinta Mountains and took us camping there every summer. It was his sanctuary

I also want to include a bird of prey, and I thought a bronze bird would be the perfect finishing touch. I spoke to one of the sculptors who shows at the gallery, and he offered to give me a bronze eagle to include. Whenever I see a bird of prey (BOP is what dad called them), I think of dad. When I was young, and saw a BOP flying in the air, I would ask dad what type of bird it was. He could tell by the shape of the wings, and the size of the bird whether it was a hawk, eagle, vulture, falcon, etc. I was always very impressed. The headstone is going to be beautiful.

XO, E

January 20, 2016

Life is good. Hayley and I went to the Midway Ice Castles yesterday. It was very cold, but fun to get out of town for a while. Going to Lava Hot Springs with my friend, Becky next week. Mame and I are firming up plans to go to Kona, Hawaii, in March. I have decided to do more thriving instead of surviving.

Namaste, Jude

January 21, 2016

Today is the first day of Sundance 2016! Mom is volunteering again. The volunteers are gifted Kenneth Cole puffy jackets every year to wear while they are on duty. This year the jacket is turquoise, one of mom's favorite colors! She was so excited to tell me all about it, and said she can't wait wear it.

We couldn't find a sponsor for Festival After Dark this year, but I was asked to host a few mini segments for the festival. They asked me to do red carpets as well, but my work schedule doesn't allow me to do both. I would really like to be able to cover the red carpets one day. Whatever we do I am sure we will have a fun 10 days of dancing in the sun.

XO, E

January 28, 2016

On Saturday, it will be a year since my dad passed. I feel so fortunate to have had a close adult relationship with him, even though the years before he died were ones of deep mental and physical decline. For some reason, the tears are flowing as I write this. Such a sad time for us all. We do love and are loved dearly.

Namaste, Jude

February 10, 2016

Tomorrow marks what would have been Mike's, 64th birthday. I am crying tonight for Mike, Gene, Don, my mother, who all died of cancer. Most of these lovely people went far too soon, without me able to tell them how very much I loved them. I go to Huntsman tomorrow for myself, and yet another infusion. I am taking helium balloons, Hershey Hugs and Kisses for the chemo nurses in Don's honor who used to dress as Cupid as he delivered smiles and laughs to all of us at Huntsman. Fuck Cancer as Don used to say.

Namaste, Jude

February 10, 2016

Dad purchased season tickets to the University of Utah basketball games with Darrell every year. I remember shedding a few tears when I received the large manila envelope filled with permits that allowed him to escape reality. It was shortly after he passed, and I could picture how excited he would have been. He and Darrell rarely missed a game, so I wanted to make sure Darrell knew they arrived. When I went to give the tickets to Darrell he offered to let Mike and I keep them. Since dad's birthday is tomorrow we made it a point to go to the game tonight. I know it is what dad would do for his birthday if he was here.

I thought of dad as I walked up the steep stairs to the red plastic chairs I knew so well as a child. A warm sensation went through my body as memories of me wearing my Utah sweatshirt and cheering on the team with my red and white pom poms flooded my brain. Dad and I would share a tub of popcorn and he would let me buy a candy of my choice. I usually chose peanut M&M's because I knew he liked them as well.

I smiled when I noticed a little girl with her father cheering on the team like I used to do. They were sharing a box of licorice and she was clutching a red styrofoam finger. I watched as the father held his daughter's hand to help her down from her seat to grab her backpack. My smile broadened. She might not realize it now, but I'm banking her dad will be there many more times to hold her hand, whether she continues to go to sporting events with him or not. Seeing them made me miss dad even more, but I am grateful I had a father who wanted to spend time with me doing the things he enjoyed so much, and be there to hold my hand when I needed him the most.

XO, E

February 11, 2016

Today is the first time we celebrated dad's birthday since his passing. I wanted to be as close to the mountains as I could, so Bella and I went to the dog park in Park City before dropping her off at Mike's work. I was having a pretty difficult time with it being dad's birthday. Since I didn't expect it to hit me this hard I tried to find comfort in calling Mike. My bottom lip started to quiver when he answered the phone. He could tell I was upset because I wasn't saying much. If I tried to say anything tears would come out instead of words. When we hung up I took a deep breath to prepare myself for a lonely, wintery walk with Bella. As I walked along the snowy path I started to feel dad's presence. I am sure we would have taken a nice walk together today if he was here. The white snow made it easy to notice a dark shadow of something following us. I squinted my eyes as I looked into the bright blue sky to see a bird of prey flying overhead. It was dad! He was there telling me he is alright. My time with dad was cut short by Bella tugging on her leash. I looked ahead and saw Mike walking towards us. He surprised me with a cup of tea and to finish our walk together. Both Bella and I ran to him like we hadn't seen him for weeks. I jumped into his arms for a hug as Bella wagged her tail. He was exactly what we needed.

When I finished up with work, I picked up takeout from one of dad's favorite BBQ restaurants and made a homemade chocolate cake. Mom and Hayley came over for to celebrate. It wasn't the same without dad there, but at least we can all be together, and remember him by doing something he would have loved.

XO, E

February 19, 2016

It is a beautiful sunny day and NO chemo this week. I am so happy to be in my home, my safe haven surrounded by all that I love and cherish. There is much going on in my life, but I prefer to concentrate on what is good, loving and serves me well. Life is for living. For learning. For letting go. For loving that what is good for our well being. There is much good to be found. You are a witness to the healing powers of love. Love you in all your glory. You are a magnificent human being full of strength, grace and honor. Know that whatever happens you are protected, you are guided, you are loved. You are a healer. You have been healed.

Namaste, Jude

March 2, 2016

Another advantage to being bald. I was reading the paper still in my robe, nightgown, and hatless at 10AM this morning. The door bell rang while

Sophie ran to the door with me shuffling behind. I cracked the door an inch or two and peered out. A group of about three Jehovah Witnesses, wide-eyed and surprised pushed a small pamphlet through the crack and hurried off the porch to the house next door without a word. Great way to start the day!

Namaste, Jude

March 8, 2016

Today was my birthday, and surprisingly, the hardest day for me since dad had passed. My parents always made a big deal about birthdays, so not having him here was another reminder he is gone. Mike took the day off work to be with Bella and I. Because I was feeling indescribably sad I was quiet most of the day, so Mike suggested we get outside to take a walk to the park I used to go to with dad.

When we arrived to the playground he took my hand, and walked me to a nearby swing set. We swung as high as we could go with Bella looking at us and wagging her fluffy tail from below. A giggle came out of nowhere. Swinging filled me with the joy I had when I would swing as a child. I felt like I could fly away from everything, including all of the stress and pain. Having a moment to feel happy was the best birthday gift I could ask for.

XO, E

March 10, 2016

Great news from Huntsman today! Bone scan was clean. CT scan stable. Tumor markers are down to 100. Doc is putting me on estrogen blockers instead of chemo. Been on chemo since September 2015. Ready to celebrate! Anyone have a private jet and a cottage near the ocean?

Namaste, Jude

March 27, 2016

Today was Easter Sunday. It was another hard day because dad always made a big deal out of holidays. We would color Easter Eggs, go to Easter brunch and although we were adults he would still hide eggs and baskets for us full of candy and little toys. We have started a new tradition of attending Easter Mass at the Cathedral of the Madeline with Mike's parents and mom. We all have an appreciation for the gorgeous stained glass windows and ornate architecture at the Cathedral. It is a treat to be able to attend mass there.

After church, we had an amazing brunch, and then back to mom's house for an Easter egg hunt and baskets. We were all sad Hayley didn't decide to join. She has been very distant since mom has been allowing her to use her car. Since dad's car is much safer than mom's we agreed to let her have it. Now, Hayley is driving her old car and subsequently hasn't been around much. She was really good about spending a lot of time with mom, going to her appointments, and helping her around the house, but the trailer park has been calling her name. We don't hear from her or see her on a regular basis anymore. She rarely posts on social media and doesn't reply to our texts or phone calls. It is a horrible feeling. Addiction truly has been worse than cancer.

XO, E

April 6, 2016

Our extended family asked Hayley and I to have our names on the back of dad's headstone. It helps when people are working on their genealogy. Hayley and I figured if our names are on the back we should also include a quote. I asked Hayley to send me a couple quotes she thought would work while I searched as well. I was surprised to get an email back from her. She sent me the same quote I found by one of dad's favorite authors, Edward Abbey," May your trails be crooked, winding, lonesome, dangerous, leading to the most amazing view. May your mountains rise into and above the clouds." When dad passed one of Mike's closest friends, Joel sent an email expressing his condolences and added the same quote because it reminded him of dad. He didn't know dad well, but knew he loved the outdoors. It is the perfect addition!

XO, E

April 10, 2016

To feel love for yourself leads to healing. It is a conscious feeling. When you speak of loving, it is a good verb. To show love for yourself must contain action. Loving yourself is not enough to do things that make you happy, fulfilled, less anxious, healthy, secure. Eating healthier is one way of showing, or giving love to oneself. Every time you take a bite of healthy food you are saying to yourself, "I am giving you a piece of love today, to help you feel good, to heal your body, to enable you to do the things you love, to feed your brain so your senses are at their peak. To feel saturated, at peace." To love oneself is to do those things that promote well being on a conscious, mindful level. To be aware of surroundings and feelings. Not out of duty, but a sense of celebration. A celebration of self.

Namaste, Jude

April 12, 2016

Hayley has been promising us she would go to detox and then rehab, but the last two times she went to check in, we would get a call a couple hours later saying she wasn't ready. We would pick her up, and then she would go back to live with Grant. We have all had enough! She was giving us false hope, and has continued to steal from mom on a regular basis. Mom needs the money for medical bills, but Hayley and Grant don't seem to care. They take her debit card without her knowing, buy something and get cash back. They have also stolen her belongings to take to a pawn shop to sell. To pay mom back for Hayley's indiscretions, I have taken money out of Hayley's savings account. I think mom told her I have been paying her back because I can't understand why she would continue this terrible behavior. It is a way for her to use her money without having it in hand.

When Mike drove past mom's house this morning the light blue Suzuki was in the driveway. Hayley was there! We hadn't seen her for weeks, so Mike did the only thing he could think of to stop her from leaving; he took off one of her tires. He sat in his car while waiting for me to see what happened. I have learned that life speaks to you in whispers. There was a little nudge telling me something wasn't right, and my pulse started to race when I pulled up to the house. I needed to talk to my sister, but was scared Grant was with her. I didn't know what Grant might do to me because he is so unstable. I ignored the nudge, took a deep breath, walked up the stairs and knocked on the back door before telling Hayley I was coming inside.

Sophie came running up to me with her tail wagging as I walked into the kitchen. I gave her some loves before making my way into mom's office, where Hayley sleeps from time to time. The door was open a crack and I said "hello?" in a soft voice before opening. Hayley said hi, like nothing was wrong. She was the skinniest I had ever seen her and the scabs on her face were worse than ever. I am so worried about her. I told her it was great to see her and asked her why she was there. She told me she was grabbing a few clothes, but the bag she was packing was too full to just be a few clothes. I knew she was lying to me because she was too out of it. She was obviously high. I told her mom asked me to call the police because she was sure Hayley and Grant were stealing from her again. Hayley looked at me with tears in her eyes. I don't think she would think that her mom, the person that loves her unconditionally would turn her in. I felt bad, so I suggested that if she goes to detox I will ask mom to not call the police. She stood in front of the mirror and examined herself a bit before quietly saying, "okay, I am ready to get better", but I don't think either of us knew if she truly was, especially her.

I should have felt relieved, but my pulse continued to race. I had a feeling someone else was in the house. When I asked her if anyone else was there she insisted she was alone, but I knew Grant was there from the way my body was reacting. I think she saw the frightened look in my eyes because she asked me to wait for her outside. I practically ran out of the house and jumped into Mike's car. I didn't know what he would do, especially now that Hayley agreed to go to detox. He won't have his partner in crime anymore. About 5 minutes later we saw Grant walk out. As he walked down the street, he said "call me when you want to come back." I felt nauseous. Seeing him made me realize how unsafe it was for Mike and I to do what we did. Grant is a dangerous and violent person. He has abused Hayley physically and mentally. She actually has a scar on her leg because he thought it would be funny to put a cigarette out on her. I really hope she can stay away from him, and he can also find the help he needs. Everyone deserves a chance to get sober.

Neither Hayley nor I said much on our drive to the detox facility. It was a hard moment for both of us. This wouldn't be the first time she has detoxed there. She knew what to expect and wasn't excited about it. She is going to be sick for days, but being at the detox center seems a lot safer than trying to detox at home, or even worse, jail. I stayed with her to help fill out paperwork and gave her a big hug before a nurse led her to the back. Neither mom nor I received a call from her two hours later.

XO, E

April 12, 2016

Mike saw my car in mom's driveway today and said that mom threatened to call the police if I don't go to detox. I am furious! Who are they to decide when I am ready to be sober? I am not ready, but I feel like I need to at least try. The other times I have gone to detox I was terrified, but this time I knew I would go to jail. Not because my family said they would call the cops, but because I knew I was headed there either way. I am so angry at my family. I feel betrayed and very misunderstood. I am at the detox facility now, terrified and not really knowing what to expect. I know the withdrawals are going to be bad because I was doing three grams of heroin to myself a day! But, I am more afraid to face the grief I haven't dealt with from dad's death. This is going to be a hard one.

-Hayz

April 13, 2016

We were able to visit Hayley at detox today. Mike and I put together a care package filled with her favorite candies and coloring books. Mom met us there so we could eat the takeout I picked up from one of our favorite restaurants together. Hayley couldn't eat much because she was still sick from withdrawals, but her eyes lit up when she opened the gifts we brought her. She seems to be doing well and has made a couple friends. There are only a few days left before she moves to a rehab facility. Mom and I are looking into a several options with the help from a social worker. Between the three of us I think we will find somewhere she feels comfortable going to. I feel so much better knowing she is in a place where she will get the help she needs. I honestly never thought this day would happen. Dad would be so happy. Hayley hasn't been receptive about the idea of getting better until I saw her a couple days ago. I just hope she isn't doing this for us again. She has to do it for herself in order for her journey to be successful.

XO, E

April 13, 2016

This has been the worst detox of my entire life. I was doing so much heroin on a daily basis the withdrawals are almost unbearable. I threw up in my sleep, and the nurses didn't do anything about it the first night I was here. I woke up with vomit on my pillow. If I was on my back, I could have died! I practically crawled up to the nurse's desk in the middle of the night to tell them what had happened, but they didn't seem to care. They didn't even look at me when they said they heard me coughing and were glad I was okay. I am so sick the doctor put me on the highest dose of a pill that blocks the opiate receptors and resists urges, suboxone. I hope the next few days are better than last night. I don't want to die in here.

-Hayz

April 17, 2016

I am wandering to southern Utah next week with the goddesses to Katies's place. Looking so forward to being in the desert, surrounded by love and laughter. Mame will stop by with her meditation group. She is doing well.

My health seems to be stable. Hair is growing back, gray for the most part. When I run my hands over my head, I feel the soft fuzziness of it. Even my eyelashes are growing again.

After six months of living with me, Hayley entered detox last week. She will be healing at a drug rehab center near the Wasatch mountains in SLC. I toured the facility last week as well as one other place. I felt the one she chose is the best fit for her. Keeping my fingers crossed that she can find the peace she is searching for.

Namaste, Jude

April 18, 2016

Mom, Erin and Mike visit every day and bring me food and gifts. I like that I can smoke cigarettes here. One of my new friends smuggled in some edible weed gummy bears. We thought arts and crafts time would be the perfect setting to eat them. We were laughing uncontrollably for at least an hour. I really needed something to get my mind off of how terrible I feel. Mom and Erin are looking at rehab facilities for me. I am scared, but feeling better about it than before. I think my new friend is going to try to go to the same facility as me. Moving on up!

-Hayz

April 19, 2016

Over the past week Hayley has done really well at detox. She has color in her cheeks again, and I can see her old self slowly coming back into light. So much has changed in the last few days; I can only imagine how much she will heal in the upcoming months. Mom toured a beautiful rehab center near the mouth of the canyons. I haven't been able to go yet, but I heard it is very nice. Hayley is being transported today. We are unable to drive her to the facility, and we won't be able to see or talk to her for about a week once she arrives. It's going to be a lot for her, but she is strong. I know she will be able to do it if she puts her mind to it. I am so proud of her, and I hope the hardest part is over. Accepting that she needs help, and detoxing couldn't have been easy. I admire her for her strength and courage.

XO, E

April 20, 2016

It was a beautiful spring day when I left the detox center, but I wouldn't take off my big puffy, down coat. The chills from the withdrawals were unbearable. Not only did my coat keep the chills away, but it made me feel safe. I am so scared to take the next step. I don't know if I am ready yet and don't feel like I belong at this rehab center. I see why mom and Erin thought this was a good place for me to heal, but everything is so nice and most of the other residents come from families with a lot of money. I just came from living in a trailer, and now I am living a posh lifestyle I don't deserve.

-Hayz

April 26, 2016

The doctor at rehab is the same doctor from the detox center. He decided it was best if he weaned me off the suboxone within a week! It usually takes at least a month! I am miserable because of the withdrawals. I feel mentally and physically destroyed, and I can't stop thinking about the one thing I know that will make it better. The withdrawals have made sleep difficult, so instead of getting some much needed rest I stare up at the black ceiling, thinking of a way I could escape this hell. When they searched my bag they didn't find my cell phone. I didn't say anything at the time in case I would need it. I have been texting friends to let them know I am trying to formulate an escape plan, so they are ready to pick me up when the time is right. I have had enough of it tonight. Part of addiction is cravings and I can't stop! I text a few friends to see if they would pick me up, but they wouldn't come because I am so far away. I was getting desperate. I started to think I should just hitchhike somewhere. The gates aren't locked at night, so all I would have to do it sneak past the people doing the night watch in the house. It would be easy, but not worth it. I have put in so much time and effort I need to see if I can do it. If I don't do it for me, I need to do it for mom. She doesn't deserve to have an addict for a daughter.

-Hayz

April 28, 2016

Got tapped at Huntsman today. 5 liters! A new record for me. I am feeling literally drained this afternoon. Tumor markers are down 30 points! The Affinitor is working. Yay!

I am off to Ivins, Utah tomorrow with my girlfriends to spend time at our friend's ranch.We carpool down there and sleep where we can find a spot. There will be 15 of us going this time. The wine will be flowing.

Gotta go mow the lawn before it gets too hot. It's going to be 80 degrees today.

Namaste, Jude

April 28, 2016

My days at rehab are taken up by four, hour long group therapy sessions a day! We get to go to the gym regularly, yoga classes and attend two-three AA meetings a week. So far the therapy isn't helping much. We sit in a circle and they ask if anyone wants to talk about something in particular. If no one volunteers a topic the therapists pick our brains until the group can agree on something to touch on. They seem to focus more on the abortion I had a few years ago than anything. I need to talk about the sexual abuse I experienced as a child, the way Grant manipulated me, and the toxic relationship we had. They also call me a victim a lot, which really bothers me. No one likes to be called a victim. It's almost like they are making me the victim by being against me, which is a common addict move, to make yourself the victim even if people are trying to help. I have decided it's best to go through the motions. I will fake my way through this until they let me leave. I have become a pretty good liar when I need to.

-Hayz

May 3, 2016

Hayley is now in rehab. I saw her this evening for family night. She looks and acts so much better. We are all cautiously optimistic about her future. We just take it day by day. This is a start, anyway.

Namaste, Jude

May 3, 2016

Mom and I were able to see Hayley for the first time in a while. It was also the first time I had been to the property. As I turned into the gated driveway, I was surprised about how beautiful it is. Mom told me it looked like a country club, but I didn't fully understand until I saw it with my own eyes. Large fountains greeted me as I pulled in. There were basketball courts, tennis courts, fire pits and a large grassy area to my right. When I looked to me left I saw huge red brick home with large windows, a balcony, and a garden out front. It is one of the two dorms for the residents. A large building stood in the middle of the property with another dorm for residents behind it. The main building is not as big as the dorms and it is where group therapy sessions and yoga classes are held. It is also the home to the offices for therapists and staff.

Family night is held every Tuesday, but tonight it was at capacity. Mom and I thought we were going to have to go home because Hayley hadn't been a resident for longer than 14 days. We weren't supposed to see her yet, but they made an exception, and allowed us to spend time with her instead of go to the meeting. It was such a nice night. We hadn't been able to be together just the three of us and her sober for years! She likes the program, the people, and says she thinks she will be able to stay sober after being there. I have a lot of hope, and for the first time I am not too worried about Hayley.

XO, E

May 3, 2016

I was excited to see mom and Erin today, but I still miss dad so much. This is the first time I am feeling the grief of his passing. I am finally facing the feelings I have been running from the last year. To say it's been hard would be an understatement. Guilt and shame are taking over my body. I just wish I could be the person I know I can be at times like this. But I still feel worthless. I want to be ready, but I don't have enough hope that life is better without the drug. I don't have hope that I can come back from all of the destruction I have caused.

On the plus side I am making some really good friends here. It's the first time I feel like I have people who know what I am going through, but I am still really sick. I want to leave, but I know it would disappoint mom and Erin. I don't want to let them down again. I have learned that I need to take it one day at a time.

-Hayz

May 8, 2016

Springtime Saturday Morning

Willie on Pandora.
Coffee almost done.
Sunshine greets me.
As if to say;
Get moving,
Go barefoot,
Feel it.
Cool splendor.
Green wonder.
Again and again.

Namaste, Jude

May 8, 2016

Today is Mother's Day! Mom loves being in the mountains, so I made a reservation at one of her favorite restaurants located in one of the canyons. Since it was a cold and rainy day we did some shopping at the mall, and then took Hayley to the grocery store to buy some goodies she could take back to rehab. She bought so much food she needed help taking it inside, so while we were there she gave us a tour of her dorm. It is gorgeous! They are coed houses, but they stay on separate floors. To help residents stay in their rooms at night, the staff looks after them 24/7.

They actually come into the rooms throughout the night with a flashlight to make sure everyone is accounted for.

After telling Hayley we loved her and how proud we are of her, Mike and I drove mom home. I stared at the light snow covering the trees on the mountaintops. It was unseasonably cold, but it didn't seem to bother any of us. I had a wonderful day honoring my beautiful mother and I am grateful both she and Hayley are here to celebrate another Mother's Day with us.

When I closed the car door to go home, I got a feeling that we shouldn't leave quite yet. Something was holding me back. I quickly realized we hadn't gotten any pictures of the day, so as Mike was pulling out of the driveway I said "Wait!" He slammed on the breaks and looked at me with a worried expression on his face. I jumped out of the car without any explanation, and ran inside to give mom another big hug and to take a selfie. She was so surprised to see me, and laughed her contagious laugh as I held the camera up to capture the moment. Celebrating holidays with mom has become even more important because I don't know when it will be her last. I want to make sure I document everyone one of them.

XO, E

May 8, 2016

Today was the first day I could leave campus. When I got into the car Mike was playing my favorite rap artist, Tech 9 to lift my spirits. They were all so happy to see me. It was good so see them as well, and I am grateful I can be with mom on Mother's Day, but I still want to leave. I have gained weight and the toxins that are leaving my body have caused my face to break out all over. I am 25 years old, but I feel like am 14 again because I have no freedom. I have to be chauffeured everywhere. I know I was slowly killing myself, but I don't want to feel like a child anymore.

-Hayz

May 10, 2016

Mom and I met at the rehab to attend our first real family night. Neither of us knew what to expect. Hayley was ecstatic to see us. She led us upstairs to the large conference room where there were several family members. The therapists take turns leading family night. The man who was in charge tonight started the session by asking us to say our names and our favorite actor/actress. It was a great way to break the ice, and get to know one another without getting too personal. After we introduced ourselves, he went right into talking about the science behind addiction, and why people become addicted. It was very interesting, and the way he explained it made it very easy to understand. The hour went by pretty quickly. I love when we get to see her. She is doing so well. She is talkative, happy, and not nodding off every 5 minutes. I feel like she is coming back to us, and I have a sister again.

XO, E

May 13, 2016

Part of Hayley's recovery is playing softball against other rehab facilities. She has always been a natural athlete, but hasn't been very active for a while, so she was a little nervous to play. Today was her first game, so Mike and I and Bella met mom at the park to watch her play. We made a huge sign that said, "GO HAYLEY" and cheered her on, which totally embarrassed her. I think she secretly enjoyed the attention.

XO, E

May 16, 2016

Hayley is rocking rehab. She is staying another 30 days! Breathing gently in, gently out. Inhaling feathers, exhaling feathers. Ever so gently as not to break or disturb each and every one. The feathers are a reminder to feel, breathe, touch, walk, taste gently with purpose not to harm or injure, but to be in the moment, thinking of intention. Going within to learn what matters. What really matters. It is a serene, peaceful place within. I don't want to leave, but am anxious to write. I am finding a voice, my voice. It is a beautiful thing, this voice of mine. I am singing and smiling at the same time. Hallelujah I say. It's about fucking time.

Namaste, Jude

May 22, 2016

Mom picked me up to get my hair done and my eyebrows waxed. It was so nice to spend one on one time with her while sober. I haven't felt like myself for a very, very long time. Getting pampered gave me confidence, and I feel beautiful again.

Music is what is getting me through most of my days, and inspires me to be better. I like to listen to Eminem because he was able to fight his addiction. His lyrics and experience gives me hope that I can do the same. I also listen to Kaskade. I love the song, "Room for Happiness" because of the lyrics, "Don't be fooled by your emptiness, there's so much room for happiness." It's a reminder that I can be happy again one day. All of the loneliness I feel will be replaced with love. I am starting to think rehab is actually starting to help. I knew I needed to do something so I can be there for mom like I want to.

-Hayz

June 3, 2016

Hayley will soon be completing treatment. We have been so fortunate to have found the perfect rehab match for her recovery. She will now go to a sober living facility which is more of a step down unit. She will work, have her own apartment, but have the support of other recovering addicts. I am amazed at how much her recovery has contributed to my overall happiness. I know it shouldn't be that way, but so it is.

Namaste, Jude

June 3, 2016

I am grateful to be in such a nice place to work on myself, but I feel like I am at a hotel. I have been here for over a month and still don't feel comfortable. I am not able to do the work I need to do because I can't be myself here. I have friends, but feel out of place. I am still lacking the confidence I need to believe I can do the things the therapists are asking of me. I am relearning social queues. I am not sure how to speak with confidence, or even meet a new person. I am lonely.

-Hayz

June 5, 2016

I woke up early this morning to cover the Pride parade. I was extremely nervous because I hadn't done anything like it before. When we arrived, I felt much more at ease when I saw two familiar faces, Brandon and Keith. I got to meet my amazing co-host, RJ. He is so easy to be around and made me feel confident that I could be a good co-host. Our job was to interview as many people in the parade that we could. RJ took the first couple entries, and then told me it was my turn. My heart was racing as I ran to the first person I could see, and asked them why they felt like it was so important to be in the parade. Even though I came up to them out of nowhere they did not hesitate in giving me a meaningful answer. They said, "The more visibility there is, the more people can see themselves reflected. They can see they are not alone." I wasn't expecting such a beautiful and honest answer. I wanted to ask them more questions, but knew I needed to keep going.

The next person I asked was a young man who was pushing his toddler in a stroller. He looked surprised and a little unsure when I came up to him. I thought I would get a one word answer, but instead he said, "I am here because I want to teach my child to accept people for who they are. I don't want him to discriminate against someone because of who they love. Equality is important." My eyes grew sweaty. Not because of the heat, but because of his answer. What he said reminded me of what my parents have instilled in me. I looked over at my mom, smiling and waving at all of the people in the parade. I ran over to her to give her a big hug to say thank you for teaching me to fight for human rights, love and equality. Just like this young father was doing for his son.

XO, E

June 5, 2016

So stoked on life today! The pride parade was filled with so much love. It was a nice change because I was feeling pretty down the last couple days. I started sober softball a couple weeks ago. I am terrible at it, but I enjoy getting out there and doing something new. At times like this I really miss dad because I know he would be at every game. I did really well at softball Friday night. When I got back to my dorm I was so excited to call dad to tell him that I had hit the ball and made a homerun, but when I picked up the phone to dial his number I remembered he wasn't here. I couldn't call him. It broke my heart knowing I wasn't going to be able to talk to my number 1 fan. He would have been so proud. I went from feeling so happy, to feeling down again so quickly. I hadn't felt that pain for a couple weeks now.

-Hayz

June 7, 2016

Today was Mom's 64th birthday! I picked Hayley up from the facility on the way home from work. I am happy they gave her permission to leave to celebrate. It is Tuesday, so she is supposed to be with family anyways. On our drive to mom's favorite sushi restaurant I put on "When I'm 64" by the Beatles as a surprise. When the first cords started to play mom quickly looked at me with a big smile on her face. We sang along and danced the entire drive to the restaurant. Mom loves the Beatles and saw them numerous times when she was a teenager. They were her boy band growing up. I wonder if she ever thought she would be singing that song with her family when she turned 64?

XO, E

June 10, 2016

Breaking the law is usually a big part of drug addiction. Over the past few years, Hayley has been arrested a few times for stealing, forgery, among other things, but hasn't spent time in jail. She has had a lot of court dates pile up and hasn't gone to any of them, which has made matters worse. A court date for one of her most recent offenses is in a couple weeks, so I needed to find her an attorney. I remembered dad recommending a particular attorney to friends, so I thought I should call him first. If dad liked him I am sure he was good. He agreed to take Hayley on as a client and will be meeting her in court this week. I hope she can get everything taken care of. She has a lot of offenses, so she may have to spend some time in jail, but if she agrees to go to drug court, maybe she won't need to.

XO, E

June 11, 2016

60 days clean has never felt so good! I finally completed something I didn't think I would ever be able to do. I have gone from wanting to run away to really wanting to stay sober this time, but I am scared. I took a tour of a sober living facility today. It looks cool, but there are only 2 bathrooms for 16 girls! It is also really expensive, and doesn't feel right. I have a lot of anxiety about moving forward. I feel like I can do this on my own and talked to my therapist about it. When I am in a structured facility I do really well and I think I can do this. I have made some great friends that I can hang out with after I am out of here. I don't feel like I need to go to sober living. I am ready to face the world on my own.

-Hayz

June 15, 2016

I Am A Crone

My bones ache. Sometimes more. Sometimes less. I snore.

I know the tenderness of the dogs love sounds. I know the delight of a belly laugh. Appearances don't matter. I know the homecoming of my bed at night.

My eyesight is limited. My eyesight is limitless. The sun is the enemy. The sun feels so good on my skin.

My life will end sooner than later. My soul is eternal. I know the sadness of a daughter made prisoner. I know the value of big brotherly love. I know the deep enduring bond of my first born. I know the loyalty of a friend.

My memory betrays me daily. A smile can alter a mood. Forgiveness works magic. Compassion is a conscious decision.

Paying it forward can change the world. There are more good people than bad. A cup of tea is the best medicine.

Namaste, Jude

June 17, 2016

Darrell asked if Bella would want to go on a hike with him, Lucy, and Cooper today. She loves them, so of course, I said yes. She gets almost as excited to see them as she did my dad. As we were getting close to Darrell's house she began to whine and pace anxiously in the back of the car. When I opened up the hatch, she shot out like an arrow. She made herself known by putting her two front paws on the door and began to whine more. Before I could get to the top of the stairs, Darrell had already opened the door and the dogs were there to greet us. Bella gave Lucy and Copper kisses while frantically wagging her tail. Lucy tried to get past Bella to come see me. She immediately burrowed her head into my body. She was giving me head hugs, which she did a lot. She loves Darrell, Corey, and Cooper, but I am sure she misses dad. The cancer bubble on her leg has gotten even bigger than the last time I saw her. It takes up about half of her leg, so she has a hard time walking, but the cancer doesn't seem to bother her other than that. I am glad she can still go on hikes, and live her normal puppy life. I told the girls I loved them, thank you to Darrell and went to work.

When I arrived, I noticed a box with my name on it. Inside was the bronze eagle for dad's headstone! The artist who gave it to me is an avid outdoorsman who loves the mountains. He reminds me a lot of dad, and I am sure they would have gotten along if they had the chance to meet. I couldn't ask for a better person to be the artist for the finishing touch on dad's headstone.

I received a distressing call from Darrell on my way down the canyon. On their hike, Lucy's cancer bubble broke open. He and Corey immediately took her to the vet where they were told that they would have to put her down. It wasn't urgent, so Darrell and Corey brought Lucy home for one last night. Mike and I rushed over after work where we saw Lucy lying on the back deck. She couldn't stand up, but wagged her tail when she saw us. I started to cry when I realized she couldn't greet us like she always used to. She was just too weak. When I looked into her big brown eyes I could tell she knew something was wrong. She looked so scared. I sat down next to her so she could put her head in my lap, while I stroked her head and told her everything was going to be okay. She and I cuddled for about an hour while I listened to birds chirping in the trees and her soft snores. Even though she lived with Darrell and Corey, she was still our family dog. It broke my heart knowing that another part of dad was going to be gone, but gave me comfort knowing they would be together again.

Nothing can prepare you for a loss of a dog. A dog is not just a pet; they are a member of the family, a best friend, a loyal companion, a teacher and a therapist. I love her so much. Bella and I are really going to miss her. Lucy and dad taught Bella how to be a mountain dog. Bella really looked up to her and is going to have a hard time. First dad and now Lucy! She is going to be put down tomorrow, which is fitting because Father's Day is the next day. It will be the first Father's Day after dad passed. Now he will have one his best friends, Lucy, with him.

Rest in peace Lucy, dad is waiting for you. You will always be remembered.

Good girl.

XO, E

June 18, 2016

Hayley finished treatment today. It was comforting to know she was somewhere safe these past couple months. While she has been in treatment, we were able to talk to her every day, and I didn't miss a family night. Mom, Mike, and I made sure she was able to leave campus every weekend. Because we were around so often, we got to know a lot of the residents. Mom is such a people person, a few of them opened up to her. They would call her mama Jude. She seems happy to take on the role of a mother figure when anyone needs her. Bella came with us almost every weekend, and become a therapy dog for many of the residents

The next step is for Hayley to live in a sober living. Hayley is very against it, and I don't know why, but her therapist agrees with Hayley's decision in not going. Mom and I aren't so sure. Mom does not want Hayley living with her again. She says it is too stressful, and there is also a higher probability Hayley will relapse if she goes back to the environment where she is comfortable using so quickly. Of course, mom wants Hayley around, but we don't feel like she is ready. She was supposed to be in rehab for 90 days, but because she did so well, the facility cut her stay short. Hayley knows how to put on an act. Since she has been lying for years she has become very good at it. Mom and I know her so well we can usually tell when she is not telling the truth, but mom needs to concentrate on her health, not Hayley's.

Because mom and I were so worried, we made an appointment with Hayley's therapist to express our concerns. Even after hearing what we had to say she wouldn't back down, and is confident day treatment will be enough for her. She is really putting mom in a tough position. It's like she is making her let Hayley live with her again without caring what mom has to say. We decided the therapist knows what she is doing, so mom agreed to go along with the plan.

To help her feel more comfortable about Hayley living with her again mom put together a contract with some guidelines. They include a curfew, her getting a job, no using drugs or alcohol, helping around the house, etc. If she breaks any of the rules mom will ask her to leave. I really hope it all works out. Mom really doesn't need to add any more stress to her life. One of her eyes has been bothering her a lot. It has gotten very dry, which can make it difficult for her to see at times. She thinks it is a side effect from the new chemo or just getting older, so she is going to ask her doc about it the next time she goes in. I hope it's nothing serious. Mom doesn't need something else to have to worry about. She has enough on her plate as it is.

XO, E

June 18, 2016

Clear headed and out of treatment! It feels so good to spend more time with my best friend that I'm so lucky to call my mom. I have missed her so much, but when I'm at home, trying to stay sober, I feel smothered by the whole family. Everyone's expectations are so high for me to remain sober that I fear making them sad or disappointed. I am afraid I will end up relapsing and lying.

My family gets too involved in something that's up to me. It becomes a huge problem, and I can't take the pressure from everyone. I'm completely stripped of my freedom at home. When again, it's my recovery, and I have to make the right choices to want to better my life. There's not much in their control unfortunately, but if there's a will, there's a way. The sky's the limit!

-Hayz

June 20, 2016

Beautiful summer's morning here. The goldfinches are eating breakfast at the feeder. Sophie is at my feet, hoping I'll drop blueberry muffin crumbs. Hayley is on her way to do day treatment. She is staying with me on a temporary basis until she can find a job and a place of her own to live. The transition is a little stressful for both of us. It's a lesson in trust and letting it be.

Namaste, Jude

June 20, 2016

I relapsed today. I was doing well in treatment because I had structure and rules to abide by, but now I don't have a sober community, or foundation. My mind is still very sick and the only way I know how to cope is to get high. I was sitting on mom's couch watching *Cops* when I started to receive texts from Grant's sister. I thought maybe I could have one last good time without any repercussions. I couldn't shake the feeling, so I snuck out, took the car and drove to her house. Once I get drugs or alcohol into my system, all I do is lie. I think mom and Erin know, but they haven't said anything yet. I need try to figure this out on my own.

-Hayz

June 26, 2016

I have been hanging out with a few of my friends from rehab. None of our families know that we have all relapsed, so they think it is fine that we spend time with one another. Since my friends wanted to say hi to mom I drove them to her house. I was talking to mom in her backyard when I looked over to see one of them hunched over in my front seat. I frantically ran over to her. Her lips had turned blue, she was not responsive, and there was a needle in her lap. She wasn't supposed to be doing anything while we were there! My other friend wanted to do CPR, but we were two blocks away from a hospital, so I put her lifeless body around me while I drove to the ER.

Somehow, the two of us carried her into the emergency room. The nurses immediately put her on a stretcher when we told them what had happened. They started to use a defibrillator to get her heart going again. It didn't work, so they gave her two shots of Narcan, but she still didn't wake up. I was so worried. What were we going to do if she died? They used the defibrillator one last time, and to my relief she woke up. She was very confused and didn't know where she was. We tried to explain it to her, but I had to get out of there. I have felony warrants out and I knew the cops were going to come. Such a scary situation! I am grateful she is okay, for now at least.

-Hayz

June 27, 2016

Darrell asked to take us on a hike to one of dad's favorite places in the Uinta Mountains. It is an area off the beaten path they nicknamed "Evans Gulch." We planned on meeting Darrell, his son, and a few of dad's friends at a campsite near the trail at 12PM. Hayley wanted to go, but because she didn't get up in time she made us all very, very late. There was no service where we were meeting the group, so we were unable to tell them our ETA. She made us two hours late! The group was pretty upset by the time we got there, but I also feel like they weren't that surprised. Being late, or not showing up is a habit Hayley has adopted. I felt so bad, but it was out of my control at that point.

Everyone brought food to share, and we had a picnic before taking the hike. When we got to the end we hung one of Lucy's collars and one of dad's hats on a tree nearby. I stood on my tippy toes to put dad's hat on the highest branch possible. As I clasped the hat onto the tree limb a tear rolled down my cheek. Before I had a chance to brush it off, a light gust of wind blew across my face, almost like it was dad wiping me tears away. Just like he did when I was little.

Our time to enjoy the scenery and the two moose that wandered into the clearing was interrupted when I saw that Bella's face was extremely swollen. She looked like the Lorax! I figured it must have been an allergic reaction to something, so I quickly reached into my bag to give her a little bit of Benadryl before Mike and I rushed her down the trail to drive her to a vet. Mom walked a little slower, so Darrell offered to take her home while we rushed to get Bella some medical attention. We were so scared it was something serious, and the closest vet was about 1.5 hours away! We packed everything up as fast as we could. As we were pulling out of the parking lot we saw mom walking across the street. She quickly hopped into the front seat while Hayley and I cuddled in the back with Bella to keep an eye on her while she slept. I held her in my lap, stroked her soft fur and kept telling her everything was going to be okay. But I had no idea if it was going to okay. My heart was beating so hard because I was scared. I couldn't lose Bella too. She is my therapy dog, my best friend and my furbaby.

The ride to the vet seemed like it took hours! We practically ran inside when we arrived. They were nice enough to take us in last minute. The vet assured us it was an allergic reaction to a sting of some sort. He gave us some meds, and said we did the right thing by giving her Benadryl. Thank goodness. I really don't know what I would do without Bella in my life.

XO, E

June 29, 2016

I recently played a small part in a movie. It was an added scene, so there wasn't much left in the budget to pay me. One of the producers, Dave asked if he could pay me in the form of photographing new headshots. I don't have any updated headshots, so I figured it was a good trade. During the photo session, I got a phone call from Hayley's attorney. Since she had court this morning I wasn't surprised to see his name pop up on my caller id. She had missed so many other court appearances before today; her attorney warned us that she would probably be booked into jail. I asked Dave if he wouldn't mind if I took the call, and I am glad I did. Her attorney informed me that the judge didn't want to give Hayley anymore chances. She went straight from court to jail. He then said that I needed to get $10,000.00 in cash to bail her out. I was shocked! $10,000.00 is a lot of money, especially in cash. How did he think I was able to do that? He said I needed to bail her out because she had another court date tomorrow, and if she didn't go she would be in even more trouble. She is supposed to get the money back when she attends court for her other cases, but because she hasn't had a great attendance record I was a little hesitant. She still has money left over from Mike and I buying her out of the house, but I had a bad feeling about it. When I hung up with her attorney Dave asked if I wanted to continue with the shoot. I don't know Dave well, but felt like it was safe to let him know what was going on. He was very empathetic and offered to continue shooting another day, but it was hard enough to find one day that worked with our schedules already. I was there, and because it didn't sound like Hayley was going to be out for another couple hours we continued.

The next hour was full of phone calls from mom and Hayley calling from jail. Mom needed to be updated on what was going on, and Hayley wanted to know if I was coming to bail her out. I kept smiling, and did the best I could despite everything that was happening. It was very hard to concentrate, but Dave did a great job distracting me. We were able to get a lot of great shots, despite all of the interruptions.

As I was pulling out of the parking lot Hayley called again. She sounded relieved when I told her I was on my way to bail her out. I was happy to help, but also very scared. She has made so much progress the last couple months. I am afraid if I bail her out she will go back to her old ways, or even worse. We think jail will be her rock bottom, and we finally have that chance to get her there, but I figured her attorney knows best.

As I drove to the bank my nerves started to get the best of me. My hands were so clammy they easily slid across the steering wheel. I had a hard time concentrating on the road because all I could think about was Hayley, and if I was doing the right thing. I almost turned around to go home, but I somehow made it to the parking lot of the bank. I took a few minutes to sit in the car to catch my breath before going in. I slowly walked through the glass doors, and made my way to the first teller I could see. He asked me what he could help me with as I handed him my withdrawal slip. He didn't seem too surprised by the 4 zeros at the bottom, but said he would need to speak to the manager on duty. I was trying not to panic. I wasn't doing anything wrong by being at the bank, but I couldn't help but think bailing Hayley out was the wrong thing to do. We can't be there to help her every step of the way. She needs to learn how to be an adult. About 5 minutes later he came back, counted out $10,000.00 and put it in an envelope for safe keeping. I smiled, told him thank you and immediately put the envelope of cash in my bag. I felt a little better at that point, but now I had a stack of $100 bills with me. I wanted to get rid of the money as soon as possible. The next stop was jail.

I hadn't been to the jail before, so I didn't know what to expect. When I pulled into the parking lot I realized that to get to the main entrance, I had to walk up a very long ramp. I started thinking about how quickly I could get inside without looking nervous. Here I am, by myself, with $10,000.00 cash in my bag, coming to bail my sister out of jail. The walk seemed like it took forever! I was walking as fast as I could without running. I am sure it was all in my head, but it seemed like everyone who walked past me was staring at me. I felt terribly unsafe because I was carrying so much cash. I made it inside, but even with several police officers around I still didn't feel secure. I waited patiently in the line that was labeled "payments." There were a few other people in line, and many others sitting on benches in the middle of the lobby. They were waiting for their timeslot to see their loved one who was a resident of the jail. When it was my turn, I was greeted by a middle aged, blonde woman. I told her I was there to bail my sister out She asked me her name, and then said it would be $10,000.00. I looked around me to see if anyone heard how much I was giving her before reaching into my bag. Her eyes widened as I pulled out the envelope full of cash. She asked me if I was sure I wanted to bail her out because it was a lot of money. I told her yes, and she shook her head as she walked over to the money counter. The officers nearby couldn't get over how much I gave her. They asked where I got the money from, and why I was bailing her out. If a new officer came by they would mention it to them, and they would all laugh. I almost felt like they were accusing me of something. I wasn't a prisoner they could push around. They were also being very loud, which I didn't appreciate because other people in the lobby could hear. I felt very uneasy. I didn't have the cash anymore, but I still had to walk to my car by myself. The woman came back with a receipt and told me it was going to be another two hours until my sister was released. Since I felt so uncomfortable I thought it was best to go home. I wanted to get out of there as soon as I could. When I got back to my car I called mom to let her know what happened. She offered to pick Hayley up on her way home from work because it was close by.

Bella was wagging her tail as I pulled into the driveway. She is always a breath of fresh air to come home to. A couple hours later I received a call from mom. Hayley still wasn't discharged! For some reason it was taking longer than anticipated. Mom was in tears and wanted to come home, which I understood. I had just been there and know how depressing of a place it is. She calmed down after talking to me for a bit and waited another 15 minutes for Hayley to make her appearance. What a stressful day for everyone, especially my sister. I really hope none of us have to visit jail again.

XO, E

June 30, 2016

All smiles after court

-Hayz

July 1, 2016

I am wondering if Hayley showed up to court this morning? She relapsed last week. I have been trying to decide whether to tell her attorney. She is due to go back to rehab today for two more weeks of inpatient treatment after her court hearing this morning. She has to test clean. I don't want to burden him with this info, but as her attorney, I feel he should know what is going on with her.

Namaste, Jude

July 2, 2016

I have asked Hayley to leave my home today. I need to put my oxygen mask on before everyone crashes and burns.

Namaste, Jude

July 2, 2016

Mom and Erin confronted me about my drug use, and mom asked me to leave her house. I know she loves me, and it is what she has to do. I don't blame her. I just don't know how to get better. I found a woman who I know through a mutual friend who will let me sleep on her couch if I give her meth and rides to work. Seems like a good deal to me.

-Hayz

July 4, 2016

Ossie

I am grieving today.
For Ossie, my dog.
He died a year ago
in my arms.
He was so sick,
I still see him
riding in cars, his
ears flying, to savor
the wind in his face,
happy to be alive.
I see him lifting his hind leg
to relieve himself
on the whiskey barrel
planter near the fence
in the backyard.
I hear his contented
dog grunts as I hold him.
His dog heart beating rapidly,
our daily morning ritual.
I see him strutting, holding
his head high as he
walks with Sophie and
me around the park.
In my mind, he lives,
A little dog
With a big heart.

Namaste, Jude

July 4, 2016

Mike helped me with another successful 4th of July party before heading to meet Hayley for her annual birthday dinner at the Dodo. The restaurant was packed because of a large celebration at the park across the street. Since we had Bella with us we needed to wait for a table near some shade. A table opened up about 20 minutes later, but there was no sign of Hayley. We were beginning to worry because no matter how sick she is she hasn't ever missed a birthday dinner. We were patiently waiting at our table when she finally called to tell us she was unable to get a ride there. She asked if one of us would pick her up, but she was about 30 minutes away, so it would be another hour until we got back to the restaurant. I have learned that she has no sense of time when she is high. If she says she will do something she usually doesn't follow through with the plans, or is an hour late. We didn't want to hold up a table, so we told her we would get it to go and have a picnic at a nearby park.

We picked her up at a small apartment complex. She is sleeping on a friend's sofa for the time being. I figure it is better than the trailer park. The car filled with the scent of perfume trying to mask the smell of cigarette smoke when she slid inside. Dry spots from the makeup she used to try to cover the up the newly formed scabs took over her face. We all exclaimed "Happy Birthday" and Bella wagged her tail to show her excitement to see her only aunt, but Hayley didn't seem to care. She was obviously upset. We tried to talk to her on the drive to the park, but all we got were one word answers. It made the car ride very uncomfortable. We walked around the park until we found a great picnic spot near a stream. We were all hangry and very tired because it was so late. We tried to enjoy dinner, but there was obvious tension. Hayley barely talked to us because she was eating her dinner so quickly. It was like she hadn't eaten in days!

As we were about to leave, Hayley started crying. Finally! I could tell she needed to get something out and couldn't understand why she waited so long to do so. Between big sobs she told us she isn't planning on getting sober. She wants us to stop trying because she doesn't want to, and if she doesn't want to there is no point in us trying. She then confessed about relapsing the day after she came home from rehab. She lied about going to day treatment. She would meet up with friends to get high instead. My heart broke as she was yelling and bawling to us. Mom was crying while Mike looked at me in shock. I knew she wasn't doing well, but had no idea she was this upset. I want to help her, but know there isn't anything I can do at this point. I have to let her hit rock bottom. We let her do most of the talking without interrupting. She obviously needed to get her feelings known. When she was done we each gave her a big hug. I told her I am here for her when she is ready before she walked away. None of us knew what to do or say on the drive home. We felt helpless. She was doing so well a few weeks ago. How could everything change so quickly? The drug has a hold on her, and she is not ready to let it go. As much as we don't want to we have to let her figure it out on her own, which I hope she can soon.

XO, E

July 4, 2016

Normally I am very excited about my birthday, but this year everything seems off. I am homeless, without a job, addicted to drugs, and it is my first birthday without dad. My family still wants to celebrate, so they brought me my favorite food at a park, but I am in such a bad place I can't pretend everything is okay anymore. I told them I don't want to get sober. I feel lonely, lost, and that life is not worth living. I have lost all hope, and I don't see a way out of this hell, so I am just going to continue to live the life I have been living, no matter how bad it is.

-Hayz

July 5, 2016

Recycle bin, scents. Delete what no longer serves you. Send to recycle bin. Can always revisit. For today, this did not serve me well. Is it in my best interest? Do I learn, grow, accept? Does this propel me forward? Stimulate my passions? Cancer and self love. What does it take to realize the wonder of you? To celebrate, appreciate healing and self love.

I am absolutely grateful for my friends. Through the good and bad times, they are there laughing and crying with me. Feeling so blessed.

Namaste, Jude

July 15, 2016

It is nice I have somewhere to live, but I also need to make some money, so I have gone back to dealing drugs. Grant used to be with me and was like a bodyguard, but now I am on my own and it is scary, but not as scary as not being sober and having to deal with the my grief.

-Hayz

July 17, 2016

My pastor reached out asking if I would be up for getting together to speak more personally about my health. I would love to chat with him about it.

Namaste, Jude

July 17, 2016

It blows my mind how we all know that today could be our last day, or our next breath could be our last breath. But why do we constantly forget it?

Remember to live EVERYDAY like it's your last. Because you never know when it will be. Or when you may lose a loved one in the blink of an eye.

Be grateful for the people in your life, tell them you love them, give them a hug or kiss, and never forget how precious each second is.

-Hayz

July 28, 2016

I co-hosted the morning show again. I was joking around about Bella coming with me with the manager of the station, and to my surprise she asked me to bring her. She is such a beautiful dog she thought she would be a hit! I got up early, brushed Bella so she was camera ready, and she made her television debut. It was fun to have her there, and since she is my therapy dog she really puts me at ease. At this point I am not very nervous about being on TV, but it always helps to have her there. A couple people were really nervous about being on television, and said her presence really helped them as well. Maybe they should have a station dog.

One reason I love hosting the morning show is getting to learn about what local people are doing to help make the community great. Much of the time they are giving back. Today I was able to speak with someone from the local rescue. They are a weekly guest, and bring a pet with them to highlight. I love animals, and I am passionate about rescuing, so when I am able to interview the person from the rescue it makes my day. I have started to produce a segment highlighting dog friendly restaurants, hotels and activities in Park City with Bella as my co host. I came up with the idea after several tourists stopped us on Main Street to ask us what they can do with their dog while they are in town. Many people bring their pets to Park City with them because there are so many great things to do with your dog. They don't call the city Bark City for nothing.

Bella and I interviewed the owners of a local, dog friendly restaurant after work. It is located near a golf course, and has amazing views of the valley. There are little stores nearby as well as a chairlift for skiing or hiking/biking in the summer. A few dogs were sitting outside with their owners. They looked exhausted from a fun day of running on the trails, and each had their own bowl of water. The owners of the restaurant were waiting for us with smiles. They led us to a wonderful seating area with a large table and umbrella where we could talk. We touched on a few things, but when I asked them why they feel like it is so important to rescue tears started to well up in my eyes. They said "There are so many that need homes. They are so beautiful and deserving. If you have an opportunity to save an animal and bring them into your family and show them what love can be, why wouldn't you?" It is comforting to talk with people who share the same values as I do. Meeting them and other rescue parents gives me hope that one day we can figure out a way to save them all.

XO, E

July 30, 2016

Cancer update: I saw Dr. Carson yesterday with Erin by my side. Tumor markers are up, scans show no progression. I am feeling pretty good, other than my left eye droops and tears frequently. I see an eye doc today to figure that one out. All in all, doing well. I have the Harvest Moon Ho Down with the goddesses to look forward to this weekend.

So good to be alive!

Namaste, Jude

August 4, 2016

I stopped to finalize dad's headstone on my way to work. It is so big I could see it from the parking lot! Dad was a tall man and had a large presence, so it is fitting. I could feel my heart beating as I got closer to the large, red rock. I should have felt relieved because finishing his headstone is one of the last big projects I have to do to close the estate, but working on it has been a welcome distraction. Now I am done I will have more time to grieve, if I allow myself to that is. I had seen pictures of the marker, but I was nervous to look at it in person. To see my dad's name on a headstone with the day of his death made it all so real. When I noticed the bronze eagle in the corner I almost fell to my knees, crying. Birds of prey remind me of dad. When I see them in person I like to think they are dad saying hi. The eagle on the headstone is him, keeping an eye on things.

Mom is still doing okay. Not great, but okay. Her eye is getting worse, which worries me. The eye doctor said it is caused by old age, and gave her some eye drops. If it continues to get worse, mom is going to get another opinion at the Moran eye center. I hope we can figure it out soon. I know it's extremely uncomfortable for her.

XO, E

August 9, 2016

On top of trying to learn more about her cancer, mom is also trying to learn about Hayley's addiction. She goes to Alinon meetings on a regular basis, and has subscribed to a few blogs about mothers of addicts. Addiction really is worse than cancer. At least with cancer, mom is taking the right steps to try to survive, while Hayley pushes us away. It has been the hardest thing our family has had to endure, and we aren't the only ones. Addiction has become a problem around the world. People truly don't know what it is like until they are affected by it in some way or another. We want to help others who are going through a similar situation, so we are very open about our struggle. When going through a difficult time, we have found that it helps knowing you are not alone.

Although Hayley is deep into her addiction I still have hope she can get through it. I have had several people say, "if she is addicted to heroin, there is no way she will get better because heroin is the hardest drug to get off of." First of all, I am astonished someone would say that. I understand that they are basing their assumptions on their experiences, but how dare they? I am not going to let their limited experience affect my expansive one. Second of all, I don't believe her addiction is going to kill her. I truly believe she will be able to get out of this alive. It is just going to take time.

XO, E

August 15, 2016

The summer has been very hot this year to the point where I have had to water trees and shrubs as well as the lawn. Looking forward to cooler weather. I am going camping this weekend in the mountains with my friend, Peggy. She has a fancy tent trailer with a queen size bed, and even a furnace if it gets too cold. My kind of camping.

I went to Park City Art Festival on Saturday to spend time with Erin, and find a birthday gift for Mame. She is leaving on Sunday to walk the El Camino in Spain. She will be gone for six weeks. I found a passport purse for here made out of plastic bags. She loved it. Erin and Mike are doing well. They are very busy, but seem happy.

Hayley relapsed shortly after leaving rehab. I had to ask her to leave my home. It got pretty ugly. I saw her last night for a little while. She is staying with a friend. Looks terrible. I hope she can find her way. The only way I can deal with her addiction is to love her, but not get involved. Life is a bitch sometimes.

My health is pretty good as of late. Hair is growing back kind of curly. I see my cancer doc next week. We shall see. I hope to stay on the meds I have been taking since April. Very few side effects, and my energy level is good.

Namaste, Jude

August 22, 2016

I first met Julie Miles during the Sundance Film Festival a couple years ago. It was a memorable night because I was interviewing one of my sister's favorite musical artists, Matisyahu. While I was listening to him play, I thought of my sister, and how much I missed her. The interview was one of my favorites. I think a lot of it has to do with how much I appreciate him for making music that was so healing for my sister growing up. When I finished talking with Matisyahu, Julie asked if I could interview her, and of course I said yes. She was decked out in beautiful pearls, which happened to be part of her jewelry line. She and I hit it off right away. As we got to talking, I learned she once had stage 4 cancer with a slim chance of survival, and Dr. Wilson was the person who saved her life. I told her mom probably wouldn't be here if it wasn't for him.

When Julie learned she had cancer, she was determined to beat it. While she was in the hospital, she promised herself she would do something she loved. She remembered the joy making jewelry gave her as a child, so she found the supplies she needed to start her own line, and the rest is history. She has traveled all over the world, and makes friends everywhere she goes. She is an inspiration, and a light to anyone she meets. It was meant to be that I meant Julie that night. We have kept in touch throughout the years, and tonight, I was thankful that I could celebrate another birthday with her. Here's to more birthday celebrations with the people we love.

XO, E

August 24, 2016

I am still working three days a week, although I have had quite a bit of time off during the month of July due to holidays and staff vacations. The summer's heat makes me weary and grumpy. Sophie is doing well considering she is 14 this month. We spent the weekend camping with friends in the mountains. We both came home in dire need of a shower. Her hind legs are dragging a bit again. I think because of her age and spinal deterioration common in small dogs. I don't think I'll ever get over losing Ossie last year.

Hayley has no desire to go back to rehab. I am working on my own recovery trying to have faith and hope she can find it in her to try again. Sometimes it is difficult to separate my daughter from the addict, but I am determined to love her through it while keeping my own boundaries. I am taking her to dinner tonight. I can't allow her to live with me anymore. The stress is just too great.

I have been feeling good on the current cancer med regimen I am on. Very few side effects for which I am supremely grateful for. I see my oncologist on Thursday with Erin. I hope I don't have to change meds.

All in all, life is good at the moment.

Namaste, Jude

September 10, 2016

The guy who provided me with the drugs I would sell quickly became my best friend. He ended up going to prison, so I had no way to get drugs. Since I couldn't pay the woman I am living with by giving her money or meth she asked me to leave. I didn't see any other option than to go to Grant's. He told me he did not want me to come back, but I know him so well I was able to talk him into letting me live with him again. I have been living in the trailer for about a month now. Grant is very jealous and doesn't like that I have friends who are men. Today, my friend who provided me with drugs called me from prison. I was in the shower, so Grant answered my phone. He was furious! He barged into the small bathroom, shoved me to the ground and began to punch me all over. I was naked, crying, and kept apologizing, but he wouldn't stop. He made me feel like I did something wrong. I hate living here, but I don't have anywhere else to go.

-Hayz

September 14, 2016

I went to Huntsman for my writing group. While I was waiting to be helped in the cafeteria, I looked up and saw a heart on the hillside made out of rocks. It was as if Mame was greeting me. She is still walking the Camino trail in Spain. I told the folks in my group about her and her trek and her heart (s).

It was only in the mid 70's today. So lovely. Went camping near Sundance with Peg and her family. I was worried I would get bored being gone for three days, but I wasn't. We laughed a lot, drank a lot, and played dominoes. We didn't know the rules for dominoes, so I had to call John a few times. Not just once, three times! When I talked to him yesterday we laughed a lot about it. He thought it was pretty funny. Hiked on Saturday through Cascade Springs. Made me think of Mike.

Namaste, Jude

September 18, 2016

Surprisingly, we are still working on the house. I have heard there is always something to do when you own a house, and I am learning more and more that is true. We have been so busy working we haven't given ourselves time for fun. We thought we should take advantage of the nice fall weather by attending a couple concerts and the Utah/BYU football game. It was much needed.

One of the concerts we went to was Mumford and Sons. When the band started to play "I Will Wait For You" a large knot formed in my belly. As the music crescendoed the knot moved to my throat and tears started to form. Mike could feel my body tense up and immediately held me. Once I felt his embrace the tears started to fall down my face. I have heard the song several times before, but there is power in live music. It gives us a chance connect with the musicians by feeling the same vibrations, and share in their joy. It's a time where I can live purely in the moment. While they played I was only thinking about how the song reminded me of the day the doctor told us mom had 9 months to live. I cried knowing it wasn't true.

XO, E

Sept 26, 2016

My doc called me today to say there was something on the MRI that needs to be biopsied. Not sure when that will be. Have to talk to my doc tomorrow. If it is cancer, the usual treatment is radiation. Trying to put on a happy face.

Namaste, Jude

September 27, 2016

Mom really wanted to go to the new musical by Sting. He is one of her favorite musicians, and it takes place in England. We made a night of it by going to dinner before and dessert afterwards. I didn't know what it was about, so when I sat down in the red, velvet seat to read the program I almost asked mom if I could leave. Much of it revolves around the death of his father. The one year anniversary of dad's death is only 3 days away. I was already on edge, and didn't know if this would push me over, making my fall into a deep despair. When I looked over at mom she was smiling. I didn't want to let her down, so I stayed. The music was beautiful, mom loved it and I didn't walk out feeling worse than before. I have begun to realize that it doesn't get any easier, but I am getting stronger. I can do this!

XO, E

September 30, 2016

Today is the 1 year anniversary of dad's death. I never knew I could miss someone as much as I miss him, and days like today are another reminder he is gone. I have noticed my subconscious knows when an important day is on the horizon. During the past year, I get a little depressed, and more anxious about a week before holidays and birthdays. I start to pick fights with Mike over the littlest things, and I have now realized it's because I don't know how to deal with the feelings of grief that are coming up. Jamie Anderson has said, "grief is just love with no place to go" and I am finding that to be truer every day. I have asked Mike to please try his hardest not to fight back, and to understand it's not him, it is the grief coming out as anger, but he has had a hard time doing so. He is so stressed out about owning a business he hasn't been able to be there for me in the way I need him to. What I need is a hug and a good cry on his shoulder.

This last week, I didn't pick any fights, but was pretty anxious. Dad's headstone still hasn't been installed. Uncle Bill came to town so we can visit the cemetery as a family to remember dad. I didn't want to disappoint the family nor did I want them to think I was irresponsible. I have been working hard on getting the headstone for almost a year now! We met my uncles, aunts, cousins, Darrell, and Corey at the cemetery. Mom wasn't feeling well, so Carol drove her to Huntsman to make sure she was okay. I am worried about her, but I needed to be there for family. Uncle Bill came all this way, and it is an important day to spend with loved ones. When Hayley didn't come to the cemetery I figured she was with mom, but she stayed at the trailer park. I hurt knowing she didn't want to be with us on such a difficult day. It is a hard day for her as well, but we are all going through the pain. It's better when we know we are not alone.

XO, E

September 30, 2016

A year ago today I lost a part of me. My biggest fear was losing a parent, which I knew was inevitable. I just wasn't expecting it to happen so fast, and at a young age. I plan on spending as much time with my loved ones because life can change in an instant, and I may never see them again.

On another note, I think it's only appropriate to celebrate my pops for the amazing dude he is. Nobody will ever live up to my dad, and I can honestly say that I feel honored to be his daughter. I miss you so much, pops.

-Hayz

October 2, 2016

I have had quite a week seeing doctors. I had an eye biopsy at the Moran Eye Center by a young doctor, who I must say is the best doctors I have had the pleasure of adding to my medical arsenal. I have breast cancer metastasis in the muscle of my right eye. This is a rare occurrence, but from what I understand it can easily be treated by radiation. I see a radiation oncologist on Tuesday. I received good news after my colonoscopy yesterday. My colon looks much better than it did a year ago, meaning that the chemo actually worked. In the midst of good news, bad news. I am supremely grateful for the outpouring of love and caring I have received from my friends and family.

I applied for early retirement last night. I am going to stop working for one dentist and only work for the dentist whose office is closer to me on Tuesdays. More time for fun!!

Namaste, Jude

October 2, 2016

Mom's doctors can't figure out why her right eye is still bothering her. After doing some research she found out it is common for lobular breast cancer to spread to the eye. I really wonder why the two ophthalmologists she went to and her oncologist didn't come to that conclusion. With her history, and the fact breast cancer is known to spread to the eye, I would have thought that they would have known that. I was angry that none of the doctors were more proactive about it, but grateful she was willing, and able to figure it out herself.

She made an emergency appointment with a doctor at the Moran eye center next to Huntsman for today. A dear friend of mine, Meghan works there, and met us in the lobby for support. After hugs, and a few tears she led us to mom's new doctor, who she said is one of the best! Mom didn't seem nervous as we were waiting. She said she was ready to get this figured out because she is extremely uncomfortable. When the doctor walked in she was very caring, yet professional. After a quick examination mom asked her if she thought it could be cancer. She put her hands on mom's when she said "yes, but I want to take a biopsy to make sure." Mom took a sigh of relief, almost like she wanted it to be cancer. It was an unknown that was finally being solved. Since she has learned how to live with the cancer that has taken over her body the last few years I think she figures she can handle this as well. The biopsy didn't look painful, but mom is going to have a black eye for a while. She had to wear a patch out of the office, and will need to do so for much of the recovery period. She doesn't seem to be bothered by it right now. It's definitely not the worst thing she has had to endure. I am just happy she found a doctor who knows what she is doing. I wish she was able to see her a few months ago. I feel like I should have been more proactive. I hate seeing her so uncomfortable.

XO, E

October 4, 2016

Neil Young was one of dad's favorite musicians. So much so, that we danced to one his songs for our daddy daughter dance at my wedding. When I saw that he was coming in concert I bought tickets the minute they went on sale. Even though I have heard his music play throughout my life, seeing him live was like hearing him for the first time. His voice is so unique, and listening to him play the guitar transported me into another world. I looked over at my mom who was swaying to the music with one of her best friends, Peggy. They looked younger to me. It was like he took them back in time, and it made me think that mom is going to be okay.

It was unseasonably cold, but we kept warm by dancing the night away. When the band played the song I danced to with my dad shivers went through my body. Not because I was cold from the bitter night, but because I felt like dad was there. I have always connected with other people when I go to a live show, but never with someone who wasn't physically around. It was comforting to know that music is going to be a way for him to make his presence known. I was one of thousands, but at that moment I felt like Neil was singing just for my dad and I.

XO, E

October 14, 2016

Saw my regular oncologist yesterday, and other than my eye, things are about the same in my stomach and colon. We are staying on the same oral medication I have been on since April. Radiation starts soon. Five minutes for 10-14 days. They made a cool mask of my face today and will do mapping via CT scan and my prior MRI. Very scientific and precise. I am in good hands.

Namaste, Jude

October 16, 2016

I saw Neil Young perform in Salt Lake City on a cold autumn evening a couple of weeks ago. It was very chilly, but we were prepared and wore our woolies. Neil was Mike's favorite musician. I felt him with me while I danced like I was a young rocker to Neil who played like he was one. What a magical evening. Neil is almost 70 years old and played for over two hours. I was on the lawn with Erin, Mike, and Peggy. The scent of marijuana surrounded our little group. For two hours, I was my younger, rocker self. I live for these moments, free for just a few hours of doctor's appointments, being stabbed and prodded in places I did not know existed before cancer. I live to be moved by the touch of a beloved friend/patient. I live to know the laughter shared with my daughters and brothers. I live to see yet another full moon rising above the Wasatch. I live to feel tears running down my face when I don't have the strength to face it all again. And then I wake up, get out of bed and remember all that I have to live for. Thank you friends and family for reminding me.

Namaste, Jude

October 22, 2016

Beautiful autumn day here in Utah. I went to our downtown Farmers Market this morning with my friend. Picked up a small carton of heirloom tomatoes that I will take to Erin's tomorrow evening for pumpkin carving and enchilada consuming. I hope she remembers the tequila!

The past month has been a bit stressful health wise. I think I am going to retire January 2017. Maybe work one day a week until I turn 65 in June and am eligible for Medicare. My left eye has been droopy for about a year. I complained to my doc and finally saw an ophthalmologist in August who diagnosed ocular cancer in the muscle behind my eye caused by advanced breast cancer. Treatment consists of 15 five minute zaps of radiation. I wear a custom fitted mask that is fastened to a hard table with cut outs for my nose and eyes. I never thought I was claustrophobic until having to wear this! At least I don't have to do chemo again. I don't really have any pain other than a burning sensation, like when you peel onions, and dry eye. I look like a fucking one eyed jack. Just when I was starting to look somewhat normal after losing all my hair, and now this. This new cancer spread is what caused me to look into retirement. I can claim Mike's social security which will help. Looks like I'll be able to do it financially. Fucking cancer.

Brother John came for a short visit a couple of weeks ago. I think he thought I was going to go blind with this new cancer. We had a lot of fun making Yorkshire Pudding for Erin and Mike with Bisto gravy, and played dominoes until the wine stopped flowing. Brother Phil and family are doing well. The Cleveland Indians baseball team is in the World Series this year. Everyone here and in Cleveland are looking forward to seeing them play. I have to admit I haven't watched any of their games, but will do so now. I think they will be playing the Chicago Cubs.

Hayley is about the same. No worse or no better. She is staying with friends at the moment. Not with me.

Erin, Mike and I went to see Sting's musical, "The Last Ship" performed here in SLC a few weeks ago. The cast had to get a special speech coach to teach them how to speak like a Geordie. I even understood them! My Grandpa was a ship's engineer on the North Sea. We are a hearty lot!

Namaste, Jude

November 4, 2016

Mom still has a black eye from the biopsy. She chooses not to wear a patch anymore, and embraces it. If she sees people stare at her she says something funny like, "you should see the other guy." She really tries to find humor in everything. Her hair is starting to grow back gray, and she gets a lot of compliments. The shorter hair really suits her. She looks great.

She had to get drained again this morning because she has been having a lot of fluid build up. I am not a doctor, but when her ascites has gotten bad in the past it meant the cancer was getting worse. I hope her doctor has another treatment he hasn't tried yet. I can feel her slowly getting worse, but it also seems to have happened so quickly. She has been doing so well, but after experiencing dad's cancer I now know it can spread without warning. It can be a silent killer, and sometimes you don't know how bad it is until it is too late.

XO, E

November 10, 2016

I just completed 14 radiation treatments on my left frontal cortex (eye). Erin told me today she wants to give me a retirement party in January.

A neighbor just came to my door with fresh tomatoes. We have had unseasonably warm temps here. I even have the back door open.

My treatment has been going smoothly, although the docs tell me my eye will be worse before better. I am still working three days a week. Glad to be off the next few days.

John sent me the itinerary for our cruise. They want to leave Seattle on Aug 5 on Princess Cruise Line ship Ruby Princess and book a mini suite w/ balcony. They have a few ideas for the land tours and are still looking at hotels before and after the cruise. I really needed some cheering up.

Namaste, Jude

November 14, 2016

Mom's social worker, Angela has been one of her biggest support systems. They have become so close, she even invited mom to her very small wedding. A local news channel asked Angela if she knew of a patient they could interview for a segment about cancer, and Angela asked mom to do it. Mom gladly said yes. She called me today to see if I had any pointers about being on TV. She was a little nervous, but I knew she was going to do a great job. It is hard not to like mom. She is fun, outgoing, and very easy to talk to. She wants to tell her story, hoping it will help others who are going through a tough time. She is one of the most unselfish, and caring people I know.

XO, E

November 18, 2016

Mom had to get drained again before her appointment today. I thought her doctor would be more concerned about her swollen belly, but since her tumor markers are only going up a little, he didn't seemed too worried. He said he may change her treatment if her tumor markers continue to rise, but he wants to wait to see. I am very confused. She has needed to go in weekly to get drained! I wish they would look at symptoms as well as tumor markers. I can understand why they feel like they are a good way to determine what treatment mom undergoes, but they aren't the only thing to determine if the cancer is growing, and mom is very, very sick. She can't eat much because her stomach hurts so badly. When she does eat, she can hardly keep anything down. It is unlike mom to not want to eat, and she is starting to lose more and more weight every week. I expressed my concerns to her doctor, but he is sticking to the regimen. I have a very bad feeling about all of this. I know my mom better than he does. Why isn't he listening to us?

XO, E

November 19, 2016

I just got back from making magic wands with some lady friends of mine. We get together once a month to create and support each other. My wand is infused with healing magic.

Mame just called me to go out onto the porch to see the vibrant, pink sunset. I can see west and around the corner to the east. What a nice end to this day.

Most everything is the same here. I hate to talk about my health, other than to say I am still here, and enjoying what life has to offer. Looking forward to taking more classes, reading and writing when I retire. Life feels good today at this very moment.

Namaste, Jude

November 24, 2016

We were invited to go to my cousin's house again for Thanksgiving. I am so grateful to have family we can spend the holidays with, but it still doesn't feel right to not be at dad's house. I shed a few tears over my oatmeal while watching the big balloons fly over 32nd street in NYC. Dad and I always watched the parade together while getting the house ready for guests. Mom called while we were on our walk to tell me she was thinking about not going because she can't eat much. It broke my heart to hear that she didn't want to offend anyone. They are family and know her situation. I assured her that everyone would want her to be there whether she ate anything or not, and I was right. The family was so happy we all came. Even Hayley was there!

My cousin has three young girls who absolutely love mom. They surrounded her with hugs as we walked in. One of her girls is learning how to play the piano, and she was very excited to perform her most recent recital piece. Listening to her softly play the ivory keys reminded me of when I was her age, and just realizing how magical playing an instrument can be. Being able to create something so wonderful is like no other feeling. You can affect the way someone feels just by the notes you play. It is an art form that connects people like no other medium can, and being able to do that is beautiful. After a standing ovation she asked me to play. Her eyes widened as she watched my fingers move quickly up and down the keyboard. It was comforting to see someone so young appreciate music as much as I do. Whether I am playing it, or listening to it live, getting lost in the music is such a great escape for me. I used to think music was a distraction, but it is more than that. Distractions are momentary, while escapes help me heal.

XO, E

December 15, 2016

I have been struggling lately with nausea and vomiting. Saw my oncologist today, and he feels the cancer in my stomach is progressing. Time to get the big guns out again. I will start weekly chemo on December 30. At least, I will be retired by then!

Namaste, Jude

December 17, 2016

I had an early Christmas present yesterday. I found a huge puddle of water in my basement laundry room the other day. My home was built in 1943 which means galvanized pipes. I called my neighbor, and he proceeded to investigate that it was the washing machine. Well, turns out it was my tenant's shower that was backing up from a clogged drain. My neighbor called another neighbor for reinforcements. They spent the entire afternoon fixing it, and even replaced my tenant's bathroom faucet which was leaking also. The only payment they would take was shortbread cookies. Why would I ever want to live anywhere else?

Namaste, Jude

December 18, 2016

Since mom has been feeling pretty tired lately I offered to host cookie making this year. Our new kitchen also has plenty of room for flour fights. As I was tying grandma's red apron around my waist I thought this could be the last year I will be making cookies with mom. I tried to push it out of my head by thinking mom was going to get over this. It was just another hiccup in her road to beating this terrible disease. I didn't want such a negative energy to be around on such a special day, but all of the happy thoughts couldn't get rid of the idea that this could be her last Christmas. I need to make it as special as I can.

I hung fresh green garland around the house, and placed Christmas decorations passed down from the family in every nook and cranny I could find. When mom walked in she oohed and aahed at how pretty everything was. Christmas Carols were playing, and a cup of her favorite tea was waiting for her on the counter. The afternoon was spent by dancing while making mom's famous press cookies. It is something I look forward to every year. She used to do it with her mom, and continued the tradition with her daughters. I only hope that if I have a child, they will enjoy this tradition as much as we do. It will be a way for me to bring mom into my child's life when she is no longer with us.

XO, E

December 20, 2016

I have been struggling with writing an obituary for myself, and wonder if I should reach out to my writing teacher at Hunstman to see if she would consider doing such a class. I am retiring in January, but may work on

Tuesdays depending on my health. I will be available for her Wednesday writing classes. Excited about that!

Namaste, Jude

December 24, 2016

Eating fondue with the Leibsla's on Christmas Eve has become a wonderful tradition. I am lucky to have such amazing in-laws who open their door to my mom and sister. Barb and my mom have known each other since they went to high school in Ohio. When Barb and Mel moved to Utah they spent a lot of time with my mom and dad. Mike and I even have a picture of us kissing on his first birthday! We didn't know our parents knew each other until our third date. Mike's parents tried to set us up a month prior, but I wasn't interested. It wasn't until I met him on my own that we decided to start dating. When we found out our parents were friends long ago we figured it was destiny.

Mom still isn't eating much, but wanted to spend time with us. I am so glad she came. It wouldn't have been the same without her and her tradition of bringing the British Christmas crackers. We ate dinner, drank champagne and then Mel surprised us all with gifts. He even got something for mom and Hayley. I am looking forward to waking up to a white Christmas tomorrow morning.

XO, E

December 25, 2016

Mike, Bella, and I woke up to a winter wonderland outside. It snowed all night, and continued to snow most of the day. We got to mom's just in time for us to help finish making brunch. Mom's house is so cozy, it is easy to relax there, and although she is so sick she is still an amazing hostess. After some much needed time at mom's, Mike and I went home to cook a Christmas feast for the family. Mom came, but when it was time to eat dinner she made her way to the door. I was close behind, worried that something was wrong. She said, "I am going to leave because I still can't eat. Brunch was already too much for me." Christmas was hard enough not having dad or Hayley there, so I begged her to stay by saying, "Please stay. I would like to have at least one parent here to celebrate." Tears came to her eyes as she smiled and nodded her head before giving me a big hug. She didn't eat, but had a little bit of champagne to make a toast with. She left shortly after and said, "thank you for making Christmas so nice for me this year. I know you put a lot of effort into it and I appreciate everything you did." I wanted mom to have a great Christmas in case it is her last. I am so happy she did.

XO, E

December 27, 2016

I am sitting in my living room, morning sun streaming through. Two elderly dogs on either side of me. My neighbors asked me to dog sit their elderly terrier mix for a week. At first I grumbled to myself, but I am reminded dog love times two is a good thing. Christmas Eve and day were filled with daughter love and laughter. Feeling so much gratitude in my life. Even though we are not close physically I feel my mom so profoundly sometimes. I could swear she so close to me. 2017 is upon us. I want to lay down underneath the Redwoods while I am still standing. I hope I can make it happen.

Namaste, Jude

December 31, 2016

We stopped by mom's to have a toast with her before meeting friends to celebrate a new year. She was already in her robe and slippers when we arrived. Mike popped open the bottle of champagne while I went to get some shot glasses. She is still very sick, but said she wanted to have a teensy, tiny bit to celebrate 2016 coming to an end. It was another tough year for all of us, especially the last few months. Mom has gone downhill, and it seems to be accelerating. I hope she can recover from this and 2017 will be one of her best years yet! Cheers!

XO, E

December 31, 2016

Mom pulled me aside to tell me she was going to stop chemo. I was sitting next to her, nodding out from all of the heroin I had just smoked. I snapped out of my delirium to her voice saying, "sometimes I wish I was addicted to heroin." I looked at her with confusion and said "why?!" She then stated "I just want to run away. I don't want to feel the hurt and the pain that this life can bring, I understand why you get high honey." That shocked me. She has hated me in my addiction, she used to tell me that she felt like I had left to a deserted island and had never returned. And here we sat; a mother succumbed by a disease with no cure, and a daughter consumed by a disease of the mind, with no hope. Here we sat, soaking in the pain, together. The unconditional love she has for me blows me away. Here she is, dying from a terminal disease, and she could care less what state I was in. She could care less of the unimaginable things I had done to betray her throughout the years. She simply just wanted me next to her. Her space was my space, we were one. Unconditional love, what a beautiful gift to be given. I can't imagine my life without her. I felt so betrayed when she told me she wants to give up, but after I thought about it some more, I realized how courageous she is to make that decision. For her to choose death over living. I know I have to do what I can to be there for her.

-Hayz

2017

In spirit, sitting next to my bed.
In her favorite green chair.
"There are fairies at the bottom of our garden,"
I whisper again and again.
Like a mantra bringing me home.

January 2, 2017

Mom has needed to be drained weekly, if not twice a week. It is extremely uncomfortable for her, so the doctor suggested they install a pump inside her stomach. A nurse taught me how to use mom's fancy new belly while I took a video. I may not be around to drain her every time, so having an instructional video will help. Mom seemed to be in good spirits on our drive home, but I couldn't shake the terrible feeling overtaking my body. Mom doesn't have the gumption she once had. I have been able to tell something is wrong, but can't pin point exactly what it is.

Bella was happy to see me when I arrived home, but not even Bella could help with the way I was feeling. I walked inside, dropped my bags, leaned against the counter, and stared at the wall for what seemed like hours. All of a sudden I started to bawl. I was crying so hard, my legs gave away, and I slowly slid to the cold floor. I sat there, holding my knees to my chest, and wept. I know I need to feel what I need to feel to get through this, but it hurts so badly sometimes. After everything mom has been through, I still want her to fight. She is the strongest person I know. It was selfish for me to think this way, but I don't want to lose her.

When the tears stopped, I sat on the floor and continued to stare at the blank wall. I just wanted to sit, and do nothing. I started to think about our relationship with time. It is one of the most difficult things to get back when we need it, yet we tend to take it for granted when we're not thinking about it. To say that my heart is breaking all over again, much like it did a few years ago would be an understatement. I selfishly want more time. More time for mom to do all her favorite things. To experience belly laughs with her friends. To sleep under the stars. To bring more beauty to the world by planting flowers. To walk around the park with Carol. To taste the indulgent sweetness of her favorite desserts. To listen to live music. To visit places she has always wanted to go. To see

Hayley get better. To watch me become a mom, and just more time to be together.

When Mike came home I was still upset. He wasn't being very understanding, and became defensive, which led to a huge fight. It was bad enough mom was so sick. Fighting with him made a bad day even worse. I am sure these last couple years have been hard for him. In the three years we have been married I have lost a parent, tried to help my heroin addicted sister, and watch another parent slowly deteriorate. I don't know how I would react if I was in his position, but I would like to think I would be there for him when he needed me. I have told him what I need from him, and he can't give it to me. Today was one of the harder days. What I needed was a hug, not for him to fight back. I really hope we can make our marriage work. We have come so far in only a few short years and have so much more to look forward to.

XO, E

January 5, 2017

Happy New Year!!! Belated. Excited for a change! No matter how crappy my mom feels she still finds the energy to take goofy pictures and laugh with me. Gotta love her!

-Hayz

January 7, 2017

I am very worried because mom went to the hospital with terrible stomach pains today. Carol stayed with her most of the day. Since her tumor markers are up the doctors are keeping her overnight. I stopped by on my way home from work to make sure she was doing okay. She has lost so much weight these past few weeks she doesn't look like herself. I stayed for a few hours before running home to get ready for Lexi's wedding. I couldn't miss one of my best friend's weddings, and of course mom understood.

Lexi was glowing, and Cole looked incredibly happy. Lexi's family treats Mike and I like we are part of their own. Both Lexi and her sister are pregnant with their first children, so there was a lot to celebrate. I love to see my friend's living their lives, but I can't help but think that that their world is spinning, while mine feels like it is standing still.

XO, E

January 10, 2017

I am having a difficult time with treatment and trying to keep my head above water.

Suicide would be

an easy way to escape

the pain of living.

A daughter addicted,

No end in sight.

Endless cancer treatment.

My end sooner than later.

What is there to live for?

This life offers me nothing.

What is the best way to die?

Stop taking the cancer meds.

No more treatment.

Aha......

Namaste, Jude

January 12, 2017

Mom made an appointment with her doctor to talk to him about what her options are. She asked for both Mike and I to join her. We were getting ready to pick her up when she called to tell us she cancelled her appointment. She asked us to come over to talk instead. When we walked inside I immediately had a bad feeling. Mom's house has always been a safe haven for me, so I knew something was up when a pit started to form in my stomach. Sophie led us to mom, who was sitting on her sofa in her favorite blue fleece pullover with a forlorn look on her face. It was almost like she learned someone had died. Mike, Hayley, I cuddled with her on the sofa. She gently grasped my hand with her cold, clammy fingers and squeezed it a little tighter when she said, "I met with my doctor this morning." A black tear started rolling down her cheek, "he told me that they have tried everything. I can continue chemo, but it's not working like they had hoped. My life will be prolonged a few months if I choose to go forward with more infusions, but because my quality of life is terrible, I told the doctor I am ready to stop treatment." She took a big breath before saying, "they predict that I have 3-4 months left to live." We were all shocked. My heart dropped as it passed the large pit in my stomach. I burst out into an ugly cry, full of dry heaving and tears. When Mike pleaded for her to talk to the doctor again She yelled, "I have fucking cancer," before breaking down into tears herself. Hayley ran over to hug her while I held her hand, and we continued to cry as a family. I told her I respect her decision, and I will be there for whatever she needs. We will all get through this.

Mike and I didn't know what to say on the drive home. We were expecting to go to the hospital to find out what options mom had, not for her to tell us she only had a few months to live! Mom has battled this disease for so long, and was so optimistic until now. It is the first time I have seen her surrender to the cancer that was eventually going to end her life too early. She deserves so much and I love her, I think more than I ever had at this vulnerable moment in our lives. Even though I am extremely upset, I will continue to be her rock until the very end. I need to give in to what she wants so she can navigate the rest of her journey on her terms.

XO, E

January 13, 2017

Sad news. I have stopped treatment and will be entering hospice ASAP.

Namaste, Jude

January 21, 2017

This is the first weekend of the Sundance Film Festival. Because I don't want to be gone from mom for a long period of time, the only thing I agreed to cover was the Women's March in Park City. It actually ended up being one of the most publicized marches in the country because of Sundance. There are a lot of celebrities in town, and several of them marched with the locals. We woke up to several feet of new snow, which continued to fall throughout the day. Thousands of people were there. They didn't seem to care about the cold, or that the snow wasn't letting up. They weren't going to let a little bad weather stop their voices from being heard.

I spoke to:

Two women who were marching because they want to bring awareness to the issues. They were there to represent minority women, and to show their children how important it is to make your voice heard.

A group of three young ladies who said they were marching to let people know they won't back down.

A transperson who is worried about their rights under the new administration. They wanted to show support to everyone for the various causes they feel strongly about.

A woman who braved the weather in her wheelchair. She was by herself, but felt safe to be there. She knew it was a place others would help her if she needed it, which they did. She wanted to attend because she believes in inclusion, and wanted to make sure that message is carried on.

A man marching with his mom. He said he is the only child of a single mother, and his mom told him if we don't support the rights of women then what do we have?

A young woman who said she is proud to be an American, and a lesbian. She told me that it felt great to be with people who believe in the same things she does.

A mom of 4 daughters marched with her family. She marched to show her daughters that there are people who still stand for positive values. Loving people, accepting people, and not propagating hate.

As I watched the large group slowly walk away, chanting, and holding signs I noticed a young girl standing on one of the balconies above. Tears pierced my eyes when I heard her let out a loud squeal when she saw the sea of pink hats below. I was so busy interviewing people I hadn't given myself the chance to be present, and realize what I was a part of. So many people from different backgrounds, showing up for themselves, and each other, looking so strong and wanting to make a difference. It was a day I will always remember.

XO, E

January 23, 2017

Today was the SLC women's march. It was snowing terribly hard again, but I was set on going. Mom really wanted to join me even though she felt horrible. When I picked her up she told me she had just taken a sip of lemonade. She was craving it, hoping it would stay down. As we were driving through the storm she asked me to pull over so she could throw it up. I rubbed her back as she held her head into the falling snow. I felt terrible. She is so sick she can't even keep a sip of lemonade down. I asked her if she wanted me to take her home. She paused for a moment to think and said in a determined tone, "no, I want to go."

When we neared the Capitol building the traffic had come to a halt. Since we couldn't move many drivers got out of their cars and walked over to where all of the commotion was. We decided to do the same. Mom held onto my arm as we walked slowly through the snow to the crowd ahead. Her eyes lit up when she heard the sounds of people chanting. She was so excited she practically pulled me to the crowd of pink hats. She wasn't well enough to march, but we were able to cheer, and clap on the sidelines. One of Hayley's friends from elementary school ran up to us to give mom a big hug. She was wearing a pussy beanie she knitted and gave it to mom to wear. Mom immediately pulled the pink knitted beanie over her salt and pepper hair. She doesn't have much energy these days, but she was giving it her all out there. Her cheers were louder than anyone around us. She was so happy. I am grateful I could share such a special moment with the woman I admire the most. I march for her.

XO, E

January 24, 2017

I unfortunately have to work the next few days. Mom is so weak I don't want her to be alone, so I made an online schedule for friends and family to help while I am gone. The time slots quickly filled up. Her friends are determined to help make her last days some of the best days. Mom's house is full of things she loves. Friends, flowers, photos with loved ones, notes of encouragement, dogs, books and music. She seems very happy. Cancer is a mixed bag. The bad news is it ravages one body like a force of nature that can't be bothered to stop. The good news, cancer shows you who loves you the most and just how much.

XO, E

January 26, 2017

Mom fell today, and I was so high I couldn't help her. She was screaming for help, but since I was nodded out from heroin, I didn't hear her. One of her friends who was scheduled to be there with her woke me up. I broke down crying. I felt worthless. I don't understand why I can't be there for mom. Heroin rules my life so much that I can't be there for the one person I care about the most. I ran out of the house with Carol right behind me. She grabbed my shoulder and asked what I was doing. I told her I don't know. I don't know how to get better. I was so embarrassed I left to go get high. The drugs numb the pain.

-Hayz

January 28, 2017

Carol has been with mom 24/7. The only time she leaves her side is to get something to eat or change her clothes. On this day, most of the family was able to visit. The youngest of my cousin's daughters, Elise took the time to have a little chat with mom. She wasn't scared of the weak woman who was next to her. She expressed no judgment, she only had empathy. Children can sometimes understand what adults have forgotten. As life goes on we can get shut down and forget how wonderful it is to love. To love freely, without expectations. Elise reminded me of that. She adores mom and didn't ask for anything in return for her love.

After everyone left, I put my head on the pillow next to mom's. We were both exhausted from all of the visitors. I asked her if there was anything she wanted to tell me or talk about. I wasn't able to ask dad before he left, and didn't want to make the same mistake with mom. She whispered "I love you and I want you to be happy" before drifting off to sleep. I don't know what I wanted to hear. I don't want to be selfish, but I wish she had more to tell me during what could be our last moment alone together. I held her cold hand as I realized things weren't going back to normal, whatever normal is. We have spent years believing she would be a miracle, and have repeatedly recited the lyrics from the song, "Three Little Birds" (aka "Don't Worry About a Thing") Bob Marley was singing to me on mom's old CD player. I wanted to believe Mr. Marley so badly, but at that moment I couldn't. I don't know what I am going to do without my mom. If she is gone I just can't believe that everything is going to be alright.

XO, E

January 29, 2017

Life goes on around me. I am on an observation deck. Far above the business of everyday life. A bystander of the mundane.

When I die. What then? Nothing will change. People will be lost in business worrying about nonsense.

What mark will I leave? A heart, a peace sign or a flower? What is my epitaph?

Here lies a woman who laughed. Will my ashes contain stardust? Will they shimmer? My ashes will be tossed to fly with the soft night wind. A little girl will catch one blinking it away with her eyelashes. She knows I paved the way for her. My path is hers.

Namaste, Jude

January 29, 2017

Carol stayed with mom all night. She didn't get much sleep because she and mom stayed up laughing and talking. Since I am off work I stopped the coming and going of friends. Mom has started to grow tired because of so many visitors. Her contagious laugh isn't as loud as it once was. She sleeps most of the day, and can hardly walk. Her body is starting to weaken, but I believe her spirit is becoming stronger. She is preparing herself to take the next step. In the last few days she has written poems, talked with friends and listened to her favorite music. I feel like it is her way to slowly say goodbye to her old life, in preparation for a new one.

XO, E

January 29, 2017

Mom has decided to stop treatment, which includes chemotherapy. We all wish she could live forever, because she is such a rare soul who has touched so many lives. Unfortunately, she has made up her mind. And I know some people may think that she is giving up, but I challenge you to realize that this is the most courageous thing I have seen my mom do. She is by far the bravest person I have ever met. Sadly, as we thought she would have more time, she isn't doing well. All I ask for now, is prayers, good vibes, whatever you believe in, that she may pass peacefully and however much longer she may have, that it's not filled with pain.

Also, take this a reminder to live every day like it's your last, like my mom did. No matter what she was doing she was having fun. We will miss you terribly.

Love you. Mom.

-Hayz

January 30, 2017

Mike and I slept in the same bed as mom last night to make sure she was okay. I was surprisingly comfortable in the middle. It was nice to have two of the people I love the most on either side of me. I didn't get much sleep because I wanted to be awake in case mom needed something. I spent the night thinking about her, and everything she had been through the last few years. Cancer, a broken ankle, a daughter struggling with addiction, the passing of her ex husband, and little stressors that don't seem so important after going through so many life changing events. She has been so positive and optimistic there would be a miracle, and that somehow she would win her battle with cancer. She has shown me that even if you are going through a tough time, the best way to cope is to embrace it, put a smile on, and fight the good fight, no matter how hard. I knew mom was going to be gone soon, and I was never going to be ready, but it wasn't the first time I lost a parent to cancer. This time was going to be different in a lot of ways, but I took comfort in knowing I had gotten through it before. I will hopefully be able to do it again with as much grace as I did the first time.

My thoughts were interrupted by a soft touch of mom's hand. I turned my head to look into her big hazel eyes glistening in the light from the rising sun outside the window. She smiled at me while interlocking her fingers with mine. With her last ounce of energy she said "I will always be here. I may not be in person, but I will be with you. When you feel butterflies in your stomach, know that is me telling you everything will be okay. Love is at the very center of life. It is the only thing that I get to take with me, and it is making it easier for me to leave this life. It's time for me to go; my mom is here to guide me home. Just like I will be there to show you the way when it is your turn." I nestled my head into her shoulder while she held me one last time. Her words broke my heart, but her touch made me feel at peace. I don't want her to be in pain any longer. My breath matched hers as I fell asleep on her chest, just like I did when I was a little girl.

Mike woke me by gently kissing me on the forehead before heading to work. I wasn't going to leave mom's side. She slept while I read, and took in the sounds of her favorite music playing in the background. We had listened to a lot of Bob Marley, The Beatles, Leonard Cohen and Willie Nelson the last few days. Music is her therapy too. It helps transport us to a place immune to anything nature can throw at us, even cancer. Mame stopped by on her way to work to check in. She whispered something in mom's ear, and gave her a soft kiss on the cheek before leaving. Hayley was there as well, but stayed in her room except to use the bathroom. It was good to see the hospice nurse when she arrived, but I could tell something was wrong when she slowly closed the doors to mom's room. I noticed her eyes full of tears when she turned to look at me and say "the end is near." My body hurt, and I was having trouble breathing. I called Mike once she walked out the periwinkle door mom was so proud of painting just a few months prior. I could hardly speak because I couldn't believe what was happening. I didn't want to put it out into the universe, so I didn't say anything, but I also didn't need to. Mike already knew and simply said, "I will be right there." I slowly walked into mom's room to sit with her. We listened to Willie Nelson while watching the shadows from the trees dancing from outside. I felt like they were putting on a show just for us and served as a reminder that light dances with the shadows.

When I heard the dogs get excited a sense of relief took over my body. Mike was back! Hayley walked in a few minutes later to let us know she was getting in the shower. I felt like I was scolding her when I told her, "no!" But I had to be firm. She would regret washing her hair over being there when mom passed. She grabbed her favorite blanket, and gently placed her head on the pillow next to mom. We quietly sang along to the sounds of Willie Nelson playing, "Just Breathe" softly in the background. The song seemed fitting because mom's breathing started to become inconsistent. It was like Willie was reminding us all to breathe. I was holding mom's hand when she suddenly opened her eyes, and took one last gasp of air as a single tear rolled down her cheek. I closed my eyes, hoping it wasn't real, but I couldn't stop the tears from gushing out from underneath my tightly shut eyelids, like water escaping a dam. Between cries I softly whispered, "I love you" into her ear before putting my head onto her chest one last time. I needed to feel the familiar comfort before her body was taken from me. The body that birthed me, fed me and held me. The body that was lucky enough to be the home to my mother's unique soul. Her soul has now been disembodied, but we share a love that cannot be destroyed. I know she will show me she is around in ways only

I will know. I promise myself to be open to those signs and learn new ways to connect with her. My greatest fear was losing both my parents, but the last few years have taught me I will never be alone. I will have guidance, protection and love from above, and have the best guardian angels a girl could ask for.

XO, E

January 30, 2017

Mom passed peacefully this morning, and I am a wreck. I went in the backyard and screamed after she took her last breath. I don't know what to do. It is all so surreal. No one has prepared me for a loss like this. No one has told me how to feel or behave. I feel utterly alone. Could I have done more to save her? Was she really gone? I am angry at the world. I am inconsolable. I am broken. I am lost.

-Hayz

January 31, 2017

When I looked into the mirror this morning the first thing I noticed were my eyes at half mast. They were still so swollen from crying the day before. Everything that happened after mom passed was a blur. I was in such a dreamlike state I wasn't able to take it all in. Almost like I didn't want to remember the traumatic events that had just occurred 24 hours earlier. I was sure there was something important I needed to remember, so I closed my eyes, hoping it would help jog my memory. Visions of the pastor coming to the front door started to appear. We were able to be alone with her for about an hour, until he arrived. He had no idea of her passing. He was there to check on her, and to talk to her about the celebration of life, not console us. I figured it was a good time for us to talk about the arrangements she already had planned, so I went right into management mode as we planned her celebration. I couldn't imagine walking into a situation like he did with so much grace and empathy.

Uncle Phil and Aunt Becky arrived shortly after the pastor left. They traveled from Ohio to spend some time with her. I felt terrible that they weren't able to see her when she was awake, but I am happy they were able to say their goodbyes before her body was taken to the University of Utah hospital. Mom asked that her body be donated to science. She had such a rare form of cancer; she hoped that donating her body would help find a cure. Aunt Marcia and Uncle Kent came over shortly after to bring dinner for all of us while Hayley went to be with friends. I figured Hayley leaving to be with friends was the part of the day that upset me, until I remember seeing mom's body being wheeled out on a gurney. When I saw her I put my hands over my eyes and buried my head into Mike's chest like I was a little girl, shielding myself from a horror film. I have seen similar scenes in movies, but I never thought I would have to watch it in real life. I sat straight up, suddenly opened my eyes and let out a loud gasp as tears soaked my cheeks once again.

XO, E

February 1, 2017

I spent the day looking over mom's finances. I had to cancel her credit cards, look into her social security, retirement and more. On top of everything I am planning the celebration of life. Which has been easy, but it is another thing I need to do. In the middle of the day Peg stopped by to make sure I was doing okay. I didn't have any makeup on, and hadn't really gotten dressed for the day, but she didn't seem to care. It was really great to see her. She is like a mother to me. Shortly after Peg left I heard the doorbell ring again. When I opened the door I was surprised to see Mame standing there with bags full of groceries. I have been in such a fog I haven't been grocery shopping, or have the energy to think about what we are going to eat. I haven't had an appetite, and honestly don't remember when I ate last. It was very thoughtful for her to think of us, and reminding me that I need to eat. She is another woman who is like a mother to me.

The celebration of life is a few days away. I still need to finish mom's obituary among other things. I asked Uncle John to write the eulogy. He was planning on coming to town to read it at the celebration, but he called me today to let me know he isn't going to be able to make it because he is ill. He is going to send his three children, Dan, Kevin and Donna in his place. He and mom grew very close over the past few years. It's only right that he reads it. While I was going over the itinerary I came up with the idea that he record it, and send it to me. He is going to record it at his friends studio tonight.

That night Mike and I opened up a bottle of wine to give us some liquid courage to look through old photos of mom for the in memoriam video Troy is putting together. I loved going through the boxes full of photos of her throughout her life. She had such a wonderful childhood. She was the youngest of three, and they did everything as a family. We found several photos of them at the lake, ice skating, and sailing. She looked so happy, especially when she was with her dad. I have heard people wait to die on a day that means something to them. Grandpa died January 30th, two years ago. Mom was such a daddy's girl I can't help but think her passing on the same day as he did was not just a coincidence.

Mom thought she was going to have months, not weeks left to live. During those months she and I planned on going through these photographs together. I would have loved to have known what she remembered of the moments frozen in time. It was nice to have Mike there with me, but it wasn't the same. Hayley was invited to come over, but declined my offer. Not being able to look through photos of our mom together breaks my heart. It is a night I cherished, and it would have meant a lot more having her there.

XO, E

February 4, 2017

Mike and I woke up to the first sunny day we have had in weeks. Even though we had a lot to do we didn't want to give up our daily walk with Bella. It is therapeutic for all of us, and if there was a day to take a walk this would be one of them. The wind blowing in the branches composed a song for us as we strolled along the sidewalks. We ran into a dear friend, Christopher who didn't know mom passed. When he asked us what our plans were for the day I looked at Mike because I didn't know what to say. It was still so surreal. As Mike told him the story, tears welled up in his eyes. He gave me a huge hug before walking a lap with us. He is a very spiritual person, just like mom. It was meant to be that we saw him today. He helped get a hard day off to a great start.

We ordered food for the celebration from mom's favorite bakery. As we were leaving a young woman came running from the back to hand me a little paper bag. She smiled, gave me a hug and whispered that she was sorry in my ear. Tears came to my eyes as I told her thank you before rushing out the door. When I sat down in the car I looked inside the bag she gave me and was surprised to see my favorite cookies. I squealed in delight. Sometimes the littlest gestures can be the ones we need the most. Acts of kindness come in all shapes and sizes. It could be smiling at someone on the street, a generous tip to a server, or a financial donation to your favorite charity. There is no right or wrong way to show up for others. The important thing is showing up at all. Your little act of kindness might just make someone's day.

When we arrived at the church we were pleasantly surprised to see the tables set up with the goddesses ready to help. Hayley hadn't shown or answered her phone. I was very worried, but had so much to do I couldn't leave to find her. After about an hour she finally called to tell me she was going to be late due to a bloody nose. A bloody nose? I thought. I told her to come either way. She needed to be there. The thought about her not attending mom's celebration made me want to cry, but I took a deep breath, held my shoulders high, and kept going. This was not a time for me to break down because of Hayley. Next thing I knew I heard, "I can pick her up." It was the voice of one of Hayley's best friends, Lydia who had just overheard our conversation. I was so relieved. I said "yes, please!" as she grabbed her coat and ran out the door. Lydia has been such an amazing friend to Hayley through everything. She even came to family night at her rehab facility a couple times. Hayley is lucky to have a friend like her.

At 11:10 the pastor asked if I wanted to wait any longer for Hayley. The celebration was scheduled to start at 11, and since I hadn't heard from her yet I told him to go ahead, hoping she would arrive soon. I was blown away at how many people were inside the chapel. Since the pews were full many people had to stand. Mom's coworkers, patients, neighbors, friends, family (including Uncle Bill and Lafe who both took last minute flights to be there) attended. The celebration was beautiful. It began with a couple singing one of her favorite songs, "In My Life" by The Beatles. The pastor spoke, and read one of mom's poems. The next song was "Hallelujah" by mom's boyfriend, Leonard Cohen before the eulogy was read over the speaker system in Uncle John's voice. I tried to take it all in, but I had a hard time being present because I was worried about Hayley. She still wasn't there. After the eulogy the couple sang, "Three Little Birds" by Bob Marley. Hayley opened the door hesitantly as they began the second chorus. Her shoulders were hunched over as she slowly walked in with Lydia close behind. She looked so defeated. I wanted to run to her to give her a big hug, but I waited until she sat down next to me. I gently squeezed her leg, signaling that I was happy she was there. She placed her head on my shoulder as her tears fell onto my navy blue dress. The service concluded with "Hey Jude" by the Beatles. By the end of the song the entire chapel was singing the chorus and clapping along. My stomach started to tighten, but it wasn't the usual feeling of anxiety or stress I have felt so often, it was a comforting feeling; it was mom. In that instant I could feel her in the room with us and my heart was full of happiness. Tears slowly traveled down my cheeks as a chill went through my body when I looked back at the crowd of friends and family, standing and singing. Mom would have loved everything about it. She wanted us to celebrate, and we did just that.

It's hard to believe mom is gone. She is a rare soul who has touched so many lives. While working as a dental hygienist for 45 years she loved her coworkers and her patients. Mom had a special way of making people smile and putting them at ease. She lived her life to the very fullest. She was a social butterfly and had more friends than anyone could hope to have in their lifetime. She loved the arts, the outdoors, music, gardening, writing poetry and being with her loved ones. Taking time to enjoy her beautiful flowers in her backyard with her dogs, her family and friends was one of her favorite things to do. Her infectious laugh could be heard blocks away, and it made everyone smile once they heard it.

Mom was a fighter, courageous and very strong. So many people didn't know she was sick because she rarely complained, and never let cancer rule her life. She was so positive and optimistic there would be a miracle that somehow she would win her battle with cancer. She taught us that even if you are going through a tough time the best way to cope is to embrace it, put on a smile, and fight the good fight no matter how hard. Our endless laughs, cleansing tears, shared travels and much more will be missed, however her bright light will be carried on forever. ONE LOVE

XO, E

February 4, 2017

The day I have been dreading is finally here. It's mom's celebration of life. I was a mess. I couldn't get ready. I couldn't move. I was numb. Lydia was blowing up my phone. She said she wouldn't go without me, so she met me at moms, and literally got me dressed. I was crying uncontrollably as she put pulled my tights over my legs. I felt like a child. She drove me to the church, and we were very late. My sister saved me a seat. Lydia sat next to me while the celebration ended. At the reception it was nice to see mom's friends, but I was ready to get back to the hotel so I could be alone and sleep.

-Hayz

February 5, 2017

In the middle of everything, our tenant at the other house had moved out, so we needed to do a walk through. The house was in terrible shape! She left clothes, personal belongings, and lots of trash all over the property. The place was filthy, and she allowed her dogs to pee in the rooms, so the carpets reeked of urine. There were beer cans and cigarette butts all over the backyard, and chicken bones in the dishwasher. We started cleaning up the house to get it ready for an open house as soon as possible. After being there for a few hours, we went to mom's house to figure out what to do next. At this point in time, we have our first house, our house, and now mom's house to take care of. It has already been a lot of work, so I am not sure if we can keep all three. Mike is handy, and I am organized, but it has already been very overwhelming. I really want to keep mom's house for Hayley, but I don't know if we can make it work.

XO, E

February 6, 2017

Cleaning out someone's house after they pass is hard. Not only because every little thing from a penny found on the ground to a family heirloom reminds you of them, but also because you can feel like you are trespassing on their life. Them being gone doesn't mean they give us permission to ransack through their belongings like an intruder, but it's something that has to be done. I have learned to try to put my emotions to the side because if I don't I will want to keep everything. It is all a piece of mom, and I don't want to give any of her away.

When I opened her nightstand I was surprised there wasn't much inside. Just a flashlight, ibuprofen, a journal, a couple books, and an old letter. I was confused as to why there was an envelope with a piece of creased, off white paper coming out of it. What letter would mom have kept so close to her? As I carefully unfolded the blue lined paper I slowly fell to the floor. It was a note she had sent to her mom a month after I was born. In her perfect cursive handwriting she wrote,

Dear Mum,

I thought since Mother's Day is approaching, and that you're probably feeling a little miserable coping with shingles that I would send you this letter. I know that I look a lot like you, but more than that especially since I have become a mother of a sweet little girl. I'm so grateful to you for teaching me how to appreciate my family, nature, friends, and so many little things. I hope that Erin and I have that kind of relationship. I hope that she thinks of me as forever young because that's how I think of you. Now that you've probably shed a few tears, I'm sorry if I upset you, but I wanted you to know how much I know you love me the same way.

Well enough mushy stuff, Erin is my left arm as I write this. She's been such a good baby lately. We've really been enjoying her.

I've come down with a cold, but not as bad as Mike's flu was. Erin seems fine. I hope she doesn't get my cold. I'm still breastfeeding her, but give her formula in preparation for work. She's had no oral reactions from the formula, and it gives Mike an opportunity to feed her.

Well, Mike is coming home for lunch soon and a girlfriend is stopping by with her two kids, so I better get moving. Hope you're doing better.

Love, Judi

I placed the piece of mom in my lap and let tears stream down my face. I wept because I was grateful to have such amazing parents who loved me more than anything, but I also cried because they are gone. I don't know if I will ever have the feeling my mom had when she held me in her arms, but reading her letter made me want to have a child more than ever. I want to love someone like she loved me. Being a mother to Hayley and I came naturally to her, and she made sure to tell us she loved us every chance she got. She taught us our love for nature, family, friends and to not sweat the small stuff just like she said she wanted in this letter. But what I will always be grateful to my mother for is helping me find my inner strength I didn't know I had, and to be a warrior in moments I didn't know I could be. I cherish the bond I had with her. She is here and always will be. I know that.

XO, E

February 6, 2017

Grant and I had just picked up a copious amount of heroin and meth. In our cracked out stupor, we thought people were after us. I had accidentally left the drugs in the car, which is a paranoid tweaker's worse nightmare. Grant asked me to run out to get them while he watched my back. He grabbed his gun as I headed out the door. The next thing I heard was a gunshot, and panic set in. My first reaction was to get low, and run back into the house. When I entered the house, I saw Grant lying on the ground with a gunshot wound to his foot. He accidentally pulled the trigger, and was screaming in pain. In that very moment, I could hear my mom telling me to "Run! You will be next if you don't find a way out of this life." I need to leave, this relationship, this addiction. I just don't know how.

-Hayz

February 8, 2017

Sophie is officially part of the Evans/Leibsla household. At first, we didn't know where to put her, but I have set up a doggy play pen for her in the living room. Since she doesn't go to the bathroom outside, she wears little diapers, and has free reign of the main floor of the house. The diapers don't hold her poop, so we need to watch where we walk. At night, I put pee pads down in her playpen, and take off her diapers. So far she has been a very good girl. She mostly stays inside because it is still very snowy. When we do take her outside, we bundle her up in one of her many sweaters, and carry her down to the park. Since her little back legs don't work she drags them while she uses her front two legs to hop. She can't go far, but I know she loves to be outside, so we let her hop around on soft surfaces as much as we can. She and Bella ignore each other for the most part, but she is a welcome addition to our home.

XO, E

February 26, 2017

Mike and I were able to get most everything out today, and boy are we tired. It was a lot of work, but we are really close to being done. It has been very emotionally, and physically exhausting. It is easier for me to clean out and move my own treasures because I know the meaning behind them. But trying to decide what is important to keep of mom's and dad's is so much harder. I don't know the significance behind it all. I was looking forward to doing this with mom. I would have loved hearing the stories behind the porcelain figurines from England. I wanted to know her favorite excerpts from the books that lined her bookshelves. I was curious to know how she felt when she made her Beatles scrapbook, and when she cut out the newspaper clippings on JFK's death. It would have been a bonding experience I would have always remembered, but instead I have had to do it on my own. There are so many questions I will probably never know the answer to.

XO, E

March 5, 2017

Mike and I decided to take a step back from everything for a bit by leaving town for my birthday. I am hoping to get some much needed clarity. Hayley wanted to come over to our house to celebrate before we left. She hasn't found the time to help with mom's estate, but at least she is answering my texts. I will take what I can get at this point. Having her around is the only gift I need from her.

XO, E

March 8, 2017

I try not to look weak because I am told to be strong, but when people ask how I am doing I want to say "Fucking terrible! I am so uninterested with a life without my parents!" But, instead I say "fine, thank you" and try to change the subject. After all, suffering is invisible to others. Addiction, grief, etc. It's easier to shut down, and pretend everything is okay in order to not make anyone feel uncomfortable.

I didn't want anyone to ask how I was doing on my birthday, so I asked Mike, Lafe and Jason to spend the day with me at the happiest place on earth. My birthday was one of the hardest days when dad passed. Now both mom and dad are gone I was expecting the worse, so I thought Disneyland would be the perfect distraction. As the day came to a close we went to Sprinkles at Downtown Disney to get a birthday cupcake. I blew out my candle on Main Street in Disneyland while the boys sang happy birthday. It was a great day to spend with some of my favorite guys, and a welcome distraction on a tough day, where not one person asked how I was doing.

XO, E

March 20, 2017

On our flight home from California, Mike and I seriously toyed with the idea of selling all three houses, and buying something in CA. We talked about it the entire flight. We have thought about the idea of moving to CA several times, but this time was different. We were more serious about it. The only thing holding us back is Hayley. I can't leave her.

Deciding whether or not I should sell mom's house is one of the hardest decisions I have ever had to make. I really want to keep it because it is a great investment property. I would really like Hayley to be able to take it over when she is in the position to be able to do so, but after thinking about it for so long I decided to sell it. There is too much work to be done. It's only been three months and it has already been very hard to take care of three houses. On top of everything, more and more medical bills are starting to come in. The house is draining us financially, our time, and energy. As much as I want to keep it, I know it is best to sell it. I want to make sure Hayley is taken care of once she gets better. She has already gone through most of the money from dad's house because she had stolen so much from mom, rehab costs, and bail money.

When we told the tenant who lives downstairs that we were selling the house he got very upset. He told me he would never sell his mom's house, and he couldn't understand why I would do such a thing. He made me feel terrible. If it were a year later, we probably would be able to keep it. I tried not to take it too personally because he doesn't know me, and has no idea what I have been through. Selling her house is like losing a piece of her. I don't want to, I have to.

XO, E

April 4, 2017

Before mom passed, she made me executor of her estate, but I still had to go to probate court. I really didn't want to go because of how uncomfortable I was the first time, but my attorney told me I had to be there. I walked into the large court house I loved so much as a child, and the feelings I had just 18 months ago year came flooding back. I didn't ask Mike to come, but wish he had offered. I could have really used a hand to hold onto while I was there. My attorney was waiting for me outside the courtroom. We walked in, and they called my case number almost immediately. It was as fast and easy as before. I thought about going to say hi to dad's old commissioner colleagues after, but I decided it was best to go home. Mike was still at home when I arrived, and I immediately started crying as he gave me a big hug. He said he should have come with me. He had no idea I would still react that way. It made me feel better that he realized I was still grieving, and could have used his support.

XO, E

April 7, 2017

Mom's writing teacher asked if she could read a couple of mom's poems to an informal gathering of doctors, nurses, therapists, patients, and their families. Her teacher emailed me today to let me know everyone was very moved by mom's poetry. My pediatrician, who has also become a family friend, was at the gathering. He spoke to her writing teacher afterwards to let her know how nice it was to hear mom's poetry. Mom was an amazing poet, and to have people appreciate it as much as she enjoyed writing it is very touching. Even though she is not here in person, she still has an effect on people.

Mom's absence has made me realize that what made her so charming was her presence and energy. It was who she was that made her so lovable, and now so missable. It made me think that I need to rely less on who I think I should be and more on who I am.

XO, E

April 12, 2017

I received a call around 11 PM from the SLC jail tonight. It was from Hayley. I talked to her for a minute before it cut out. She tried calling a number of times, but we continued to lose connection. When we were finally able to talk she told me she had a number of warrants out for her arrest, and the police came to the trailer to take her to jail. The police didn't arrest Grant because his foot is infected from a gunshot wound. They are afraid it would get worse in jail. She sounded scared, but okay. I was frightened for her, but told her everything was going to be alright, and I will call her attorney to see what the next steps are. She asked me to put some money in her account, so she could purchase a few things at the commissary, make phone calls, and write emails. I know it's harsh, but we were all waiting for this. She needs to hit rock bottom in order to get better. Hopefully her being in jail will do just that. She is going to have to detox in jail, which doesn't sound like fun at all, but Hayley is strong, and makes friends everywhere, so I know she will find a way to make it through. I will look into everything tomorrow. I am glad I can be here for her.

XO, E

April 12, 2017

Well it finally happened. The trailer got raided and I'm in jail. I called my sister and begged her to bail me out, but my bond is set at $50,000 cash only. This is going to be a long night. The chills are already starting to hit me, it won't be long before full withdrawal kicks in.

All I can think about is Mom. She left just a few months ago, and look where I end up. I'm so sorry momma, I'm going to be the woman you taught me to be. Please give me the strength to get thru this pain.

-Hayz

April 13, 2017

Hayley's attorney advised me not to bail her out. The jails are very full, so she will probably be released on ankle monitor very soon. I went on the jails website to order her snacks, a pillow, a tooth brush, and other essentials. I also surprised her with a few goodies I know she will like. She called me to tell me how she is doing. I was right, she has already made a few friends, and she has been able to survive detox so far. She said it has actually been easier to detox in jail than in the detox center, which I don't understand, but as long as she is doing okay. She knows she won't be bailed out anytime soon, and said she is going to make the best of things. I really want to see her in person to make sure she is okay, but I can't visit her for a couple days because of the visitation schedule. I am glad I can at least talk to her on the phone, and buy her what she needs from the commissary. Since her commissary items won't arrive for another week, her cellmate has shared a few items with her. She asked me to buy a couple more things to pay her back with. What an ordeal. I was told my life is like a movie, but I didn't feel that way until the last couple years.

XO, E

April 13, 2017

I am sitting here in jail finally dealing with the death of both of my parents. I am hugging the disgusting, jail toilet for dear life as I throw up from withdrawals. I have pins and needles, hot sweats, and all I want to do is sleep, but this dirty rubber mattress with no pillows makes sleep near impossible. I look in the foggy mirror. I can't see my reflection, just an outline of my head, and I am questioning whether I want to live or die. I need to make a change, or I need to end it now.

-Hayz

April 17, 2017

Mike and I visited Hayley for the first time in jail today. Him being there made the hike up the long ramp a lot less threatening. When we checked in an officer gave us each a key to a small locker for our belongings. We can't have anything with us when we see her, not even a book or magazine. There weren't many visitors at first, but many people came in as it got closer to 8. Since they seemed to know the drill Mike and I followed their lead.

A metal detector was the entryway to another large waiting room. There were long skinny benches for us to sit on, and a TV in the corner with a few toys for children next to it. They don't allow us to change stations, so whatever is on is on. People raised their hands as an officer called out their name, and told them what cell block to go to. It was like he was a teacher taking roll call, except this teacher had a badge, and we were going to see someone in jail, not take a math test. During our 45 minute wait, Mike and I discussed what we wanted to talk to Hayley about. Our visit is only 30 minutes long, so we wanted to make sure we touched on everything.

We were soon escorted into a large hallway where there were arrows pointing towards the different cell blocks. Hayley was in cell block C, so we turned right and walked down another very long hallway. There were so many twists and turns we felt like we were in a cement labyrinth. It took so long to find our way we didn't know if we were going to get to her in time. When we arrived to her cell block, we walked into another room with several doors. We found the door to get to Hayley, but it was locked. At this point I was getting anxious to see her, so I waved to the camera pointing at us. We heard a buzzing sound, signaling us that we could enter. There were five plexiglass windows with metal chairs in front of them. Hayley was sitting on the other side of one of the windows in the second stall. I practically ran to her when I saw her. She can't wear makeup in jail, so the scabs on her face stood out more than ever. So did the dark circles under her eyes and her pale skin. She looked exhausted, but her eyes lit up, and she smiled when she saw us.

There are holes in the plexiglass, but it was still difficult to understand what one another is saying. We had to raise our voices to be heard. We mostly talked about how she is doing, and what jail is like. Even though she has gotten to know a few other women in her cell block, she wants to get out of there ASAP! I told her the court dates have been scheduled, but nothing could be done right now. To put a positive spin on things I made sure to tell her that there is a good chance she might get out on ankle monitor. I jumped when a loud voice came over the intercom telling us that our 30 minutes were up. Our time went by so quickly! I wanted to give her a big hug goodbye, but instead I put my hand up to the plexiglass as she did the same. It was the closest thing to a hug we could do. I hate seeing her there, and I felt terrible leaving her. Hopefully this is the beginning of a new chapter in her life. One where heroin isn't the author.

XO, E

April 20, 2017

Jail fucking sucks. I finally have an appetite, but the food portions are so small, I'm ALWAYS hungry. The only thing I have to look at is the clock. The girls in here are super nice, but they get annoying. The best part of my day is eating, and when we eat they herd us like cows. I've never felt so much like an animal in my life. There's at least 90% of us in here with a drug problem. It seems like they should have some sort of alternative for bettering our mental health than locking us in a cage? I don't understand our justice system.

I don't sleep. All I think about is drugs, cigarettes, and how much of a piece of shit I am for the way I treated my parents on their last days. My sister is keeping me alive in here, I don't know what I'd do without her. I'd honestly probably end my life if I didn't have her constantly holding me up. I don't feel like I have anything to live for anymore. I just don't get why? Why am I like this? Why do I allow heroin to control my whole entire fucking life?

-Hayz

April 24, 2017

I heard from Hayley's attorney today. He said the prosecution has offered to have her plead guilty to one of five felony possession of forged documents, and to dismiss the rest. On the facts, it seems they have a very strong case because they discovered four altered Utah driver licenses, two altered Utah ID cards, and one altered US Passport on her person as they were searching her incident to an arrest warrant. Her photo appeared on all of these government issued documents.

In the past we have discussed finding a local substance abuse program for Hayley. He said now is the time to figure out whether it should happen. He spoke to Hayley about participating in Drug Court when he went to visit her. She hasn't wanted to do in the past, but I hope he can talk her into it. She has a lot of court dates, and now she is in jail she can get to them because the jail transports prisoners every week to court. She and her attorney get along very well. He has her best interest at heart.

XO, E

April 25, 2017

Hayley was released from jail today on ankle monitor/work release. She is back at the trailer park again, and is using mom's old car while she is there. Her job assignment is to work at the horse stables for the jail. I really don't want her to fall into the same habits. Work release is pretty strict, so I am sure there will be consequences if she does relapse.

With everything going on I am back fight or flight mode. The trauma of my parents passing isn't going anywhere, but I can't allow myself to grieve because I have no choice but to keep moving. I want to feel what I need to feel, but between having to support Mike with his new business, and helping my sister, I have to put myself to the side. I wish Mike could be there for me, but he isn't allowing himself. I feel like I have to be there for him most of the time. He is depressed because his new business venture isn't what he thought it would be. I have kept us afloat financially, and I am his shoulder to lean on when he has a bad day, but he isn't capable of doing the same for me. I really want to surrender to the grief I need to feel, but no one will let me, including myself. It's funny how I surrender all of the time without thinking. When I go to a concert, cross a busy street or drive my car. Why can't I surrender to this? I know that when I am able to succumb to the pain I will finally be able to work through it, but not until then. In a way I think it is like Hayley's struggle with addiction. When I am ready I will be able to do it, but not until then.

XO, E

April 27, 2017

I'm back in jail. Because I relapsed. But I've BEEN relapsing. I can't handle these emotions sober and the only thing I know how to do to suppress these emotions is get high. Especially when I have cravings and it's all around me! It's like I'm in the devil's playground, and I don't know how to get out! I really liked working at the equestrian park with the horses. Even though we cleaned up their shit, they were so cute! It helped remind me of the innocence that's still in our world, when my world feels so gray and gloom. The animals made me smile.

I guess I just have to continue to deal with my repercussions. I'm a junkie and that's what it is. Who knows if my life will ever change.

-Hayz

May 2, 2017

The last time I heard from Hayley was when she called me a couple days ago to let me know she is back in jail. It is unlike her to not call every day, so Mike and I were anxious to visit her today. While we were sitting on the cold metal stools, waiting to see her pop up on the other side of the plexiglass window, I heard my name on the intercom asking me to come to the front desk. The officer told me that Hayley refused to see us. I asked why, but they didn't have an explanation. They only said I had to go home. I didn't know what was going on. We had driven down there, waited for about an hour to see her, walked to her cell block, and to have them call us back to say she refused to see us was very upsetting. It is very unlike her to not want to see me.

To get my mind off of Hayley I decided to do some much needed yard work at mom's house. Mom found solace in her garden, so I figured I could as well. Mike and I spent the evening weeding, mowing the lawn, and making the outside look immaculate for the open house this weekend. I haven't had much experience gardening, but would like to get more. Mom's garden was the perfect place to start. I know she was looking down on us, happy we were working on it.

Hayley called me later that night to tell me there was a lice scare, so they wouldn't let people out of their cells. She couldn't even call me. She felt terrible, and said she would never refuse to see me. I assured her that I wasn't upset with her; I told her I was more worried than anything. I was just glad she was okay. I hope I can see her soon. Since she gets a few chances, she will probably be on work release again soon. I have a feeling I am going receive a few calls from the jail in the next couple months. This won't be the first time she will be in and out of work release.

XO, E

May 5, 2017

Signs for an open house led me to mom's. Chills went through my body when I saw a for sale sign, and strangers walking in and out. Cleaning out mom's house was hard, but this made it all so real. Selling her house isn't like giving away a small trinket. Her house was a big part of her and our family. We created so many memories there. It is going to be the hardest thing to let go of.

The realtor called me this evening to let me know the open house was very busy and we already had three full price offers. One of the couples even wrote a letter about how much they loved her home. Tears came to my eyes as I read their sweet words, and I immediately told him they were the ones. Mom loved her house, and we didn't want to sell it to just anyone. From what they told me in the letter, I think they will cherish it as much as she did.

XO, E

May 10, 2017

Erin told me mom's house has sold when I called her this morning. I'm in jail, without any control. I'm not able to help her, nor am I able to see my mom's house one last time. I don't blame my sister, but that house has a piece of my heart. There are so many memories I have with my sweet mom there. This addiction is something I will never understand. The things that were once so important to me, seem like nothing when I'm high.

The guilt and shame that I feel sitting in the jail cell are indescribable. I am not a bad person, and I know that. But why do I continue to hurt myself and EVERYONE around me. Who am I?!

-Hayz

May 16, 2017

I received the due diligence from the inspector yesterday. There are a few repairs that need to be done before we sell, but the big problem is that they found traces of meth. I was shocked! Mike and I immediately thought it was Hayley, but mom has also had several tenants living in her mother in law apartment over the years, so it could be from one of them. At this point it didn't matter who brought meth into the house, we just needed to get it taken care of.

I was able to talk to a few local decontamination companies today. When I told them what the inspector said they told me they would have to take out the flooring and drywall. The house would essentially be ruined! My heart dropped at the idea of destroying mom's house. I already have to give up a big piece of her. I don't want to have to demolish it as well. It would cost a lot for the cleanup, but even more to put it back together, which they don't do. Mike and I would have to do all of the repairs. I felt defeated and wanted to cry until Mike came up with the idea to test the house ourselves before hiring someone. He knows of a local lab that has self testing kits, so we are going to stop by there this week. I feel a bit more relieved, but I am still on edge with everything going on. I don't know if I can take anymore.

XO, E

May 17, 2017

Hayley's attorney called to ask me to find her a rehab facility. He said they would let her off work release, and she won't go back to jail if she is in the custody of a rehab. At this point I was burnt out. We are dealing with a meth house, selling the house, her in and out of jail, etc. I had no idea what to do. I felt like screaming! I wished dad was here because he would have known what to do. I closed my eyes, took a deep breath, and started my research on rehab facilities. I already know I don't want to waste money on the rehab facility she went to last time. It was so expensive! I reached out to a few people I know who have worked with many of the local rehabs, but no one had a good answer. Every facility I looked into seemed like a scam. I was about to give up until I found, Serenity. I somehow stumbled across Serenity, which is a nonprofit rehab facility about a mile away from our home. Their website said "Serenity is a residential drug and alcohol treatment program, which requires a minimum of 100 days. It includes daily Alcoholic Anonymous meetings, group therapy, community service, work and peer confrontation. It also requires involvement in the family program, participation in group activities, and adherence to strict set of residential rules. It is a therapeutic community, and as such, confrontational, demanding and rigorous." It is perfect!

I spoke to a sweet woman who was able to answer all of my questions, and told me they have a bed available, but not for long. When she mentioned that they will need a couple days notice I didn't know if it would work. I have no idea on when Hayley will be ready because her situation changes weekly. I thought letting Hayley know that I may have found an option for her would help motivate her to make a plan. She sounded a little reluctant because it wasn't where she went before (which where she wants to go because she knows it and is comfortable there), but I told her it was a great option. We were supposed to visit today, but she didn't show up. I put so much effort into finding somewhere for her to heal, and for her not to show up was like a slap in the face. She isn't taking this seriously, which makes me thinks she will be back in jail again soon.

On a brighter note, Mame called me to tell me her daughter got a message from mom via Facebook messenger. It was an emoji. I still have her phone, so I checked her messenger to see if other people received messages from mom. Sure enough, about 5 other people did. They were all different emoji's. I thought it was strange that the other people who received a message didn't say anything. Mom taught me to look for signs that someone is there. Mame and I both think it was mom telling us she is still here and watching over us. She is the best guardian angel we can ask for.

XO, E

May 24, 2017

Hayley had too many strikes from being late to work, so she is back in jail. I visit her on every visitation day. I usually go by myself, but Mike joins me once in a while. The days of the week switch because each cell block has a different day for visitors. She gets transferred to different cell blocks regularly, so it can be difficult to plan a time to see her, but I have made it work. She is always so happy to see me. I am the only person she has asked to visit her. She doesn't want her boyfriend there or her friends. It feels good knowing she trusts me, and I bring her comfort when she needs it. Hayley looks much better than just a few days earlier. It's amazing how fast our bodies can recover, even after years of hard drug use. She still wants to get out as soon as she can, which I don't blame her. She likes her new cell mate even more than the last. She said the last one committed first degree murder! I am glad she has learned to be able to adapt to her environment, and she is doing well, but it was still very hard to leave her again.

XO, E

May 24, 2017

My sister and I haven't gotten along the past couple of years because of my addiction. But right now, at this very moment, I'd be so lost without her. She has saved my ass, once again. I just hope that I can be there for her like she's been here for me. She mentioned that she found a rehab that I can smoke cigarettes at. It's not the treatment center that I went to before, but everyone in jail says it's the best place they've ever gone. I'm so nervous, and I DO NOT want to go. But I don't know what else to do.

It's either prison or treatment. I'm going to choose treatment.

-Hayz

May 26, 2017

Since mom donated her body to science, she asked to have a tree dedicated to her at one of her favorite places, Red Butte Garden. She spent a lot of time in the garden. This is where she took Tai Chi classes, saw many concerts, took walks with friends, and just enjoyed the beautiful landscape they have to offer. It is a peaceful place and perfect for mom's tree.

When someone donates a tree, the garden doesn't plant a new one, because if it would be terrible if it doesn't survive. They let us pick out an existing tree instead. Mom and Mame visited the garden together regularly, so I asked her to help us pick it out. Mom specifically asked for a dogwood tree. The gravel paths led us to different areas with several beautiful trees, but none of them spoke to us. We were about to give up when turned the corner to see two bronze deer in front of a dogwood full of pink flowers, and a butterfly floating in front of it. I took the butterfly to be a sign that it was mom showing us the tree she wanted to have in her name. It is just right.

XO, E

May 29, 2017

Mike and I took a quick trip to Yosemite to celebrate a friend's birthday. I received a call from Hayley on our way. She said she was out of jail again on work release. I was so stressed because we were out of town, and I had no idea what she would do while we were gone. I still can't trust her or the people in her life. I was really hoping she was in jail while we were gone. It is easier on me because I know where she is, and that she is somewhat safe. I don't like to be far away when she is still so sick.

I had a hard time not thinking of Hayley the remainder of the drive. I told Mike I should take the next flight home because I wanted to be there in case she needed me. He asked me to sleep on it before making any rash decisions because we were close to Yosemite. All of my stress went away as we pulled into the park. I couldn't think of anything but what was surrounding me. We were enveloped by huge slabs of rock towering overhead. Around every turn were waterfalls, bigger than the next. Seeing the water gush over a cliff, and fall close to 1,500 feet, reminded that nature controls itself. It doesn't rely on anyone to survive or move forward. It just does. I have little control over what happens to me, but I can decide how I respond. I can be as forceful as a waterfall breaking stones in its path, or as still as water in a teacup, bringing comfort and warmth. At that moment I decided I would like to be more like water. It can take any form without changing who it is. I am going to try harder to take the shape of my environments and circumstances. I can only fully help myself. I can't do everything for everyone. I need to let my sister figure it out on her own. Prioritizing my personal growth and wellness is essential. It is necessary that I take some time for myself because my energy feels lost, the magic is gone, and my anxiety is high. Escaping to nature is the best thing I can do to feel at peace.

XO, E

May 30, 2017

We woke up early to take a quick walk to a waterfall near our hotel before the crowds came. The water splashed onto the bridge when it hit the rocks at the bottom. Most of the tourists would shield themselves from the water as they ran over the bridge, but when I crossed the bridge I stopped, closed my eyes, and felt it splatter onto my face. I imagined it washing my worries away as it touched my cheeks. I was sopping wet when I found Mike. He smiled, and shook his head while I took his arm to lead him to the magical bridge. We stood there together for a few minutes, giggling at how cold it was and how funny we may have looked, but we didn't care. We were present. I was able to rid the residue of yesterday, and clear my mind of the fears of tomorrow. I was only thinking of us, and the waterfall.

On our way home Mike started to feel very sick. I felt terrible because we had a 9 hour drive ahead of us, and he was in a lot of pain. I took over driving so he could try to sleep it off. I listened to my favorite music while taking in the beautiful scenery. I thought a lot about dad during the drive. He loved taking us on road trips and exploring the gorgeous landscape our country has to offer. We traveled to mountain towns, camped in deserts, ran on the beaches of Oregon and so many other places. He made me the adventurous person I am today. I miss him so much and all of the stories he would tell. Like the one about falling rock. Whenever we passed a falling rock sign I would ask him to tell me the story over and over again, and he would happily oblige.

As the setting sun bathed the valley in a rosy light, I could really feel dad's presence. He wasn't with me physically, but he was there. My eyes grew foggy from the tears that were forming as I said out loud, "I know you are around, but I wish you were here with me." When I blinked the tears out of my eyes I saw a bald eagle flying overhead. I smiled as the tears started to gush down my face like the waterfall I was so enamored with earlier. It was dad, guiding me home.

XO, E

June 5, 2017

Working at the Equestrian Park. The baby horse and his momma are soooo cute! He's getting more and more social each time we see him.

-Hayz

June 6, 2017

A couple weeks ago we bought a few do it yourself meth kits and tested areas all over the house. The results from the DIY meth test kits came back today, saying there was little meth in the house, phew! The person who agreed to do the cleaning came to take tests of his own, and I received an email today saying he did not find methamphetamine residue over the Utah State Standard. Double phew! He is still going to clean the HVAC system to make sure everything is out of the house, but he won't need to destroy the house like he originally thought. This is such great news for everyone! We hope to close on the house at the end of the month.

XO, E

June 7, 2017

Uncle John and Aunt Bonnie came to town to celebrate what would have been mom's 65th birthday. Since they hadn't seen mom's tree yet we met Peg, Mame, Carol, and Hayley at Red Butte Garden to walk around the garden she loved so much. I was pleasantly surprised to see Hayley there. I didn't think she would make it on time. During our stroll Uncle John and Aunt Bonnie reminisced about the times mom would take them there to show them her favorite flowers. Mame shared stories of she and mom walking around with champagne disguised as water in their aluminum water bottles, laughing about the fun weekends they had. When we arrived to her tree I was excited to see the pink flowers were still in bloom, and a plaque that reads "In Memoriam of Judi Evans" was already in place.

As we were leaving Hayley said she couldn't come to dinner, but asked for $20 for gas. I told her I didn't have any cash, so Aunt Bonnie handed her $20. I told her she didn't need to, but she said "if I want to give my niece $20, let me give her $20," I knew she was just going to buy drugs with it, but didn't have the heart to tell my Aunt. She wants to help, and I appreciate her for doing so. We all drove up the canyon to go to Ruth's diner to sit on their patio for dinner. I miss my parents every day and days like this make me miss them even more, but nights with family and friends make hard days a little easier.

XO, E

June 10, 2017

They keep releasing me on ankle monitor, but I can't stay sober. I swear every time I am going to stay sober, but every time they let me out I can't do it.

-Hayz

June 11, 2017

Hayley tested dirty when she showed up to work release last Friday, so she is back in jail, and this time we expect it will be for a while. She told me that in order to be released to Serenity for inpatient treatment, the judge has to release her into their custody. I spoke to Serenity today to let them know Hayley is back in jail because her intake date was yesterday. As far as I know, they still have a bed for her, and they said they are willing to write a letter stating that if her attorney needs them to. They have been very understanding. I feel like I call them once a week telling them Hayley will be there, and then she either doesn't show up or she is in jail. I am sure they deal with situations like this on a regular basis, but I hate to be so flaky.

Ever since Mike and I were married people have asked when we are going to have kids. We waited so long to get become husband and wife I think they figured we should have kids right away. We thought about it right before dad died, but a lot has happened since then. It has been hard to think about starting a family while I am losing mine. Mike likes to say we were in the middle of the dust storm. It was really dusty, settled down for a bit and got really dusty again. We are waiting for the dust to settle before we do anything. I also feel like we have a 25 year old child. Since Hayley was an addict in her early 20's she missed a lot of formative years. She is learning how to become an adult. My dad taught me, and I am trying to teach her. She is our child right now.

XO, E

June 18, 2017

I met with my lawyer, and he said the courts were offering me drug court. When I first got in trouble with the law dad had mentioned Drug Court to me. It sounded super scary, and unobtainable. I have always resisted it, especially hearing my friend's talk about it and how it's a set up for failure. And here I am. Felonies hanging over my head, which could mean potential prison time. I have a choice to go back on probation, or I can take Drug Court, and eventually get my record expunged, once I complete the program. I feel conflicted and terrified. I heard that if I mess up in drug court, even once, they will throw me back in jail. I'm not sure what to do right now. The only way I can imagine me completing drug court is if I go to a treatment center first. My sister has been a godsend this whole time. She visits me regularly, and is actively searching for the right treatment center. My only requirements are that I can smoke cigarettes, and that it is coed. She mentioned this place called Serenity which is right by her house. She has a very good feeling about it. I trusted asking the girls in jail what they thought, and I only got good responses.

-Hayz

June 20, 2017

I received a request of entry for the health department today from the decontaminator. There isn't a trace of meth in the house, so we can now close the case on the property. Since he only had to go through the HVAC system there wasn't much of a mess when Mike and I went to clean everything up. It is heartbreaking enough to have to sell mom's house. I am so relieved it didn't need to be destroyed. I don't know what we would have done if Mike didn't think of testing the house ourselves.

In order for Hayley to be released into the custody of Serenity, I had to get a letter from them to the judge presiding over her case. Hayley's attorney contacted me to let me know he sent the letter from Serenity to the judge, and he is waiting to hear back. He said he may need to schedule a hearing, so to tell Hayley could be another week before she is out.

I went to the facility today to hand them a check for her first month. I quickly received a letter stating her treatment has been paid for, and they have a bed available upon her release. So far it seems like a great place for her. It is in an historic brick house in a great part of the city. The offices are in a small building separate from the main facility in the back (Hayley actually went to preschool in these building years ago, coincidence?) When I arrived, residents were playing basketball in between meetings in the parking lot and showed me where I needed to go to pay. The two people who take care of intake are sweet, but to the point. I can tell they don't take any shit from anyone. They know the process because they have both been residents at Serenity before. One of them went to school when he finished treatment, and is now one of the therapists at the facility. I have a very good feeling about it. Now I just need to get her there. I think after her time in jail and being a resident at Serenity with drug court on the side she will be able to succeed. It's what mom and dad wanted most, and I am going to do my best to make it happen. I know this sounds morbid, but death leads to birth and I feel like they gave their lives to save hers.

XO, E

June 26, 2017

Mike and I went by to do one last walk through of mom's home. We sat at her little, iron bistro table on the deck to eat dinner, and admire the backyard she loved so dearly. We reminisced about the many BBQ's we had on the deck, picking apricots off the tree, playing with the puppies, and her 60th birthday party. We then walked through the house before stopping in the living room where we sat down on the floor and cried. I was losing a very big piece of mom, and didn't want to leave. We all loved mom's house. It was home. I was happy we sold it, but heartbroken at the same time. Mike helped me off the floor, and led me to the back door. I looked behind me before I walked out of mom's kitchen one last time. A memory of her sitting at her kitchen table in front of her bay window in her turquoise robe with Ossie on her lap, and Sophie looking up at her from the floor appeared. Then a rainbow came out of nowhere. I looked around to see where it came from and saw a crystal prism hanging on a ribbon over the sink. I gently took it off its hook, said goodbye to her house once last time, and placed it over the rearview mirror in my car. Mom will make rainbows wherever I go.

XO, E

June 27, 2017

I went to court this morning, and took the drug court plea. Something in me told me it's the right thing to do. But, from experience, I know that I will not be able to successfully complete the program, unless I get away from the trailer, get away from Grant and start over completely. I told my sister today that I accepted the plea, but I need to get into treatment right after jail or I won't be able to successfully stay out of jail. I really hope this is the last straw, I don't want to waste any more time behind bars. I'm ready to experience life to the fullest, like my parents would want me to. I will be released into the custody of Serenity tomorrow. I am starting to get comfortable in jail. It has been fun and more like a girl's camp than a place to be punished, but I know I need to take the next step. I am ready.

-Hayz

June 28, 2017

Before I left jail I was put into a holding cell where I could change into my street clothes. It was a small, 6x6 room, which smelled terribly from the pee all over the walls. They held me there for an hour and a half while they tried to find my clothes, which they never did. I couldn't wear my jumpsuit or go naked, so they gave me some donated clothes. Since the clothes were made for a young boy, they didn't fit my 5'9" body. I had to go with it, and was mortified when I walked into Serenity for the first time. My hair was crimped from the braids I wore to court, I had short slacks that barley fit me, a little boys baseball thermal which showed my belly, white jail tube socks topped off with bright orange crocs. Here I am the first time socializing with sober people out of jail, and I am dressed like this. It was humbling to say the least.

-Hayz

June 29, 2017

I am at Serenity, and thank goodness my sister brought me a bag of clothes, makeup, and other essentials. She wasn't allowed to transport me here, but I am glad she could at least drop off some necessary items. I haven't talked to anyone, which is rare for me. The residents keep hugging me, and I can't understand why.

-Hayz

July 2, 2017

Anxiety attacks have become more regular since my parents passed. They usually only happen in the morning and a pilates or yoga session is a quick cure, but they have now been occurring before I leave to run errands. Even though I have gone to the grocery store several times I am scared to go by myself. I wasn't afraid of many things when I was younger. I moved to NYC without knowing anyone or having any worries. Why have I adopted this fear now? With my parents being gone so has my independence.

I really didn't want to run errands today, but knew I had to in order to get over my fear. As I was tying my shoes Bella put her head on my lap and looked up at me with her big brown eyes. I started to feel a little more at ease. Bella hasn't just changed my life, she has saved it. During good times and troubled times she has been my consistent. The gentle touch of her wet nose and a loving lick is enough to make me feel brave again. With Bella by my side I know I am not alone. She gives me comfort, friendship and unconditional love. Everyday I tell Mike how happy I am that we can make her "furever" home a loving one. We rescued each other and I am lucky to be able to call her our furbaby. I gave her a kiss on her head, told her thank you before walking out the door.

When I arrived at the store the anxiety I was feeling earlier came back. My body started to shake and I was having a difficult time breathing. I walked as quickly as I could, grabbing items off the shelves and throwing them into my basket. I was moving so swiftly I felt like I was a contestant on the game show, Supermarket Sweep, not running a dreaded errand. While I was waiting in the long checkout line my nerves creeped up to an all time high. I almost left my cart full of groceries behind and walked out of the store until I heard "Just Breathe" on the speakers overhead. It was a sign from mom, telling me to breathe. I took a deep breath, allowing the anxiety that was deep down in my belly to escape. After a few inhales and exhales I felt lighter. I have been so busy I haven't allowed myself to be aware of the signals mom has been sending, but this one was hard to ignore. She knew I needed her. A feeling of gratitude overwhelmed my body. I am grateful I was finally able to decode a message from mom. I am grateful Hayley is doing well. I am grateful I have been able to be there for my family when they needed me the most. I am grateful for the wonderful people who have been there to support me. I am grateful for life.

XO, E

July 5, 2017

Serenity has a speaker come to the center to tell their story every week. The speaker has been through addiction, and has over a year sober. I will never forget the first time I heard someone speak. I understood everything they described, and all of a sudden, I don't feel so alone. For the first time, I realize I have found a community of people that understand me. They are my family. They don't judge me for my mistakes. We are all on a mission to overcome our demons, and work together for a better future.

-Hayz

July 11, 2017

Today was a great day. Our goddaughter was born! She is perfect and looks so much like her mama. She has a full head of dark hair and big blue eyes. I never thought I would be a godmother, and I am honored to take on the role. I can't wait to watch her grow up and be a big part of her life. Lexi said we are already a part of their family, but with my parents being gone she wanted to make it official.

We also got to see Hayley today! It was our first family night at Serenity. Every Tuesday, they invite family and close friends to come to family night. When Hayley saw us, she ran up to us and gave me the biggest hug. The therapist who moderates family night chooses a different topic to talk about every week. About 30 of us sat in a large circle. Each person introduces themselves as either an addict or as support. The residents tell the group what their drug of choice is, and the people who are there as support tells the group their name and who they are supporting. Then the entire group says "SUPPORT." I almost jumped out of my chair the first time they said it because they were so loud. It was refreshing to listen to a group of people be so honest about their addiction. Their life has been hard, and they aren't hiding from their experiences. They are facing them. We all have a personal story and our stories help shape us into the people we are today. They start when we are born and follow us through our lives until we are ready to work them. I think this will be a good place for Hayley to recover who she once was.

After the group, we were able to visit with Hayley for another hour. Hayley introduced us to her new friends before sitting down under a big tree. Since we didn't get to see her on her birthday, I brought her a few birthday gifts and a piece of her favorite chocolate cake with a sparkler to celebrate. She looks so happy. I don't feel like she is faking it this time. She genuinely seems ready.

XO, E

July 13, 2017

My therapist is doing EMDR therapy with me to help me overcome the trauma I've had in my life. We started with the abuse I've experienced with Grant. I REALLY, REALLY don't want to do it. It seemed weird to me. EMDR therapy is supposed to release the emotion from the trauma so when you think about it, it doesn't affect you the same. I don't have PTSD that bad, but sometimes it causes me major anxiety. I trust my therapist, we'll see if it works. I just don't want to relive a lot of these moments. Ignorance is bliss?

-Hayz

July 18, 2017

Serenity has eight AA meetings a week! I was upset about it at first because the mention of god and prayer makes me cringe, and that's all they talked about. I expressed my feelings to a friend, who said I don't need to think of my higher power as god. It can be whatever I want it to be. I thought about it and said I want it to be my parents. I feel so much better going to the meetings with this mindset. My parents are my higher power. They are my guardian angels.

-Hayz

July 30, 2017

We picked Hayley up from Serenity to come to our house for dinner. From now on, she can leave the facility for 6 hours one weekend day. They also allow her to leave for the entire weekend three times during her stay there. We have planned a camping trip for one of those weekends, and will allow her to stay with us the other two. When she is with us she uses my phone to catch up on social media. That night, I noticed that she changed her profile picture to one of her and mom.

XO, E

August 12, 2017

It's been hard for me to acknowledge the sexual abuse I endured when I was young. Mostly because I feel like I have suppressed it for so many years. My therapist asked if we could do EMDR a couple days ago, but it was too hard. With EMDR, they ask you to explain what happened exactly and what images you store in your brain. I started talking about it, and I got super uncomfortable. She was okay with putting it off until I feel more comfortable. These images I permanently have in my head make me sick to my stomach. A part of me wonders if I had never experienced this, would I still be a drug addict? Trying to run from every bit of emotion? I knew facing reality wasn't going to be easy, but shit just got REAL.

When I got to Serenity, I was scared. The last thing I was ready to do was get vulnerable with my secrets with a bunch of strangers. As I've built a family here, and have heard some other people's experiences, I feel open to express my truth. Today we did an exercise where we write a letter to our abuser. We write it, forgive them, and then read the letter to our group. It was not easy. The last person I want to forgive is the person that caused my soul so much turmoil. As I sat there, with my leg bouncing, and my heart racing, my friend next to me read her letter about her brother sexually abusing her when she was young. Although our stories weren't identical, I didn't feel alone. For the first time, I felt like someone understood me in a way that nobody ever had before. I felt relief. I'm not alone, my story, the tragedies I've experienced don't need to suffocate me anymore. I am so grateful for this group and Serenity. It's like they understand that addiction is just a symptom to what is really going on in my soul.

-Hayz

August 14, 2017

Hayley was driving mom's old car while she was living at the trailer. When she was in jail, Grant would drive it, and still does. We thought about trying to get it back, but were worried about our safety. We spoke to Hayley's attorney who suggested we talk to the police. They offered to give us a police escort, but we were still too scared. We didn't know what he would do if he knew we took the car. Our safety was more important, so we let him keep it for the time being. A couple days ago, I received a notice saying the car had been towed because Grant was pulled over for a DUI. This was the perfect time to get the car back into our possession. Hayley had a court date today and the rehab facility allowed me to drive her to and from her hearing. This was the first time we had been alone in years. I felt like she was a stranger sitting in the passenger seat. We were silent much of the drive. I have no idea who she is anymore. It made me sad realizing that my only living family member is someone I don't know. I really hope we can find a way to reconnect. I would love to have a sister again.

XO, E

August 17, 2017

Drug court isn't turning out to be all that bad. I have to go to court every 2 weeks to check in with the judge. I meet with my case manager once a month, and I meet with a therapist twice a month. I also get drug tested 2-3 times a week. It can be overwhelming at times, BUT I know that I need this kind of intensive babysitting. I did an orientation with the Drug Court admissions lady today so they could determine what level of care I would need. She was a very sweet older woman, she asked me about my past and what led up to me to using drugs. I gave her a brief history, and what had happened most recently with the loss of my parents. She looked shocked, and full of compassion. She then said "I'm rooting for you sweetie, and one day your story could change the world." It didn't occur to me until that moment, how much strength I have in me. This disease doesn't need to consume me anymore; I do get to live the life I crave, because I am resilient. My past doesn't define who I am today.

-Hayz

August 20, 2017

Dad started the Divorce Education Program for Children in Utah in 2003. He developed this in an effort to help children of divorce learn coping skills taught in the courtroom by mental health professionals and judicial officers. The program is still going strong and growing! Dad did a lot during his time as a court commissioner, but this program was very close to his heart, and today it won an award! My sister and I were honored to be at the luncheon on his behalf. We really enjoyed hearing about how many families the program has helped. I am so lucky to be able to call him my father and miss him every day, but I am happy knowing his hard work is still making a positive impact on our community.

XO, E

August 26, 2017

This was the second full weekend Hayley spent with us. Before starting the fun weekend we had planned, we sold her car to her friend at Serenity who was scheduled to go to sober living in a couple days. I tested the car with the at home meth tests, and it came back negative. I also had it professionally detailed and checked by a mechanic to make sure it was safe for her to drive. Hayley had a bit of a hard time saying goodbye, but I feel like it is a way of putting her past behind her. The car is full of terrible memories, and having it gone will help her move on to the next phase in her life.

After we said our goodbyes to mom's car, we went to a celebration of life event. The University of Utah donation center holds an event to commemorate the people who donated their bodies to science each year. We felt like it was important to be there because the glass plaque with mom's name engraved in it had recently been placed. The event consisted of music, and a couple speakers. One of them was a young girl whose life was saved by a donation of an organ from someone who donated their body to science. Mom really was a hero in so many ways. Her organs may not have been able to save a life of a little girl, but since her cancer was so rare I hope her body will help doctors, and researchers find a cure.

We rushed home to pack the car for a quick trip to the Uinta Mountains to do some camping. I have found that we need to get away from the stress of the world as often as we can, and the silence found in nature is a relief to our busy minds. It was just the three of us in a landscape where almost nothing has changed. Trees might have fallen, new ones may have grown, but otherwise we looked out on a stretch of calm water, green forests and towering mountains that have remained the same for years.

Hayley retired to bed early while Mike and I stayed up to stargaze. I had tingles, not from the cold, but from how peaceful it was. The pace of life slows in the mountains. There is no traffic to cover up the sounds of nature, and on a clear night, without light pollution from the city, I can count the stars. As I stared at the sky I thought about how each tiny star is actually a raging sun, and started to feel small by comparison. I closed my eyes to feel the heat from the fire, as a chill came through the air. I felt a way I hadn't felt in a long time. Not only was Hayley coming back to us, but the true me, deep down inside was returning as well. I have been lost because I have felt numb for so long. The two people who were there to show me the way are gone, but I am beginning to forge my own path. A change is coming, but this time it is for good.

XO, E

August 27, 2017

Serenity is the best treatment center I've ever been to. Granted I've only been to two, but they are hard on me! A friend called me out, and prompted that I needed to discuss my mom's death in a therapeutic setting because I haven't talked about it. They call me the "ice queen" because I don't cry. I don't feel like I know how to process emotions anymore. So, the doctor did something called an "empty chair" exercise. He had me talk to the empty chair as if my mom was sitting in it. I broke down, closed my eyes, and just started talking between grunts of tears. Meanwhile, the therapist was rubbing my back probing questions as if he were my mom. I had never felt so hurt and heartbroken. So many emotions were rolling through me all at once, although I did feel a little bit of freedom, and relief. I forgot I was in a room with a group of people. When I opened my eyes everyone was bawling with me. They all hugged me and we cried in a circle together. It was at this point that I knew I can't do this alone. I need a group of like minded people on the same mission as me to get thru this.

I have found a family. I am not alone.

-Hayz

August 30, 2017

We haven't missed a family night since Hayley has been at Serenity. We have gotten to know the residents, and since we take Bella with us every week she has become a therapy dog for everyone there. I recently found a poem mom wrote that I thought the group would like to hear. Hayley gave me the permission to share it with everyone, but I was a little nervous. I didn't know how Hayley would react in front of her friends. I took a deep breath and read:

I Hate Heroin

I am struggling today.
My daughter,
addicted maybe forever.
The reality breaks my heart
again and again.
I am so tired of living this way.
I do not want to live this way.
The grief is never ending.
Would her death bring peace?
I am afraid to think that.
Am I selfish to think of my own grief
and not her pain and suffering?
No, I need to think of myself.
What is good for me at this time.
I hate heroin.
It has abducted my daughter, my love.
She is not herself when she is using.
It's as though the devil inhabits her soul.
The darkness overwhelms me.
I long for peace.

When I looked up from the white paper I saw my sister crying. She ran up to me to give me the biggest hug she had ever given me as we wept together. I felt terrible that I was the one to make her feel that way, but knew it would help with her sobriety. She wants to get better this time, I can tell. Knowing how much pain she caused mom will give her motivation to never cause pain like that again.

XO, E

August 30, 2017

Erin read a poem mom wrote about my addiction tonight, and it really got to me. When I first read it I didn't let it sink in, but as she recited it out loud to the group my heart sank. It broke knowing I hurt mom so much. I knew I upset her, but not in that way. Everyone in the group was affected by it. We all cried together, and the therapist leading the group was speechless. Family members don't usually share such raw emotions. It was something we all needed to hear. We need to know how our loved ones feel when we abuse drugs. Hearing how badly we hurt others is only motivation for us to stop. We know we are slowly killing ourselves, but forget that we are also killing those who care about us the most. I am going to get better. I am determined.

-Hayz

September 2, 2017

While I was at work today a wife of one of the artist's came in with her daughter. They have become very close friends and I love them dearly. Her daughter is pregnant with her first baby, and their first grandchild. They are so excited! When I heard her talking to her other daughter on the phone I almost asked if I could call her when I needed some motherly advice. I miss mine so much. A few moments later I noticed her touching her daughter's belly from across the gallery. She looked up at me with a huge grin on her face. She was so happy. I smiled back at her as a lump grew in my throat, but I pushed it down deep, as I have done for years. My skin felt hot, and prickly, and there was a dull ache in my chest. I was ready to cry happy tears for her, but I also wanted to cry sad tears. Seeing her and her expectant daughter made me miss mom more than ever. Mom wanted to have a grandbaby so badly. If Mike and I ever have children neither she nor my father will be able to meet them. It breaks my heart knowing my child won't ever know the most important people in my life.

XO, E

September 30, 2017

I've been working a 12 step program. And step 9 is supposedly one of the hardest steps, "Make direct amends to such people wherever possible, except when to do so would injure them or others." Meaning, to reach a certain level of peace, I must take accountability for the things I've done, and make it right with the people I have harmed in my addiction. Unfortunately, the people I need to make amends to most are no longer on this earth. My mom and dad have passed away. After a lot of thought and networking, I've decided to write two letters. One to mom, and one to dad. Owning my part, and telling them that I choose to live a life worth living. The life they have always wanted me to have.

Adam, my boyfriend, and I went to the dollar store, purchased 10 balloons, figured out how to tie the letters to the strings, and drove to Red Butte Garden. Mom's tree was nearby, and I had a gorgeous view of the Salt Lake valley. It was gray and gloomy outside, the air was brisk and the city inverted with pollution. However, it felt so peaceful up there. Adam was sweet enough to give me space. He handed me the balloons before I walked up to the edge, said a prayer and asked my parent's for strength and courage. I said, "I love you" as I let go of the balloons. Watching them fly into the clouds brought tears to my eyes. I miss them both so much, but for some reason, this visual representation to let go of my past, brought a feeling of newness all throughout me. I felt a sense of freedom, but most importantly, unconditional love. I will never forget this day.

-Hayz

October 12, 2017

I'm graduating Serenity today. I have 124 days sober, and I actually want to stay sober this time. I'm scared to start this new chapter in my life, but I am so excited. The family that I've created in this treatment center, and in the rooms of this 12 step program are something that I could've never dreamed of. From here I move into sober living. I'll have my own apartment with my best friend I am graduating treatment with. I've never had my own place before. I'm so excited! I've haven't felt this excited about starting life again. I feel like I'm just learning how to be an adult at 27 years old. My soul feels alive for the first time in so many years.

I've committed to working a 12 step program with my sponsor. My sponsor has been through almost everything I've been through, and she just picked up her year sober chip. I look up to her so much, and if she can do it, I know I can do it too! The people that surround me give me hope. They've conquered the same demon I have, and they look genuinely happy.

I am building back my relationship with my sister and brother in law. They are finally starting to trust me again. I love feeling like I am a part of the family, and making new memories. My sister and I share a bond that can never be broken. We are each other's rock's. I just hope I can be there for her one day the same way she's been there for me.

My mom and my dad's energy have surrounded me throughout this whole process. I now understand how much power there is in love. Although they are not on this planet anymore, they surround me with unconditional love. That's what keeps me going. I love you Mom and Dad, thank you for guiding me and watching over me through this monumental chapter in my life. My addiction brought me so close to death, but now out of love, I am finally free.

THANK YOU

-Hayz

October 12, 2017

Today was Hayley's graduation from Serenity! We asked family members to attend, as well as mom and dad's closest friends. Since our parents can't be here in person, their best friends are the second best thing. All of them have been like parents to us growing up. During the graduation, the residents give a short speech about what they learned while being at Serenity, and what they hope to achieve. Afterwards family and friends say a little something. I am so proud of her. There was so much I wanted to say, but thought it was best to keep it simple, so I said:

"Addiction is harder than cancer", this is what our mom said to me while she was battling a rare form of breast cancer, which was what she died from a year and a half ago. Being a family member who has watched her loved ones go through cancer and addiction I would have to agree with our mom. Addiction is a disease that we truly didn't understand. We couldn't fathom why Hayley wouldn't take the steps to get better. We would get upset because we didn't know what she was going through. Cancer was something my parents had more control over. They did what they could to live a quality life while being sick, where addiction was all up to Hayley. We couldn't force her to make healthy decisions until she was ready. Hayley was deep in her addiction for years. She missed holidays, birthdays, and barely made it to my wedding. She would stay with our mom from time to time, gain her trust, and then steal from her when she could barely pay her medical bills. As much as we all wanted to help her we had to step away. We had to allow her to go down the path that was destroying her life. I didn't feel like I had a sister, and then we found Serenity.

After a few weeks at Serenity, I could see Hayley's outgoing personality slowly coming back. The scabs on her face went away, and she had color in her cheeks again. She talked about doing things that made her happy, and started taking care of herself. When she was deep into her addiction her teeth were in terrible shape. Since our mom was a dental hygienist this was very difficult for her to watch. She would make appointments for Hayley, but she would rarely show up. When I heard she was making appointments on her own to go to the dentist, and actually got there on time, I knew Hayley was on the right path.

The time we really got to see Hayley shine was when she would stay with us on the weekends. We would have family dinners together, go to the farmers market, and even went camping. We have been able to bond again. I finally feel like I have a sister again.

While Hayley was at Serenity she started drug court. Before she went to jail an attorney told me drug court was the best thing for her. When I would mention this to her she said, "no way." She was afraid to go because of what her friends had to say. They told her it was too hard, but it has been a great experience for Hayley. She has been incredibly successful in her recovery, and I feel like much of it is because of drug court. Having an assigned therapist, case worker, classes, Vivtitrol shots, a judge who truly cares, and the chance to have all of your felonies expunged once you graduate has been very beneficial to her staying sober. She has done so well I like to tell her she is the valedictorian of drug court.

I love hearing that Hayley has already helped others in recovery by sharing her story. I admire her for her strength and working through what has been one of the hardest things I have ever witnessed anyone accomplish. I know recovery is going to be difficult. It is something she will have to work on the remainder of her life. To become close to people and lose them to addiction won't be easy, but I am grateful for the community she has found. Having friends who support her in her recovery has been essential to her battling this horrible disease. I will always be here for her, but it's not the same. She needs to have people in her life that understand the struggles of addiction and Serenity as helped her find people who want to see her succeed. It's been amazing to watch her realize her potential. She told me she would like to go back to school, so she can get a job in the community where she can help others. I can't wait to see what she does in the future because her future is bright, and will continue to get brighter.

That night Mike and I took a walk around the block. I felt a comfortable warmth in my stomach as we were walking along the dirt, tree lined path I used to walk with my father. I put my left hand on my heart, right hand on my stomach, and closed my eyes. Tears started to slowly roll down my cheeks. Mom was there with me. I looked up to see two little birds. They started to sing a familiar song I heard when I was a child. I smiled through the tears knowing they were mom and dad. Two little birds, telling me that everything was going to be alright, and this time I believed it to be true.

Both my parents have died within 18 months of each other. The words remain surreal. Life has incredible highs and lows. Perhaps feeling it all at the same time is the art. The last few years have made me learn to trust time. Five seconds turn to fifteen. Fifteen turn to thirty, and then before I know it, I'm healing for a minute. Minutes become hours, which becomes days. And suddenly it's been months I have been mending my broken heart. I find myself randomly crying, thinking about how grateful I am to have such amazing people in my life. I have been told that life will move on, just differently, and as most families do, we have begun to get used to a life after death. I still miss my parents dearly, but the days full of crying have become less and less. Things have settled back into their traditional rhythms, season after season, and I have gotten used to having Hayley in my life again.

Before everything happened I would worry about the smallest things. I would touch on what could go wrong, but not what could go right. I have realized that the real troubles in life are the things that never crossed my mind. I never worried that my parents would be gone so soon. I thought both of them would live for a long time. I never thought Hayley would be a victim to heroin, and there we were.

I am trying to love every minute of life, and not take it for granted. I was moving so fast I had forgotten to stop and relish it. I find more joy in the simple things. I am opening my heart, and being present in every moment because moments are too precious to waste. I listen more intently to my favorite songs, feel the squeeze from my friends when they hug me, stop to watch birds of prey glide across the sky, taste the indulgent sweetness of a glass of red wine, and take in the fragrance from the flowers mom loved so much. I now wake up and live because tomorrow isn't a guarantee.

XO, E

There Are Fairies at the Bottom of Our Garden

Night is full of unknown creatures.
I am awake, covers over my head.
Like a tent about to collapse.
"Mummy" I call into the darkness.
Will she be angry or kind this time?
I wait holding my breath.
There.
She comes and gently peels back my covers.
To expose me to the night.
"There are fairies at the bottom of our garden"
Her whispers lull me back to sleep.
The fairies will protect me.
I am safe again.
Cancer is full of unknowns.
I am awake with eyes wide open.
Like a wild animal alert to danger.
"Mum", I call into the darkness.
She has been gone for many years.
Our cancers are the same.
She visited me once at my father's house.
In spirit sitting next to my bed.
In her favorite green chair.
"There are fairies at the bottom of our garden"
I whisper again and again.
Like a mantra bringing me home.

Namaste, Jude